*Woman and Society in
Eighteenth-Century France*

Woman and Society in Eighteenth-Century France

Essays in Honour of
JOHN STEPHENSON SPINK

Edited by

EVA JACOBS
W. H. BARBER
JEAN H. BLOCH
F. W. LEAKEY
EILEEN LE BRETON

LONDON
THE ATHLONE PRESS
1979

Published by
THE ATHLONE PRESS
at 4 *Gower Street London* WC1

Distributed by Tiptree Book Services Ltd
Tiptree, Essex

USA and Canada
Humanities Press Inc
New Jersey

British Library Cataloguing in Publication Data
Woman and society in eighteenth-century France.
  1. Women—France—Social conditions—
18th century—Addresses, essays, lectures
  I. Jacobs, Eva   II. Spink, John Stephenson
301.41′2′0944   HQ1613
      ISBN 0 485 11184 5

Printed in Great Britain by
WESTERN PRINTING SERVICES LTD
Bristol

Preface

It has become a general practice among publishers to require that essays collected as a tribute to a respected scholar should form as far as possible a book with a unified theme. The Editorial Committee set up to prepare such a volume in honour of Professor J. S. Spink readily acquiesced in the Athlone Press's request that the scope of the essays be delimited in advance, regretting at the same time that this necessarily implied that some of Professor Spink's colleagues, friends and pupils would not feel able to contribute. The subject of the book almost suggested itself to the editors. Professor Spink's main, although by no means only, field of specialization is the eighteenth century. His commitment to the history of ideas seemed to exclude a purely literary approach. But why the emphasis on women? When Professor Spink retired from Bedford College, he spoke with feeling of the particular happiness that he had experienced in his twenty-one years as a member of that institution. The origins of Bedford College lay in the movement towards the emancipation of women in the nineteenth century. Founded in 1849, it is the oldest university college for women in the country, and as such contributed greatly towards the general acceptance of women into university life. When Professor Spink joined the College in 1952, it still had only women undergraduates, although male postgraduate students were admitted. It was at that time still conscious, as a community, of its secular, progressive traditions, and Professor Spink felt himself to be very much in sympathy with its aims and its 'spirit'. The world changed, and the College was opened to male undergraduates in 1965. But Professor Spink continued to uphold the principle that students had to be accepted into the College purely on merit, and he never attempted to achieve an artificial balance of the sexes in his own department. He has thus personally contributed in no small measure to women's education, and he has always shown himself a determined believer in the intellectual equality of women. The theme of this book reflects therefore at least some of Professor Spink's central preoccupations, and pays homage not only to his scholarship, but also to his effective action in the field of women's education.

The contributions fall into three main sections, although there is some overlap between them. The first, and longest, deals in general with the attitudes of various eighteenth-century writers and thinkers towards the second sex. Some rather unexpected facts emerge. It is not necessarily those eighteenth-century figures most usually considered progressive who held the most progressive ideas about women. Nor was it always women themselves who were the most enlightened in their understanding of their own situation, or in their readiness to examine it. The detail of the discussions upon which these writers embarked inevitably recalls modern debate on the subject of women, but perhaps the lines of division between them were then not so clear-cut as today, when political prejudices have a tendency to warp the issues. This section of the volume may well help to add a further historical perspective to the current interest in the subject of the equality of women.

The second section of the book looks at women in literature, both as writers and protagonists. Here, we see women in action, either real or imagined, rather than in the more theoretical framework of ideas. But attitudes emerge none the less that have a bearing on any assessment the reader may wish to make of the more general problem of woman and her place in eighteenth-century society. At times consciously, at times unconsciously, each writer suggests a view of woman, as well as of particular women. This section prompts further consideration of the oft-stated opinion that literature reveals a society at least as well as, and perhaps better than, contemporary historical documents.

The third and last section is about five individual women who have particularly interested the contributors in question. Here again, readers may wish to set specific examples of women, one of whom was already very old at the beginning of the century and another of whom lived on well into the nineteenth century, against the more general, theoretical discussions earlier in the book. What is the relation between individuals living out their lives in a given society and that society's beliefs and assumptions?

Without any expectation that a single book can give final answers to questions of this kind, the editors hope, nevertheless, that these essays, from a diverse company of scholars, will be agreed to be a worthwhile contribution to Enlightenment studies, the field in which Professor Spink himself has pursued such a distinguished career.

Because this collection of essays has a central theme, a number of contributors have naturally dealt with related aspects of the subject, and certain writers and books appear in more than one essay. Cross-referencing has been supplied by the editors in the form of an index of proper names and selected subjects.

The editors would like to thank the staff of the Athlone Press for encouragement and help in the preparation of this volume. They would also like to take this opportunity to express their gratitude to all those contributors who have joined with them so readily in this tribute to Professor Spink.

Eva Jacobs
W. H. Barber
Jean H. Bloch
F. W. Leakey
Eileen Le Breton

Contributors

JEAN H. BLOCH
Lecturer in French, Bedford College, University of London

E. R. BRIGGS
Emeritus Professor of French, University College of Wales, Aberystwyth

J. H. BRUMFITT
Professor of French, University of St Andrews

COLIN DUCKWORTH
Professor of French, University of Melbourne

JOHN FALVEY
Senior Lecturer in French, University of Southampton

DENNIS FLETCHER
Professor of French, University of Durham

ELIZABETH J. GARDNER
Lecturer in French, Bedford College, University of London

P. M. HALL
Lecturer in French, King's College, University of London

EVA JACOBS
Senior Lecturer in French, Bedford College, University of London

P. D. JIMACK
Professor of French, University of Stirling

SHIRLEY JONES
Senior Lecturer in French, University College, University of London

JOHN LOUGH
Emeritus Professor of French, University of Durham

H. T. MASON
Professor of European Literature, University of East Anglia

SHEILA MASON
Lecturer in French, University of Birmingham

VIVIENNE MYLNE
Professor of French, University of Kent

ROBERT NIKLAUS
Emeritus Professor of French, University of Exeter

ROBERT
SHACKLETON
*Bodley's Librarian, and Fellow
of Brasenose College, Oxford*

JEAN VARLOOT
*Professeur à l'Université de
Paris-Sorbonne*

MARK WADDICOR
*Lecturer in French,
University of Exeter*

Contents

II Women in Literature

III Five Women

John Stephenson Spink

It is entirely fitting that the present volume should be a tribute to Professor J. S. Spink on the occasion of his seventieth birthday, rather than an offering to mark his retirement. For, although he retired from the Chair of French Language and Literature at Bedford College in the University of London in 1973, there is an obvious sense in which he has not retired at all. The flow of publications from his pen has, if anything, increased since his release from the heavy burden of teaching and administration that he undertook as Head of the Department of French. With his energy and brilliance as a scholar, he continues to make major contributions to research in the field of eighteenth-century French studies, as is shown by the accompanying Bibliography of his publications. An international reputation keeps him in demand as a speaker at conferences, and he is heavily involved as an editor in the current enterprise to publish Diderot's complete works: retirement, indeed, seems an inappropriate word to use to describe what is merely a change in emphasis in his academic activities. His colleagues and friends have chosen, therefore, to give him a birthday present, as a token of their admiration for his past and present achievements.

John Stephenson Spink was born in Pickering in North Yorkshire in 1909 and educated at Pickering Grammar School. From there he went on to the University of Leeds, where he obtained in 1930 first-class Honours in French language and literature. During his undergraduate course, he spent one term and two vacations at the University of Geneva, and became particularly interested in Jean-Jacques Rousseau. He began postgraduate research under the direction of Daniel Mornet, while working in Paris as an *assistant* at the Lycée Henri IV, and as a *lecteur* at the Sorbonne. His M.A. thesis for Leeds was a presentation of the manuscript text of Rousseau's *Lettres écrites de la montagne*, with a study of the genesis of the work. In 1934 he obtained the Doctorate of the University of Paris with a thesis entitled *Jean-Jacques Rousseau et Genève*, which was awarded a share of the Prix Marcelin Guérin of the Académie française. His first appointment as a university teacher was in 1933, in his own university. In 1937 he moved to King's College, London, as a Lecturer, and he remained there until 1950, when he was appointed Professor of French and Head of the Department of Romance Languages and Literatures in the University College of Southampton. In 1952, he succeeded Professor Gladys Turquet in the Chair of French at Bedford College, and he remained Head of Department until his retirement.

During his forty years as a university teacher, Professor Spink took part in every aspect of university life. One might be tempted to infer, from the extent and depth of his scholarly work, that he must have been remote from the more mundane concerns of the academic community, but this is far from being the case. Actively involved in his profession, he was Secretary of the King's College branch of the A.U.T. for a number of years, and a member of the A.U.T. committee at Southampton. He did not seek after office, but his colleagues elected him to many key positions. He was Chairman of the Board of Romance Languages and Literatures from 1953–7, and Dean of the Faculty of Arts of the University of London from 1960–4. He was also Dean of the Faculty of Arts of Bedford College from 1964–6, and Vice-Principal from 1965–6. His interest in student activities led him to accept the Presidency of the University of London French Society, a position which he held for many years. He was also, in 1959–60, Chairman of the Association of Heads of French Departments.

The generations of students who benefited from his teaching will remember above all his inspiring lectures. They were pitched at a high intellectual level, and gave his listeners a true perception of academic discussion at its best. He held firm views about the nature of university studies, and in particular believed that a language department should offer, in the broadest sense, a 'philological' discipline. Thus, much of his own research and of the research he has directed with postgraduate students has been based on an approach to the history of ideas from a lexicological point of view. It would be misleading, however, to suggest any narrowness in his attitude. His interests range from semantic studies to cultural history, from detailed genetic studies to comparative literature. He is best known, no doubt, for his many contributions to the history of ideas, especially the history and development of free-thought in France, a field in which his book *French Free-Thought from Gassendi to Voltaire*, published by the Athlone Press and translated into many languages, remains a standard authority.

Outside his special and professional interest in France, Professor Spink is deeply interested in the Soviet Union. A long-standing member of the Society for Cultural Relations with the U.S.S.R., he became its Vice-Chairman and twice visited the Soviet Union as a delegate at conferences. He has also travelled extensively in the U.S.S.R., mostly driving privately with his wife. His many contributions to the *Anglo-Soviet Journal*, and his translation in 1944 of Krimov's *The Tanker 'Derbent'* for Penguin Books, bear witness to his familiarity with Russian life and letters. His other 'leisure' interest, which he shares with his wife, Dorothy Knowles, who is a specialist in that field, is French theatre, and particularly the avant-garde theatre, an interest he first developed during his years in Paris as a postgraduate student.

Professor Spink and his wife each year have spent as much time as they could in France, where they have many friends. They have never lost touch with the latest developments there, and it is always illuminating to speak with them about French cultural, literary and political life. In 1973, in recognition of his devotion to France, Professor Spink received the high honour of nomination as an Officier de l'Ordre National du Mérite. Inveterate travellers, Professor and Mrs Spink have driven thousands of miles together not only in France and the U.S.S.R., but also through most of Europe and North Africa, and in the Middle East. All those who have had the opportunity to come into contact with them have profited from the example of openmindedness, intellectual liveliness and ready acceptance of the modern world. No one looks back with less nostalgia or forward with more enthusiasm than John Spink and Dorothy Knowles. We wish them both many more long and fulfilling years of travel, scholarly research and writing.

Eva Jacobs

List of Publications
by J. S. Spink

I CRITICAL EDITIONS

1 'La Première Rédaction des *Lettres écrites de la montagne*', *Annales J.-J. Rousseau*, xx (1931), 9–125, and xxi (1932), 9–156.

2 Jean-Jacques Rousseau, *Les Rêveries du promeneur solitaire* (Paris, Société des textes français modernes, 1948).

3 Jean-Jacques Rousseau, *Mémoire présenté à Monsieur de Mably sur l'éducation de monsieur son fils (Projet pour l'éducation de monsieur de Sainte-Marie)* and *Emile, première version (manuscrit Favre)*, in *Œuvres complètes de Jean-Jacques Rousseau*, iv (Paris, Pléiade, 1969).

4 (With P. Casini) Diderot, *Essai sur le mérite et la vertu*, in *Œuvres complètes*, i (Paris, Hermann, 1975).

5 Diderot, *La Suffisance de la religion naturelle*, in *Œuvres complètes*, ii (Paris, Hermann, 1975).

In the press

6 (With J. Varloot) Diderot, *Suite de l'apologie de l'abbé de Prades*, in *Œuvres complètes*, iv (Paris, Hermann).

II OTHER BOOKS AND ARTICLES

1 *Jean-Jacques Rousseau et Genève* (Paris 1934). Ouvrage couronné par l'Académie française, prix Marcelin Guérin.

2 'Mademoiselle Clairon à Ferney', *Bulletin des historiens du théâtre*, 3e année (juillet-août 1935), 65–74.

3 'Un Document inédit sur les derniers jours de Jean-Jacques Rousseau', *Annales J.-J. Rousseau*, xxiv (1935), 155–70.

4 'La Diffusion des idées matérialistes et anti-religieuses au début du XVIIIe siècle: le *Theophrastus redivivus*', *Revue d'histoire littéraire de la France*, 44e année (1935), 248–55.

5 'A *prêtre philosophe* in the Eighteenth Century—Jacques-Joseph Le Blanc', *Modern Language Review*, xxxvii (1942), 200–2.

6 'The Strategic Defeat of the Left', *Horizon*, vii (1943), 11–20.

7 'The Teaching of French Pronunciation in England in the Eighteenth Century, with particular reference to the diphthong *OI*', *Modern Language Review*, xli (1946), 155–63.

8 'Libertinage et "Spinozisme": la théorie de l'âme ignée', *French Studies*, i (1947), 218–31.

9 'J.-J. Rousseau dans la rue Plâtrière', *Mercure de France*, no 1021 (1948), 36–44.

10 *Literature and the Sciences in the Age of Molière*, Inaugural Lecture, Bedford College (London 1953).

11 'Les Premières Pages de l'*Emile*', *Cahiers de l'Association internationale des études françaises*, no 3–4–5 (1953), 185–9.

12 'Form and Structure: Cyrano de Bergerac's atomistic conception of metamorphosis', *Literature and Science* (Proceedings of the 6th Triennial Congress of the International Federation for Modern Languages and Literatures) (Oxford 1955), pp. 144–50.

13 *French Free-Thought from Gassendi to Voltaire* (London 1960). (French edition, translated by Paul Meier, 1966; American edition, 1969; Italian edition, translated by Luisa Sacerdote, 1974; Polish edition, translated by A. Neuman, 1974).

14 'L'Echelle des êtres et des valeurs dans l'œuvre de Diderot', *Cahiers de l'Association internationale des études françaises*, no 13 (1960), 339–351.

15 'Les Premières Expériences pédagogiques de Rousseau', *Annales J.-J. Rousseau*, xxxv (1959–62), 93–111.

16 'A propos des drames de Beaumarchais: tragédie bourgeoise anglaise, drame français', *Revue de littérature comparée*, 37e année (1963), 216–26.

17 'Diderot devant la religion et la libre-pensée', *Europe*, no 405–6 (1963), 89–94.

18 'La Vertu politique selon Diderot', *Revue des sciences humaines*, nouvelle série, fasc. 172 (1963), 471–83.

19 'La Phase naturaliste dans la préparation de l'*Emile* ou Wolmar éducateur', *Jean-Jacques Rousseau et son œuvre*, Actes et Colloques 2 (Paris 1964), pp. 171–82.

20 'Rochester, Dehénault, Voltaire and a chorus from Seneca's *Troades*: negation as a source of lyricism', *Problèmes des genres littéraires (Zagadnienia rodzajòw literackich)*, viii (2) (1966), 5–16.

21 'Chronologie et composition thématique dans les ouvrages à forme biographique et autobiographique au XVIIIe siècle', *Cahiers de l'Association internationale des études françaises*, no 19 (1967), 115–28.

22 'Un Abbé philosophe à la Bastille (1751–53): G.-A. de Méhégan et son *Zoroastre*', in *The Age of the Enlightenment, Studies presented to Theodore Besterman* (London 1967), pp. 252–74.

23 'The Reputation of Julian the "apostate" in the Enlightenment', *Studies on Voltaire and the Eighteenth Century*, lvii (1967), 1399–1415.

24 'The Abbé de Prades and the Encyclopædists: was there a plot?', *French Studies*, xxiv (1970), 225–35.

25 'Un Abbé philosophe: l'affaire de J.-M. de Prades', *Dix-huitième siècle*, iii (1971), 145–80.

26 'The Clandestine Book Trade in 1752: The Publication of the *Apologie de l'abbé de Prades*', in *Studies in Eighteenth-Century French Literature presented to Robert Niklaus* (Exeter 1975), pp. 243–56.

27 'The Social Background of Saint-Preux and d'Etange', *French Studies*, xxx (1976), 155–67.

28 '*Sentiment, Sensible, Sensibilité*: les mots, les idées, d'après les moralistes français et britanniques du début du dix-huitième siècle', *Problèmes des genres littéraires (Zagadniena rodzajòw literackich)*, xx (1), 33–47.

29 'From "Hippolyte est sensible" to "Le fatal présent du ciel" ', in *The Classical Tradition in France, essays presented to R. C. Knight*, ed. H. T. Barnwell and others (Lampeter 1977), pp. 191–202.

30 'Marivaux: The "Mechanism of the Passions" and the "Metaphysic of Sentiment" ', *Modern Language Review*, lxxiii (1978), 278–90.

In the press

31 'Les Avatars du sentiment de l'existence à l'époque des lumières', *Dix-huitième siècle*.

32 'Rousseau and the problems of composition', to appear in a forthcoming *Festschrift* for Professor R. A. Leigh.

III TRANSLATION

Yuri Krimov, *The Tanker 'Derbent'* (Penguin 1944).

Reviews in *French Studies, Modern Language Review, Revue d'histoire littéraire de la France, Times Literary Supplement, Romanic Review*—about seventy in all. Reviews and longer surveys relating to Russian literature and philosophy, in *Anglo-Soviet Journal*.

I
WOMEN IN SOCIETY

Women and the Reform of the Nation

JEAN H. BLOCH

The second half of the eighteenth century produced an upsurge of interest in the position of women and their role in society. Much of the debate focussed on the question of women's education.

This was, of course, by no means new. The seventeenth century had produced a wide range of suggestions concerned with the opening up of new possibilities for women and the extension of their field of study. The most radical of these was undoubtedly that of the Cartesian Poulain de la Barre[1] who, applying his thesis that sexual differences being purely physical they can in no way affect the intellect, argued that women would be perfectly capable of holding posts in the Church, army, judicature and so on, normally reserved for men.

It was, however, not Poulain, but the more conservative Fénelon, who was to become the authority on girls' education for many eighteenth-century writers. Fénelon, like his contemporary Fleury, accepted that women would have little or no public role or office. Unlike Fleury, however, who consequently focussed on the education of women for the domestic sphere[2], Fénelon felt that this was wrong, particularly as so much emphasis was placed on the importance of boys' education for the public good.[3] He therefore stressed the compensating importance of women for the family, posterity and, hence, society as a whole, arguing that in this way girls' education is just as important to the public interest as boys'. However, although he suggested a wide reading syllabus for girls, Fénelon placed emphasis primarily on extensive religious and moral education. This was partly because he saw a woman's principal role as that of a *moral* influence within the family, and, more generally, because as a churchman he placed moral matters above purely intellectual ones for men and women alike.

In 1730 the Abbé de Saint-Pierre took the argument concerning the social usefulness of girls' education further. In his *Projet pour perfectionner l'éducation des filles* he argued that the aim of boys' and girls' education alike must be 'le bonheur de leur patrie'[4], an argument striking in the context of the 1730s for its new emphasis on a truly public and patriotic education for boys and all the more so for extending this notion to girls. For the Abbé de Saint-Pierre the education of both boys and girls must be useful, aiming at virtues which will increase both personal and *public* happiness. Earlier educationalists had normally stressed personal happiness and salvation. Because of his emphasis on the social utility of women's education, the Abbé de Saint-Pierre preferred a convent education for girls to private education at home, a preference which was to prove markedly less popular in the second half of the century as the convent schools came under attack.

Despite his identification of the basic social aims of education for both boys and girls, the Abbé de Saint-Pierre, like Fleury and Fénelon before him, continued to accept that women would not be destined for public office and that their influence would be through the home and family. His vision is essentially that of a society reaping the benefits of a better educated womenfolk who would thus become virtuous and intelligent mothers, enlightened widows and guardians of children, informed advisers of husbands, some of whom would hold high public positions. He thus emphasized the need for an improved moral education for women, though this was to be backed by an introduction to almost all branches of knowledge to prepare women for their role as enlightened wives and mothers. But although he went far in defining the social and even patriotic orientation of education, this was not an entirely secular ideal. Throughout his work the Abbé de Saint-Pierre makes it clear that the goal is double: the achievement of salvation *and* the improvement of society. We have not yet reached the period when education can be separated from Christian morality and the Church.

A widening interest in the status, role and education of women becomes apparent around the mid-eighteenth century. Now, not simply major authors, or writers ahead of their time like Poulain, take up the discussion, but also a plethora of often rather minor writers all eager to publish works on the merits, position or possible education of women. As one might expect, opinion was divided. In 1744 a writer named Boquel prepared a treatise to demonstrate women's inferiority (*Supériorité de l'homme sur la femme*), but, in contrast, the Abbé Dinouart argued in 1749 that women are equal to men (*Le Triomphe du Sexe*), while in 1753 Philippe Joseph Caffiaux attempted to draw attention to Poulain's arguments, which he declared to have had little effect and whose work was now hard to come by.[5] Women too wrote in defence of their own sex, Mme d'Archambault and Mme de Puisieux, both in 1750, the latter, like Poulain, advocating equality even professionally.

By the time Rousseau published *Emile* in 1762 the debate concerning women's education was not only well under way, but there is evidence that, whatever public opinion may have been, among those who chose to write on the subject of women's education many now favoured improved intellectual education for girls. Even a conservative writer like J. H. S. Formey, while following the traditional notion that women are made to please, nevertheless argued that they could only please by showing an intelligent mind and acquaintance with the greatest works of literature.[6] Rousseau's argument in *Emile* that the education of women must be entirely relative to their relationship to men and that equality is, therefore, unnatural, was, in some respects already behind the times. The formulation of his ideas is, however, of great importance in the light of the subsequent development of notions concerning the role, education and, above all, the moral influence of women.

Like most of his contemporaries, Rousseau denied any public or professional role to women, but closed the gates even more firmly by 'demonstrating' in a quasi-rational manner that this exclusion is in accordance with nature. Women are manifestly different from men and, subsequently, not only physiologically, but also socially different. The natural differences between the sexes necessarily imply differences of role within the social order. A woman's natural role is manifestly one of dependence: 'la dépendance étant un état naturel aux femmes, les filles se sentent faites pour obéir (*O.C.* iv, 710).[7] Rousseau thus builds up an argument which demonstrates the differences and inequality of the sexes. Although the strength of his approach in the analysis of inequality in the *Inégalité* had been to unite the moral and political spheres, he did not extend this approach to women. A woman is to be educated to take her place in the physical and moral spheres, which are closely connected. As a woman's natural physical role is to be a mother, so her moral role is (as Fénelon had also stressed) primarily concerned with her husband and children. Book V of *Emile* stresses the importance of virtue for women and through them to the whole of society. Teach women to love and desire virtue and men will want to merit them: the moral regeneration of society will thus become possible.

It is Book I of *Emile*, however, that presents the clearest and most impelling arguments, and that was to obtain the greatest success with upper-class French women over the next twenty years. It is through mothers that the moral regeneration of a corrupt nation can be effected. If mothers were once again to breast-feed their own babies and thus forge again the bonds of natural affection and all this entails, moral reform would become possible: 'Ainsi de ce seul abus corrigé résulteroit bientôt une réforme générale, bientôt la nature auroit repris ses droits. Qu'une fois les femmes redeviennent méres, bientôt les hommes redeviendront péres et maris' (*O.C.* iv, 258). But if Rousseau stressed moral regeneration through women, he did not believe that this would come about as a result of making women more knowledgeable. Throughout his work he shows that he prefers virtue to knowledge, indeed, it was this that distinguished him from the main stream of Enlightenment thought, which saw virtue as stemming from greater knowledge. Nowhere, however, was Rousseau's emphasis on virtue to prove more significant than in its application to women. For him, women should be educated only in so far as their role as wives and mothers requires, they should not attempt to emulate men. Even the enlightened Julie of *La Nouvelle Héloïse* does not attempt to go too far. Once her sons are older they will be educated by men, and preferably by their father: 'Je suis femme et mere, je sais me tenir à mon rang. Encore une fois, la fonction dont je me suis chargée n'est pas d'élever mes fils, mais de les préparer pour être élevés.' (*O.C.*, ii, 578).

Neither did Rousseau stress, as the Abbé de Saint-Pierre had done, the necessary social orientation of women's education. This was partly because at this stage he had rejected all possibility of educating boys to become citizens in the corrupt society of eighteenth-century France and had therefore concentrated in *Emile* on the education of natural man for whom Sophie is destined as a companion. It was also because the desired regeneration was to come from the family unit which, although he saw this as a micro-society and the basis of the social state, he tended to see more on the side of nature than of the community. The social implications were certainly there, but not stressed as they had been by the Abbé de Saint-Pierre.

After Rousseau the debate continued. Some writers sought simply to point out existing injustices (e.g. Mme Riccoboni in *L'Abeille* of 1765) or to maintain like Joseph de la Porte in his *Histoire des femmes françaises* of 1769 that women have already achieved works which demonstrate that their intellectual powers and their talents can equal those of men. The most significant contribution of the 1760s, however, was probably an article on national education published in 1766 in the *Ephémérides du Citoyen* which maintained that *all* French girls should receive public education. The author, Baudeau, one of the physiocrats, now emphasised the desirable social and patriotic orientation of girls' education in a totally secular context: 'Il ne faut pas oublier que l'une et l'autre institution [i.e. boys' and girls' schools] doivent tendre au meme but, et concourir au bien de l'Etat . . .' (*Ephémérides du Citoyen*, iv, 57). At the same time, however, he firmly anchored women's apparently new social role, that of *Citoyennes* (which he linked with the example of Ancient Sparta) to the traditional role of wife and mother: 'Il faut poser pour maxime fondamentale, que les Filles de la Nation sont destinées à devenir chacune dans leur condition, Citoyennes, Epouses et Meres. Ces trois idées doivent servir de boussole aux Spéculateurs qui voudront s'occuper du système d'études et d'exercices qui leur convient.' (ibid., p. 58). In many respects Baudeau was obviously ahead of his contemporaries and it was really only during the Revolution that these three allied notions were to become commonplace.

By the 1770s, however, the general debate concerning women's education clearly begins to develop a fairly well-defined set of arguments. In 1772 the Abbé Fromageot attempted, in his *Cours d'études des jeunes demoiselles*, to get down to practical reform and put forward the elements of a coherent socially-orientated argument. This was of course the period when the ideal of motherhood was fast gaining ground. In 1767, for example, the Comte de Caraccioli had spoken admiringly of a mother instructing her children in *bienfaisance* by her own example;[8] in 1772 an ardent campaigner for divorce, M. de Cerfvol, maintained that it is motherhood that makes women particularly respected, the childless woman merits only the respect shown to fellow human-beings;[9] while the mid-1770s saw the fashionable return to maternal breast-feeding. At the same time the condemnation of the allegedly unsuitable education offered by the convent-schools was steadily growing[10] and in this context it is not surprising to see Fromageot suggesting as a desirable alternative to convent-school education a good education at home from a 'mère tendre'. Although he accepted that women would be excluded from government and associated fields he maintained, as the Abbé de Saint-Pierre and Baudeau had done, that they can and should serve society. Fromageot believed that they could best do this by being better equipped intellectually to educate their own children. Now this is important, because it indicates not simply the fusion Enlightenment thought made generally between intellectual progress and social utility, but, in this particular case, the extension of this notion to women. Indeed, Frederick the Great had made a similar point in his *Lettre sur l'éducation* of 1770, stressing the need to train women's minds so that they might better educate their progeny.[11] Though Fromageot implies that women can equal men intellectually by suggesting that his detailed proposals for their education will be equally useful for boys, basically his ideal for women is still that of a faithful wife and tender mother, though, like Baudeau, he adds the wider social role of a good citizen. In Fromageot's case, however, the term 'bonne citoyenne' turns out to mean simply someone who will not disturb the order of society.[12] This is in itself interesting because this is precisely the period when writers on boys' education were beginning to elaborate the notion of the secular education of the citizen, emphasizing not simply the notion of the common good but the more particularized notion of the good of one's fellow citizens.[13] It may be that Fromageot is a particularly conservative writer, but it would appear on existing evidence that the term *citoyenne* in pre-Revolutionary France was to be firmly anchored to the notions of a good wife and mother. The distinction between men and women in this respect fits very well with the notable opposition in this period between emphasis on the desirability of public education for boys and the contrasting emphasis on domestic education for girls. This was obviously in part the practical result of the conviction that convent education was bad and did not fit a girl for life in society, but there is no doubt that there was at the same time an ideological backing for this preference which continued to link women to the domestic sphere. At this point the notions of nature, virtue, motherhood and, in some cases, enlightenment, fuse, whereas when boys' education was discussed although the role of the father in his children's (and especially his sons') education was often stressed and the notion of the good father joined to that of the good citizen, it was the *public* education of the citizen in its full civic and patriotic sense that was to come significantly to the fore in pre-Revolutionary France. In this respect Rousseau's *Emile* was often seen as anti-social and out of line with current preferences.[14] This is not to say, however, that the theory behind women's education was untouched by the new civic and patriotic consciousness that had slowly penetrated French thought during the first half of the eighteenth century and which spread considerably among educational reformers from the middle of the century on. On the contrary, we have already seen the Abbé de Saint-Pierre employing the word *patrie* in relation to girls' education and the term *citoyenne* being introduced. We shall also see writers on women's education speaking in terms of not simply the good of society as Fénelon had done in the seventeenth century, but also in terms of the State, the nation and national education. Like men, women are to play their role in a patriotic sense, and indeed, to bring about the reform of the nation, but they are to do it through the home and by means of their moral influence on their husbands and children.

1777 brought several interesting writings on girls' education which serve in part to show the growing importance of the ideal of motherhood and also Rousseau's influence in this period. Mme de Montbart, for example, an ardent disciple of Rousseau, fully accepted that women's education should be based on the role they play in relation to men and suggested preparing them both to please and to perform their domestic tasks with pleasure. She defended Rousseau against possible criticism of anti-feminism and maintained that women would like what he had to say about motherhood,[15] a remark which was certainly confirmed by the attribution of the return to maternal breast-feeding to his influence.

Bernardin de Saint-Pierre's essay for the Académie de Besançon of the same year also stressed the mother's rôle in her daughter's education. Believing that a mother must teach her daughter virtue, he developed his essay, as one might expect, along the lines of Rousseau's argument of education according to nature, but Bernardin made a significant point when he criticised Rousseau, albeit rather mildly, for *not* showing how women's education could be useful to society, maintaining that one would think education should be national, not seeking isolation.[16] This was, of course, a point commonly made with reference to *Emile* by writers on boys' education, but it is interesting to see Bernardin de Saint-Pierre using it in the context of education for girls. Firstly, it suggests that he did not fully understand Rousseau's complex reasons for opting for the education of the individual in *Emile*; secondly, and more important for our present discussion, it provides further evidence that the ideal of 'utilité publique' was becoming an increasingly common notion for writers on the education of women in this period. Bernardin de Saint-Pierre also identifies the *bad* education women receive with general social corruption, an idea that was often repeated in the years leading up to the Revolution and the negative side of the Academy's question: *Comment l'éducation des femmes pourrait contribuer à rendre les hommes meilleurs.*

Manon Phlipon, who became Mme Roland, answered the same question. She, rather surprisingly, also emphasized the natural inferiority of women but saw this as an actual means to their social utility. She argued quite clearly that better education for women must be used to influence men for the good and to direct the education of young children. Though she would not deprive women of knowledge, the future Mme Roland placed greater emphasis on the value of *sentiment*, which is, of course, what lies behind Rousseau's notion of virtue. Unlike Rousseau, however, and like Fromageot, she saw virtue as resulting from knowledge, though, like Rousseau, she saw a woman's main role as inspiring men to virtue through goodness. In this way she saw families achieving happiness and thereby ensuring the happiness of the State: 'que les sublimes transports d'une vertu douce et pieuse allument dans leur âme la noble ambition de régner par les mœurs, en leur donnant toute la bonté dont elles peuvent être susceptibles, et la félicité des familles deviendra le gage assuré de celle de l'Etat.' (*Mémoires de Madame Roland*, ed. M. P. Faugère (Paris 1864), ii, 356).

Through writers such as these one sees how women acquired at the ideological level an essential role in the Enlightenment struggle for the moral reform of society, but what is interesting at the same time is the variation apparent from one writer to the next. What looks at first sight like a coherent ideology, the moral regeneration of families, and consequently the nation, through the better education of women, turns out to contain crucial distinctions. While Rousseau emphasizes virtue, others see knowledge as a means to virtue; Bernardin de Saint-Pierre seems surprised to find Rousseau omitting a social emphasis, while Manon Phlipon accepts the co-existence of basically different attitudes to virtue and knowledge. What seems to happen is that such notions as motherhood, virtue and the regeneration of the nation come through clearly, but the means of achieving this are blurred. Distinctions which can have significantly different effects on the direction women's education can take do not seem to be clearly perceived.

The dominant argument, however, was fast taking shape. The belief that women can benefit from better intellectual training had been growing. The Abbé Le More had maintained in his *Principes d'Institution* of 1774 that, small differences aside, girls should have the same education as boys. In 1778 the Comte de Golowkin had suggested ambitious studies for upper-class girls (*Mes idées sur l'éducation du sexe*). Now, in 1779, in his *De l'Education physique et morale des femmes*, Riballier put the argument in even stronger terms by insisting, as Poulain had done over one hundred years before, on women's natural rights to knowledge. Riballier united this conviction with the emphasis on moral regeneration through women in much more positive terms than Fromageot had done in 1772. He argued that the degeneration of the nation resulted from the bad education imposed on women by men. Women could, however, teach virtues to young children from birth and thereby become the means of the regeneration of the nation. The reform of women's education was therefore essential. And in this case the reform of women's education is clearly meant to imply greater knowledge: in Riballier's treatise the notions of moral regeneration and enlightenment stand quite clearly united.

Riballier added an encouraging reminder that the reform of women's education will not destroy society (an argument sometimes raised by the opponents of improved education for women and complementary to Rousseau's arguments that education along male lines will only serve to denature them).

Mme de Genlis may have been one who had fears for the effects such reforms would have on society. Certainly she expressed in her *Adèle et Théodore* of 1782 the fear that education could remove women from their proper status in society and cause them to dislike it. Whether she meant this simply as a threat to personal happiness or gave it wider social implications is difficult to know, but, at all events, she dismisses genius in women as 'un don inutile et dangereux' (op. cit., i, lettre ix). Like many of her contemporaries, however, Mme de Genlis suggests a wide selection of studies for girls.

In the following year, 1783, the Académie de Châlons set the essay question: 'Quels sont les moyens de perfectionner l'éducation des jeunes demoiselles?' The fact that the academy chose to word its essay in such positive terms suggests that by now the subject of improved education for girls was seen less as a matter for contention than as a practical problem to be solved. That such a question was likely to be answered in terms of improved intellectual rather than simply moral education is borne out by the reply received from a M. Dumas, who had no hesitation in stating that with the same education women can equal men, but spent more time on what one should *not* do rather than on outlining a positive programme for reform. The most interesting response (which took the form of an unpublished fragmentary reply only) was, of course, from Laclos, who raised the subject to a higher philosophical level in his *Des femmes et de leur éducation* on the subject of the opposition of nature and society. His direct reply to the academy's question, however, represents a rare appreciation of woman's predicament. He argues that given the state of present society a woman receiving a good education would either be unhappy or dangerous to society. Women in society are in fact slaves and there can be no 'improvement' without a revolution. Because women have no freedom they cannot act morally; without morality there can be no education. Thus Laclos reaches an intellectual impasse which he abandons in favour of a discussion of natural woman, rather as Rousseau, reaching an impasse over political and educational reform, opted in *Emile* for private education away from corrupt society.[17]

As the Revolution approaches we find few innovatory ideas. The campaign seems to lose impetus and there are signs of reaction to the proposals for reform in the publications of Joly de Saint Vallier and Lezay-Marnésia. One still finds, however, continuing emphasis on the basic importance of a woman's relationship to society coupled with the need for the reform of her education. This is certainly true of the Abbé Reyre whose *Ecole des jeunes demoiselles* of 1786 acknowledges the importance of women for their families and the whole of society. Indeed, it was precisely on such ideas that the women campaigners on the eve of the Revolution were to seize.

Interesting as the development of a socially-oriented but nonetheless domestic ideal for women's education is in its own right, it is by no means the only thing that strikes one when one looks at the profusion of pre-Revolutionary publications on women's education. One of the significant things to emerge is that it is often the women themselves who are the most conservative, not necessarily in the actual suggestions they make for improved syllabuses, but in their general approach. Admittedly the period saw some overtly anti-feminist works written by men, but of those writers who favour improvement or at least show a sensitive appreciation of woman's predicament, it is often the women who suggest the more moderate change and who approach the subject more circumspectly.

Mme d'Epinay, for example, in a letter to the Abbé Galiani of 20 January 1771 felt that women were prevented from being useful to society by their exclusion from the professional field and consequently looked to study for women as a purely personal reward. The future Mme Roland accepted the notion that women are naturally inferior. It is only fair to add that she made it quite clear that an ignorant woman was a curse to her husband and family, but she accepted that women are made to please rather than govern and wrote her essay entirely in terms of woman's supportive role. Mme de Miremont, writing in 1779, thought it was ridiculous for women to try to be erudite or witty or aspire to a public role, while the ultra-conservative Mme de Montbart was anxious to avoid being called a 'bel esprit' for writing. One can appreciate that such comments may be the inevitable result of necessary discretion and the feeling that more will be gained by a moderate approach, but the attitudes of the women contrast sharply with the attitudes and vocabulary of some of the men. Poulain and Caffiaux had spoken in terms of exploitation and enslavement, Diderot of enslavement and debasement, Fromageot of debasement and degradation, Laclos of enslavement and lack of morality. Many, like Joseph de la Porte, spoke of injustice and prejudice, others, like Riballier, blamed men for the bad education women receive. Condorcet, on the eve of the Revolution, went further than any in claiming educational *and* political rights for women. It might be argued that some of these pre-Revolutionary attitudes in fact encourage defeatism or reinforce prejudice concerning women (especially something like Laclos's approach), and that writers like la Porte and Fromageot are rather conservative in their actual suggestions for women's education, whereas in this respect some women go quite far in seeking significant improvements in studies for girls or in maintaining they can equal men intellectually (Mlle d'Espinassy, Mlle Chanterolle, Mme de Miremont and particularly Mme de Puisieux). The fact remains, however, that it is usually the men who formulate the problem most clearly and in so doing take the issue further than the rather more compromising suggestions of many of the women writers of the period.

If we emphasize this point it is because it combines rather interestingly with the developing ideology of women as essential agents in the reform of the nation and may help to explain how Rousseau, apparently unfavourable to wider intellectual studies for women, nevertheless became associated with the campaign for improved education of girls for the women of the early Revolution.

When one looks at reactions to Rousseau's ideas on Sophie's education one finds that what criticism there is usually comes from men. True, Mlle d'Espinassy criticized Rousseau's restriction of studies for girls, but she also approved much of what he said. The material presented by Professor Jimack later in this volume is very revealing. When there is criticism of Rousseau it is from Formey and especially Riballier and contrasts sharply with what we ourselves have seen in the admiring enthusiasm of a Mme de Monbart. Indeed, as Mme de Genlis points out in *Adèle et Theodore* and as much contemporary comment justifies, Rousseau owed much of the *popular* success of *Emile* to women. Mme de Genlis is, in fact, exceptional amongst the women of her time in pointing out the paradoxical nature of this enthusiasm: 'C'est aux Femmes qu'Emile a dû ses plus grands succès; toutes les femmes en génèral ne louent Rousseau qu'avec enthousiasme, quoiqu'aucun Auteur ne les ait traitées avec moins de ménagemens' (op. cit., Pt. I, p. 190).

What seems to have happened is that Rousseau's controversial treatise, which from the start provoked both enthusiasm and indignation, aroused fervent support in the 1770s for its contribution to the field of childcare and physical education in particular. Though pedagogical writers had at first been slow to recognize his work as an educationalist, by the 1780s he had become an established authority mentioned in the same breath as Montaigne and Locke.[18] By this date it becomes apparent that his work was less precisely known and that in some cases early misconceptions (particularly that of the cold bath from birth) had become firmly associated with his name. By the Revolution *Emile* stood for general values: humanity, motherhood, virtue, freedom and reform, and was known for only a selection of details in line with contemporary desires for change: breast-feeding, a healthy diet and regime and, at worst, a *laissez-aller* in instruction coupled with tender parental affection. Thus it was that his reputation was ready for popular acclaim and enthusiastic simplification on a large scale.

As far as the education of women was concerned, in many ways he fitted perfectly. As we have seen, by the eve of the Revolution the dominant ideology among writers on women's education was that it was through them as wives and particularly as mothers that the nation could be reformed. A recent article by Ruth Graham, 'Rousseau's Sexism Revolutionized' states that the women pamphleteers of the early Revolution almost unanimously called for moral regeneration and claimed a better education for themselves as wives and mothers, reiterating the formulae which had been developed for them by the pre-Revolutionary writers and stressing their role as inspirers of virtue and the force behind the moral regeneration of the nation.[19] Now, however, the vocabulary became noticeably patriotic and the term *citoyenne* commonplace in the writings of both men and women. However, just as in the pre-Revolutionary period, the term was to be constantly accompanied by the notions of the good wife and mother.

Ruth Graham claims that many of the women's pamphlets show obvious (and sometimes professed) association with Rousseau. Certainly many of the Revolutionary writers on education refer to Rousseau and *Emile* even when discussing the education of women: a point which seems paradoxical to the twentieth-century mind. What seems clear is that the precise details of Rousseau's ideas concerning the education of women were little heeded by the women of the pre-Revolutionary and early Revolutionary period. The sentimental generation of pre-Revolutionary France had readily espoused the notion of women as the virtuous inspirers of men and posterity. Moreover, as Professor Jimack's essay emphasizes, Rousseau was also the creator of the unquestionably enlightened Julie (despite her own modest claims), and we know from contemporary comment that Julie was much admired by women. Even the picture of Sophie offered a glimmer of hope: Riballier expressed amazement at the apparently paradoxical contrast between Rousseau's principles on women's education in *Emile* and the delightful portrait of Sophie herself. Above all, Rousseau was the acknowledged inspiration of the fashionable return to breast-feeding of the 1770s. No doubt all these factors contributed to his success with women and help to explain the extremely small amount of contemporary criticism one finds (especially from women) of his insistence on the inequality of the sexes. Moreover, we have also seen that many educated women of pre-Revolutionary France even when they were not simply disciples of Rousseau tended to be generally rather conservative in their attitude to the underlying principles of the campaign for reform.

In addition to these various factors, however, it looks as if the rather uncritical building-up of a socially-orientated ideology for the education of women also helps to explain Rousseau's success. After all, he stood for the major elements of the campaign: motherhood, virtue, moral regeneration and, for more direct disciples, nature. It does not seem altogether surprising that the women of the early Revolution ignored the lack of emphasis given to knowledge when the main stream of pre-Revolutionary writers saw virtue as stemming from knowledge and equated the notions of knowledge, virtue and a better education for women. In this way Rousseau's insistence on the moral superiority of women could fuse quite easily with the general reputation of *Emile* as the symbol of humanity and virtue.

Indeed a similar thing happened with regard to Rousseau's emphasis on private education. Later writers freely incorporated popular notions from *Emile* in treatises on public education,[20] while, as far as the education of girls is concerned, Mme de Genlis readily incorporated details from Emile's education in her programme for them. Far from provoking criticism, jarring elements are often disregarded in favour of assumptions more in line with the prevailing attitude of the time.

Emile was, however, a two-edged sword. Mirabeau and Talleyrand both seized on the popularity of Rousseau to restrict women to the domestic sphere, allowing them civil but not political status,[21] and an ardent admirer of Rousseau's, Labène, elaborated a plan designed to educate women for entry into the *ménage* while boys were to be educated for the nation.[22] The backing these writers gave to their proposals was precisely Rousseau's most formidable argument: the claims of nature.

It is not surprising that the more critical middle-class English-women of the period expressed dismay at Rousseau's popularity and saw him as a man who had bewitched some of the greatest minds in Europe.[23] It is only occasionally that a French voice shares their opinion: Mme de Genlis in 1782 and in 1792 the deputy of the Hérault, J. Courdin, who, in his *Observations philosophiques sur la réforme de l'éducation publique* emphasized once again the need for better intellectual education for women. Courdin saw that attitudes like that of Talleyrand went back to the opinions of major writers and maintained that both Molière and Rousseau 'ont retardé de plusieurs siècles le développement de leurs [i.e. des femmes] facultés morales et intellectuelles, le progrès de la raison et de la vertu' (p. 97).

2

The *Philosophes* and Women: Sensationalism and Sentiment

ELIZABETH J. GARDNER

Feminism was not a cause espoused by the *philosophes*, with the obvious exception of Condorcet, who is anyway not always included in their ranks. It is not sufficient, however, merely to claim that women were naturally included in the general programme of amelioration these thinkers envisaged. For the views of the *philosophes* on women must be considered within their own terms of reference; and while it would be anachronistic to labour any supposedly anti-feminist remarks culled from their disparate writings, it is of interest to examine the various theoretical conclusions which writers like Helvétius, Diderot, D'Holbach and Condorcet drew from a common premise—sensationalism. We can then see how this doctrine was applied to one half of the human race.

The works of Helvétius provide a starting point for this discussion, since in his rigid expression of sensationalism we find some of the logically egalitarian implications of this theory applied to the subject of women, although not in a systematic or coherent fashion.

All men, Helvétius claims, are equal, at least in potential, at birth, and therefore subsequent inequality is the result of differences in education and environment.[1] If women do not achieve eminence in the Arts and Sciences it is because they are hampered even more than their male counterparts by the type of education they receive and their life-style. Thus when accounting for the relatively small number of great minds in Paris, Helvétius automatically disqualifies women: 'Or, de ces huit cent mille âmes, si d'abord l'on en supprime la moitié, c'est-à-dire les femmes, dont l'éducation et la vie s'opposent au progrès qu'elles pourraient faire dans les sciences et les arts . . .'[2]

Helvétius side-steps the question of educational reform in *De l'esprit*, arguing that since the possibility of reform is so remote, lengthy proposals would be superfluous.[3] He returns to the theme of women's education and its ills in *De l'homme*. However, if Helvétius strikes a more constructive note on the subject of male education, little mention is made of the female of the species when he draws up plans for public education and professional training.[4] There is, Helvétius states, a basic incompatibility between what is taught to the child or adolescent and what is expected of him or her in the world. This dichotomy is particularly blatant in the education girls receive in convents: 'C'est dans les maisons religieuses et destinées à l'instruction des jeunes filles que ces contradictions sont les plus frappantes.'[5] For instance, girls are taught to be truthful but they are not allowed to express their opinion if their parents' choice of husband does not please them.[6] They order these things differently in Turkey where at least women receive training appropriate to their future submissive role.[7] Helvétius insists on the primacy of education. Intelligence is not proportionate to the degree of refinement of the senses. Women, for instance, have a more acute sense of touch but are not thereby more intelligent than, say, Voltaire.[8] By the same token the intellectual inferiority of women cannot be related to specifically female characteristics. Helvétius leaves us in no doubt whatsoever about this: 'L'organisation des deux sexes est sans doute très-différente à certains égards: mais cette différence doit-elle être regardée comme la cause de l'infériorité de l'esprit des femmes? Non: la preuve du contraire, c'est que nulle femme n'étant organisée comme un homme, nulle en conséquence ne devroit avoir autant d'esprit. Or les Saphos, les Hyppathies, les Elizabeths, les Catherines II, etc. ne le cedent point aux hommes en génie. Si les femmes leur sont en général inférieures, c'est qu'en général elles reçoivent encore une plus mauvaise éducation.'[9]

The optimism prevalent in such aspects of Helvétius's thinking on women was far from being commonplace at the time, as Diderot's comments constantly show. In his notes on *De l'homme* Diderot offers a much narrower interpretation of the facts. He seems to suggest that exceptions do not affect the norm, otherwise

one swallow would make a summer.[10] Similarly, 'Le petit nombre
de femmes de génie fait exception et non pas règle', and moreover,
as he churlishly asserts, the standards expected of women are
lower than those expected of men; like the rich they are surrounded by flatterers.[11] He is equally sceptical about the role of
education as a universal panacea. Helvétius, Diderot states, had
claimed that 'les femmes sont susceptibles de la même éducation
que les hommes'; Diderot's contention is far less radical: 'Dites:
on pourrait les élever mieux qu'on ne fait'.[12]

Although Helvétius, unlike Diderot, makes no distinction
between male and female potential, he fails to implement his
theory of the absolute equality of the sexes when he rhapsodises
on the role women would play in an ideal society. Reforms in
education, changes in marriage laws and sexual mores seem to be
inspired chiefly with the benefit of men in mind. Not only does
woman fail to emerge as an independent entity—and we should
not be too harsh on Helvétius for this—but the only means of
acquiring status allowed to her is to submit her one source of
power, sex, to the control of the state. Helvétius is obviously less
concerned with being consistent with his own theories than with
seizing every available opportunity of attacking the Church's
views on sex and morals. Women's education should be improved,
he argues, because of the deleterious influence they have on men.
Women are a distraction and prevent some men from fulfilling
themselves intellectually. If sex were demystified, the power
women exercise over their lovers through the cult that is demanded of the latter would be lessened and men could indulge
their pleasure and be free to pursue intellectual matters as well.[13]

Helvétius reiterates this point in De l'homme where he advocates
a more matter-of-fact approach to sex, particularly for busy men:
'Il faut donc des coquettes aux oisifs, et de jolies filles aux oc-
cupés;'[14] and again: 'La chasse des dames comme celle du gibier,
doit être différente selon le temps qu'on veut y mettre.'[15]

Since men are motivated chiefly by a desire for sexual gratifica-
tion, the solution to the problem that women pose for men would
be, in Helvétius's view, to put women at the disposal of the state.
Helvétius wistfully speculates that the Spartans would have been
even more heroic if their goal had been sexual favours rather than
mere glory. Woman's lot too would have been enhanced: 'Tout

concourait, dans cette législation, à métamorphoser les hommes en héros; mais, pour l'établir, il fallait que Lycurgue, convaincu que le plaisir est le moteur unique et universel des hommes, eût senti que les femmes, qui partout ailleurs semblaient, comme les fleurs d'un beau jardin, n'être faites que pour l'ornement de la terre et le plaisir des yeux, pouvaient être employées à un plus noble usage; que ce sexe, avili et dégradé chez presque tous les peuples du monde, pouvait entrer en communauté de gloire avec les hommes, partager avec eux les lauriers qu'il leur faisait cueillir, et devenir enfin un des plus puissants ressorts de la législation.'[16] This is pure sophistry: being a tool of the state is scarcely an active role. Woman, however venerable, however revered, is still an object, as Helvétius makes abundantly clear in *De l'homme*: 'Qu'une belle esclave, une concubine devienne chez un peuple le prix, ou des talens, ou de la vertu . . . les mœurs de ce peuple n'en seront pas plus corrompues.'[17] In *De l'homme*, Section II, Chapter IX, an unrepentant Helvétius answers his critics, expanding the theory he had tentatively expounded in *De l'esprit*. He implicitly rejects the theoretical equality he accorded to women. Ideally women would be owned communally and would be taught to favour only those men who had distinguished themselves intellectually, physically or morally. How could this be implemented, one wonders? Helvétius is hazy about details; 'exiger', for example, is suitably vague but leaves plenty of scope for a fertile imagination: 'Supposons . . . un pays où les femmes soient en commun . . . Tout ce que l'on pourroit encore exiger d'elles, c'est qu'elles conçussent tant de vénération pour leur beauté et leurs faveurs, qu'elles crussent n'en devoir faire part qu'aux hommes déjà distingués par leur génie, leur courage ou leur probité. Leurs faveurs par ce moyen deviendroient un encouragement aux talens et aux vertus.'[18] In addition, what would be the lot of those women who, although desirous of implementing the state's policy, found that they were undesirable?

It would, however, be unwise to make too much of Helvétius's fantasies. He was similarly naive about the condition of peasants. He paints a somewhat rosy picture of their marital bliss and harmony, which he attributes to the fact that they are mutually dependent on each other for their livelihood and also so busy that they do not see each other very much! In contrast, the boredom of the rich leads to infidelity.[19] Condorcet, for instance, found his own experience proof enough against Helvétius's theories: 'Il ne me fera pas croire que, si je résous des problèmes, c'est dans l'espérance que les belles dames me rechercheront; car je n'ai pas vu jusqu'ici qu'elles raffolassent des géomètres.'[20] Helvétius's muddled and inconsistent statements on the subject of women should be seen not as a conscious attempt to debase woman herself: they stem rather from his desire to relate all activity to his system of interest and male sexuality. They should not obscure his great merit, which lies in the fact that like true feminists he makes no *a priori* assumptions about women. This is particularly refreshing in view of the very different conclusions his contemporaries Diderot and D'Holbach infer from a sensationalist framework.

Diderot for his part was quick to recognize the additional subjection of women inherent in Helvétius's schemes: 'Quelque avantage qu'on imagine à priver les femmes de la propriété de leurs corps, pour en faire un effet public, c'est une espèce de tyrannie dont l'idée me révolte, une manière raffinée d'accroître leur servitude qui n'est déjà que trop grande.'[21] On a different occasion, when expressing ideas very similar to those of Helvétius, Diderot was careful to introduce the element of choice: 'dites un mot, et promettez un baiser, élevez moi comme un jeune spartiate; conduisez moi au temple de l'honneur par le chemin du plaisir, et je crois que j'arriverai. Ah! si les hommes me ressembloient et que les femmes voulussent, on n'auroit pas besoin d'une autre institution publique.'[22]

Yet Diderot himself introduces a form of subjection not found in Helvétius's work when he rehearses the age-old theme of feminality. He bases this not on divine ordinance but on female anatomy and physiology, from which he derives psychological differences between the sexes. Women are victims of 'leur organisation délicate' and hence incapable of the sustained effort and concentration required in the making of a genius. They are unfulfilled sexually because of their inferior organs: 'Organisées tout au contraire de nous, le mobile qui sollicite en elles la volupté est si délicat, et la source en est si éloignée, qu'il n'est pas extraordinaire qu'elle ne vienne point ou qu'elle s'égare.'[23] Furthermore they are prone to hysteria and other excesses which, it would appear, are female characteristics rather than by-products of repression or education: 'C'est de l'organe propre à son sexe que partent toutes ses idées extraordinaires'.[24] While criticizing contemporary institutions and practices which govern women, Diderot is careful to point out their natural disabilities, including the fact that specifically female organs such as the uterus and breasts are prone to incurable diseases; the cruelty of society is merely a continuation of the cruelty of nature.[25] The predominant impression which Diderot conveys in *Sur les femmes* is that women could not be any different. Thus his solution to their dilemma is no solution at all: 'Femmes, que je vous plains! Il n'y avait qu'un dédommagement à vos maux; et si j'avais été législateur, peut-être l'eussiez-vous obtenu. Affranchies de toute servitude, vous auriez été sacrées en quelque endroit que vous eussiez paru.'[26]

D'Holbach adopts a more practical stance. In the *Ethocratie* he complains about the education girls receive in convents—a familiar theme of the age. They learn nothing useful, that is to say their education is not functional since it does not equip them for their future role as mothers and citizens. It would be beneficial for women themselves and society at large if improvements were made in their education.[27] Since women are constitutionally unsuited to abstract thought, sensibility and sentiment must form the basis of their moral education: 'Les femmes, par la foiblesse de leurs organes, ne sont pas susceptibles des connoissances abstraites, des études profondes et suivies qui conviennent aux hommes; mais la sensibilité de leurs ames, la vivacité de leur esprit, la mobilité de leur imagination, les rend très susceptibles d'adopter avec chaleur les sentiments du cœur.'[28]

Elsewhere in the *Ethocratie*, D'Holbach places the responsibility for women's irrationality on their education rather than on physiology and psychology: 'On remarque que pour l'ordinaire les femmes sentent très-vivement, mais raisonnent fort peu. Ce défaut en elles vient de ce que l'éducation ne les habitue point à réfléchir, ne donne pas des idées de justice propres à modérer les fantaisies, les saillies subites de leur imagination, leurs caprices inconstants.'[29] But feelings on their own in fact do not provide an adequate foundation for morals; they must be kept in check by reason and justice, which are both surely male preserves. Although D'Holbach does not insist on male superiority, his system does imply a hierarchy. Supremacy in the realm of feeling is thus, as always, a poor substitute for equality; and it is ultimately of no more use to women than pie in the sky is to the poor. D'Holbach, like Diderot, laments woman's inferior status; yet he nevertheless basically accepts it, subject to suitable modifications to the conditions governing her lot.

Condorcet recognized the difficulty besetting the discussion of women and the amount of convention and prejudice surrounding the subject. He expresses his diffidence about the reception his views on the equality of the sexes will have from women themselves. After all, they worship Rousseau in spite of what he had said about them: 'J'ai peur de me brouiller avec elles, si jamais elles lisent cet article. Je parle de leurs droits à l'égalité, et non de leur empire; on peut me soupçonner d'une envie secrète de le diminuer; et depuis que Rousseau a mérité leurs suffrages, en disant qu'elles n'étaient faites que pour nous soigner et propres qu'à nous tourmenter, je ne dois pas espérer qu'elles se déclarent en ma faveur. Mais il est bon de dire la vérité, dût-on s'exposer au ridicule.'[30] This aside highlights a problem that neither Condorcet nor, for that matter, Mary Wollstonecraft resolve: What if women prefer to exercise their charms rather than compete with men on equal terms?

Condorcet shares with Helvétius a belief in the potential equality of the sexes, but unlike Helvétius he is actually prepared to take this into account in his writings. In the opening paragraphs of the *Esquisse d'un tableau historique des progrès de l'esprit humain*, Condorcet expounds his sensationalist theory which he derives from Condillac and Locke. Epistemology as such is not his main concern. Nevertheless these basic principles of sensationalism provide the cornerstone of his egalitarian society, which includes women. Woman's political rights, her right to education and equality before the law have the same basis as man's. Able to receive sense impressions, she is potentially rational and can acquire moral ideas: 'les droits des hommes résultent uniquement de ce qu'ils sont des êtres sensibles, susceptibles d'acquérir des idées morales, et de raisonner sur ces idées. Ainsi les femmes ayant ces mêmes qualités, ont nécessairement des droits égaux.'[31] Men's rights are derived 'non de leur sexe, mais de leur qualité d'êtres raisonnables et sensibles, qui leur est commune avec les femmes.[32] Condorcet emphasizes the similarities rather than the differences between the sexes and therefore their equal rights to education: 'On propose une éducation commune aux hommes et aux femmes, parce qu'on ne voit pas de raison pour la rendre différente; on ne voit point par quel motif l'un des deux sexes se réserverait exclusivement certaines connaissances; on ne voit pas pourquoi celles qui sont utiles généralement à tout être sensible et capable de raisonnement, ne seraient pas également enseignées à tous'.[33] Condorcet resolutely refuses to perpetuate the myth of woman's exclusion from political rights on the grounds of her irrationality and reliance on sentiment, which he sees as a circular argument: 'Eloignées des affaires, de tout ce qui se décide d'après la justice rigoureuse, d'après des lois positives, les choses dont elles s'occupent, sur lesquelles elles agissent, sont précisément celles qui se règlent par l'honnêteté naturelle et par le sentiment. Il est donc injuste d'alléguer, pour continuer de refuser aux femmes la jouissance de leurs droits naturels, des motifs qui n'ont une sorte de réalité que parce qu'elles ne jouissent pas de ces droits.'[34] He likewise finds menstruation and pregnancy insufficient justification for her exclusion, attributing to these no more importance than the fluctuations in health people in general suffer.[35] The case against women is by no means proven and Condorcet demands more substantial evidence: 'qu'on daigne réfuter ces raisons autrement que par des plaisanteries et des déclamations; que surtout on me montre entre les hommes et les femmes une différence naturelle, qui puisse légitimement fonder l'exclusion du droit.'[36]

Condorcet believes in the intrinsic value of equality. Primitive man acted against his own interest and the general interest when, with the division of labour, he assumed that his role as defender and hunter entitled him to moral ascendancy. Unlike Rousseau, Condorcet laments the passing of equality; he dwells on this in the *Fragment de l'histoire de la Ire époque*: 'L'homme et la femme commencent à se partager les travaux. Les dangers auxquels expose le soin de la défense commune, les occupations qui exigent une plus grande intensité de force, furent réservés à l'un. L'autre fut chargée des travaux qui ne demandaient que du temps, de la peine, de la patience. Dès lors l'homme a pu abuser à la fois et de la supériorité physique, et de l'avantage de pouvoir seul rendre à sa famille les soins les plus importants et les plus périlleux. Des préférences, une autorité plus grande, lui parurent conformes à la raison même. Le sentiment de la justice, tel qu'il pouvait l'éprouver, s'unit à l'intérêt personnel pour l'écarter de la douce égalité, aux dépens de la félicité commune, et surtout de son propre bonheur.'[37] An integral factor of the progress Condorcet envisaged would be the re-establishment of the natural order of equality between the sexes, which he saw as the true foundation of happiness and morality. Inequality is detrimental even to those whom it purports to favour: 'Parmi les progrès de l'esprit humain les plus importants pour le bonheur général, nous devons compter l'entière destruction des préjugés, qui ont établi entre les deux sexes une inégalité de droits funeste à celui même qu'elle favorise. On chercherait en vain des motifs de la justifier par les différences de leur organisation physique, par celle qu'on voudrait trouver dans la force de leur intelligence, dans leur sensibilité morale. Cette inégalité n'a eu d'autre origine que l'abus de la force, et c'est vainement qu'on a essayé depuis de l'excuser par des sophismes.'[38]

Every age, it seems, clothes perennial myths in contemporary phraseology. Diderot and D'Holbach were no exception when they sought to establish woman's particular place in sensationalist epistemology. Helvétius and Condorcet each in his own way drew strictly egalitarian conclusions from very similar premises. As is well known, supposed equality in the case of Rousseau does not include the other half of the population, namely women. Condorcet recognized the thorny nature of the subject when embarking on the question of woman's rights: 'il est difficile même à un philosophe de ne pas s'oublier un peu lorsqu'il parle des femmes'.[39] That he avoided many of the pitfalls is no mean achievement.

3

The Riddle of Roxane

SHEILA MASON

Much critical discussion of Montesquieu's attitude to women is undermined by the inadequacy of its supporting framework of textual and historical reference. Montesquieu, the misogynist, steps boldly from the non-fictional works along the traditional path of Puritan denigration initially cleared by Pastor Jacob Vernet in his Index to *De l'esprit des lois*;[1] Montesquieu, the feminist, largely a by-product of intensive thematic and structural analysis of his fiction, shines forth from the *Lettres persanes*. Montesquieu, the creative thinker, remains inscrutable, most consistent it appears in his objective stance as political sociologist, his legacy in this respect brilliantly acknowledged by Diderot's imagery in *Sur les femmes*: 'suspendez-les sous mes yeux, comme autant de thermomètres des moindres vicissitudes des mœurs et des usages.'[2]

Thematic investigation has recently culminated in Michel Delon's fertile article, 'Un monde d'eunuques',[3] where the unity of the *Lettres persanes* is shown to reside in a sustained antithesis of power and impotence. The presence and activity of the eunuchs is juxtaposed to 'un discours bougeois' implicit in the topics constituting the political and economic commentary on Western Europe, through which Montesquieu rehabilitates pleasure and profit and exhibits the commerce of fulfilled sexuality as a source of demographic, economic and cultural progress. This thematic polarity is epitomized in that of the central couple, Usbek-Roxane, in which Roxane exercises the more galvanic power, since she alone in the work transforms criticism into action.

Delon's thesis would seem by its synoptic coherence to set the seal on the *Lettres persanes* as a feminist work. Radical feminism acts as a catalyst for the political message of the book, accepted in its totality as combining historical testimony, scientific doctrine and anti-despotic propaganda. Roxane's heroic suicide assumes literal as well as symbolic force. Yet, aesthetic and ideological cogency notwithstanding, such an interpretation confronts us with the double necessity of pausing to assess the bias introduced into our evaluation of Montesquieu's opinions by our own historical standpoint, and of producing a study comprehensive in its use of materials, so that his doctrine on women, whatever its features, may be seen to fit into the broader pattern of his social and political thought.[4] By presenting the *Lettres persanes* in a perspective originating in our own view of the socio-economic role of women, Delon begs the key question of Montesquieu's precise philosophical relationship to the phenomenon of bourgeois capitalism with the moral dynamic C. B. Macpherson has so aptly baptized possessive individualism.[5] Moreover, he overlooks the substantial evocation in the *Lettres persanes* of the frivolous social life of aristocratic womanhood and her all-powerful, subterranean and entirely capricious political influence, upon which certain critics have placed, not illogically, a hostile construction, since it most obviously complements important details of the analyses of monarchic and despotic government in the *Lois* (e.g. *Lp.* LII, XCIX, CVII, CX; cf. *L.* VII, 9; XIX, 12).[6] The scope of the desired study would far exceed the limits of a short essay; all that can be attempted here is an account of certain critical and historical insights which might attenuate the apparent inconsistency and discontinuity of Montesquieu's thought.

Contradiction in his attitude to women, taking a broad view of his works, can be reduced to the opposition between the assertion in Letter XXXVIII of the equality of the sexes in natural law and the seeming indifference, even contempt for the claims of their essential dignity as human beings manifest in his treatment of their civil and domestic condition in the *Lois*. Letter XXXVIII, which Montesquieu ends, one should notice, on a deliberately inconclusive note,[7] puts the argument for regarding male ascendancy as a tyranny, founded and perpetuated by superior physical strength alone, a tyranny irregular in its incidence moreover, in both historical and geographical terms, and universally counterbalanced by the unvarying power of feminine beauty. Where intelligence is at issue, there is potential equality, inhibited in women only by discrimination in educational opportunity. At the end of the *Lettres persanes*, Roxane in Letter CLXI, seems to vindicate the claims of natural equality by overthrowing the régime of the harem, having first exercised in secret her right as an intelligent, sentient being to give herself freely to a lover of her own choosing: 'J'ai pu vivre dans la servitude, mais j'ai toujours été libre: j'ai réformé tes lois sur celles de la Nature, et mon esprit s'est toujours tenu dans l'indépendance' (Gar. 334). Her subsequent words make it clear that in her mind virtue and enforced subjection are utterly incompatible.

Turning to the *Lois*, if one combines VII, 9 on the condition of women under various régimes, with XIX, 5 where Montesquieu sets forth the maxim: 'c'est au législateur à suivre l'esprit de la nation, lorsqu'il n'est pas contraire aux principes du gouvernement', it emerges clearly that women are in fact, if not in nature, double prisoners: of *les mœurs* and of the political order. Where the concordance of these two factors permits, i.e. in the monarchy, women's behaviour is regulated by the prevailing 'esprit de liberté'; that is to say, they participate freely in a characteristically competitive society, indulging the vanity which is their dominant trait, and thereby promoting luxury and a healthy economy. In the despotism and the republic, socio-political factors dictate, it appears, the subjection of women. In the first, they are mere objects of luxury, though Montesquieu hastens to express his disapproval, 'dans ces États les princes se jouent de la nature humaine'; in republics, women, free in law, are constrained even more effectively by the austere moral climate which stifles corrupt tendencies and inhibits luxury. We are confronted then, it seems, with a modified account of the nature of women and a conception of their 'freedom' emptied, or nearly so, of the moral and political content deriving from an abstract consideration of individual capacity and dignity.

Two points must be made immediately regarding the evaluation of these materials. First, it is easy to overlook the purely domestic framework within which Roxane acts: on the evidence of the text, her revolt has moral and social implications only, and the latter are limited. This is confirmed by reference back to the *Histoire d'Ibrahim et d'Anaïs* (*Lp.* CXLI), where, even though the supernatural usurper of the jealous Ibrahim's place styles himself a citizen, he liberates the household only to the extent of dismissing the eunuchs and instituting free social intercourse for his wives. Roxane's monitory act acquires a political dimension only in relation to the tragic momentum of events in Regency France. Similarly, the declaration of female equality in Letter XXXVIII entails no demand for the reform of women's legal or political status, and, indeed, is incorporated into a narrow discussion of the merits of monogamy where the European voice assumes for women exactly the sort of freedom that Montesquieu later allows his fashion-conscious *vaniteuses* in the monarchy. Secondly, taking up the pejorative stereotype of female character deployed in the *Lois*, it in no way contradicts the social and economic role French women are presented as playing in the *Lettres persanes*.[8]

Like his precursor, Poulain de la Barre, Montesquieu may denounce male domination as a usurpation, he may deplore the poverty of women's education as Fénelon and Fleury had done,[9] but there is no evidence, even allowing for the predominantly descriptive register of the *Lois*, that he ever envisaged any radical transformation of the domestic role allotted them in contemporary society, still less the extension to them of political rights. Indeed, he would have been far in advance of his time had he pursued the logic of the equality of persons to the extent of including women in the active processes of democracy, an expectation by which Rosso at least is prepared to gauge his attitude.[10] The republic of the *Lois* he regarded in any case as an archaic phenomenon, primarily of historical and scientific interest. Beyond this, it should not be overlooked that manhood suffrage, even on the limited scale existing in England, was a mere dream in France.[11] The structure and machinery founding and regulating the freedom of the *monarchy* as Montesquieu establishes it in the *Lois* derive nothing from representative governments other than the feudal model in which *class* interest was paramount; and this must be taken to reflect the situation in which he was writing and also, to a degree, his political projections.

Montesquieu's inability to conceive of women as political creatures is unsurprising. The English Levellers of the seventeenth century, arguably the most seminally radical democratic theorists prior to the Revolutionary epoch, while inferring from the natural equality of the sexes an equal consent to government and an equal interest in civil liberties, excluded women, like servants, from political rights, assuming that these were tacitly included in those of husbands and masters.[12] Montesquieu's own contemporary, Morelly, remote in spirit from English individualism but acclaimed as the utopian precursor of Babeuf and mentor of the early communists, in isolating the family as the original and elementary unit of society, reinvigorates patriarchalist conceptions and entrenches paternal authority as the archetype and correlative of political power.[13] Women pass unmentioned in the *Code de la nature* outside the section devoted to 'Lois conjugales', an omission moderated perhaps by Morelly's initial redefinition of freedom as interdependence within the organism of society. Indeed, in relation to the ambiguous freedom which Montesquieu concedes to women in the *Lois*, it is worth recalling his conception of political liberty in turn. Like Morelly, Montesquieu isolates it rigorously in *Lois* XI from any notion of individual right or claim. It is specific to moderate governments, which are distinguished above all by the possession of a particular institutional structure. Viewed from the angle of the citizen, Montesquieu attributes two aspects to it: as a condition it consists in the sense of security afforded by the protection of the constitution; as an active process it involves, in a manner which anticipates Rousseau, the voluntary internalization of the law: 'la liberté ne peut consister qu'à pouvoir faire ce que l'on doit vouloir' (ch. 3). This aspect of the phenomenon, profoundly philosophical despite Montesquieu's disclaimers, and austerely reminiscent of the evocation through Books II to VIII of the moral climate of the republic, would perhaps place it as a political discipline beyond the aspirations of the mass of women as Montesquieu is wont to present them; nevertheless, the terms of his definition so far, while not positively including, do not exclude women from the enjoyment and pursuit of political liberty. For it is elsewhere, and largely by inference, that the link between liberty and participation in legislative activity, for particular reasons an exclusively male prerogative, is established. The 'freedom' associated with women in monarchies, not discounting the constitutional variety, is clearly generically different, a matter of social climate, as Montesquieu's comment on English women reveals: 'Dans une nation où tout homme, à sa manière, prendroit part à l'administration de l'État, les femmes ne devroient guère vivre avec les hommes. Elles seroient donc modestes, c'est-à-dire timides: cette timidité feroit leur vertu; tandis que les hommes, sans galanterie, se jetteroient dans une débauche qui leur laisseroit toute leur liberté et leur loisir' (*L.* XIX, 27; Pl. II, 582). It also emerges from the definitions of XI, 3, that political liberty is not primarily for Montesquieu a function of personal equality.

Now it is impossible to ignore the allusions scattered through the whole corpus of Montesquieu's work to the incapacities of women, incapacities which can be and have been taken as the clinical documentation of their physiological inequality and the justification of the 'dépendance' which surfaces every now and then in the text of the *Lois* as their natural civil condition.[14] Physical and moral factors in combination incline women to marriage, which is their only social destiny and the only institution capable of emancipating them morally and spiritually. Thus, Book XXIII, chapter 9: 'Les filles, que l'on ne conduit que par le mariage aux plaisirs et à la liberté, qui ont un esprit qui n'ose penser, un cœur qui n'ose sentir, des yeux qui n'osent voir, des oreilles qui n'osent entendre, qui ne se présentent que pour se montrer stupides; condamnées sans relâche à des bagatelles et à des préceptes, sont assez portées au mariage: ce sont les garçons qu'il faut encourager' (Pl. II, 688). In the preceding chapters Montesquieu vindicates the paternal regulation of marriages, and his approval of the exception to the rule, England, where women frequently evade this authority in order to marry as they are able, on the grounds that their religion denies them recourse to the convent, makes his undeviating assumptions regarding their social role abundantly clear. Paternal authority is and should be perpetuated in the marital power of the husband, just as it was in Roman law and continued to be in the southern provinces of France: 'Il est contre la raison et contre la nature que les femmes soient maîtresses dans la maison . . . l'état de foiblesse où elles sont ne leur permet pas la prééminence' (*L.* VII, 17; Pl. II, 348). Adultery is a punishable offence only in women because it signals their rejection of natural dependence: '. . . la femme, en violant les lois du mariage, sort de l'état de sa dépendance naturelle' (*L.* XXVI, 8; Pl. II, 759). The husband's administration of joint wealth in marriage is justified, since women have natural incentives to marry: 'Comme les femmes, par leur état, sont assez portées au mariage, les gains que la loi leur donne sur les biens de leur mari sont inutiles' (*L.* VII, 15; Pl. II, 347). One could not hope for a more thoroughgoing endorsement of the *status quo* at least in its legal aspect.[15]

However, if it emerges that matrimony is in Montesquieu's estimation the natural, limited and lowly estate of woman, it is no less evident, again from the *Lois*, that it largely produces and conditions the rights and duties of man, even in a political context. It is also clear that side by side with the legal dependence which Montesquieu allots women in marriage, he reserves for them a personal equality grounded in the reciprocity of mutual affection which could be envisaged as the continuation of their original natural state. Certainly, taking a broad view of his social theory, neither sex is allocated rights or functions on the merits of gender alone; while, on the other hand, a substantial amount of material suggests that for Montesquieu, no less than for Morelly, and no less than in ancient legal systems, Roman law having particular relevance in Montesquieu's case, the individual enjoys rights by virtue of his membership of a family and in extension of this through his access to a given patrimony.

This is especially significant in the case of citizenship. Book XI, chapter 6, projects a view of citizenship as participation in legislative activity and prescribes manhood suffrage; but on returning to the earlier examination in V, 5 of the legal foundation of equality in the republic, one finds set out the basic equation of citizenship with the proprietorship of an equal share of land, the importance of maintaining intact this simple and static patrimony being stressed in the surrounding discussion of ancient laws relating to marriage and inheritance. Book XXIII on population, introduces the further notion in chapter 4 of the family as a sort of property with ideas of continuity and stability attaching to it, and relates the drive to procreate to this particular quality. Now it is against the background of such remarks, indicative by their random but complementary nature of fundamental assumptions on Montesquieu's part, that his treatment of masculine and particularly paternal prerogatives must be judged. For they imply that the crucial qualification in matters of public as of private right was proprietorship rather than sex. And, as if to bear this out, Montesquieu indicates in his chapter on the family that he sees no inconvenience in matrilineal succession, the drive to perpetuate the line remaining constant whichever sex prevails. Further evidence of the key role of the family as a source of social cohesion and by extension as a determinant of status and right, a function in fact adumbrated in the *Traité des devoirs* (*P.*, Bkn. 616 (MS 1267)) is to be found in the very treatment in the *Lois* of domestic slavery. Thus, the divisive effect of polygamy is counteracted by enclosure, but enclosure creating an artificial family: 'De là dérive pour les femmes toute la pratique de la morale: la pudeur, la chasteté, la retenue, le silence, la paix, la dépendance, le respect, l'amour, enfin une direction générale de sentiments à la chose du monde la meilleure par sa nature, qui est l'attachement unique à sa famille' (XVI, 10; Pl. II, 515).

It is to this family that eunuchs in the nature of things also belong. Out of it, being deprived of issue, they have no status and hence: 'ce n'est que par une espèce de fiction qu'on peut les regarder comme citoyens' (XV, 19; Pl. II, 507). The link between proprietorship of a family and authority is most explicitly confirmed when Montesquieu examines the arranged marriage of the Western hemisphere: 'Le consentement des pères est fondé sur leur puissance, c'est-à-dire sur leur droit de propriété' (XXIII, 7; Pl. II, 687).

This assimilation of family with property must be of considerable importance in plotting Montesquieu's relationship to the Patriarchalists proper on the one hand, and to Locke on the other. But the analogy drawn by Patriarchalism between paternal and monarchic power is, we know, rejected in *Lois* I, 3, which for our purposes at least implies the absence of any strict adherence to male-dominated archetypes. The norms in law and custom are fixed rather by the family group seen as the natural origin of society; and, in spite of ascribing unvarying importance from *Lettres persanes* CXXIX onwards to the moral force of paternal authority, it seems that at one stage Montesquieu viewed the location of such authority as an historical accident. He certainly accepts for most analytical and theoretical purposes the patrilineal family of common experience, but close inspection of his treatment of matrimonial and family law reveals that it is the conservation of the group rather than the sanctification of male ascendancy that preoccupies him. Dealing with incest in both the *Pensées* and the *Lois*, he discovers the reason for its universal prohibition in the insoluble conflict between the intimate equality promoted by the conjugal bond and the submission and respect inhabiting family relationships. For the good of society the respect due to the *paterfamilias* must prevail (Bkn. 1928, 1931 (MS 205, 377) and *L.* XXVI, 14). In the matter of divorce his priorities remain constant, while the precedence of the sexes is strikingly reversed. His promotion of the facility proceeds paradoxically from the conviction that nothing should inhibit marriage seen as the universal estate of adults (*L.* XXVI, 9). Repudiation, which after the fashion of his ancient models Montesquieu retains, should be a prerogative of womankind, above all of the polygamous wife whose only recourse it is against an uncongenial and unproductive union. So anxious is he to advance the cause of women here that he goes out of his way to invent an origin for their right in the ancient Roman law of the Twelve Tables (*L.* XVI, 15, 16).[16]

Identical principles inform the wider treatment of demography where the laws of succession and inheritance come into play. The bias of his doctrine can be described as anti-feminist only to the extent that he recognizes the overwhelming need when pleasure can be freely bought for financial inducements and penal sanctions to encourage men rather than women to marry. His ardently pro-populationist objectives, inspired by the Augustan laws *Julia* and *Papia Poppaea* which adjusted civil status and economic privilege to family size, are most menacingly expressed in an early entry in the *Pensées* comprising a comprehensive plan of legal reform.[17] Here, with radical insensitivity, he overrides all considerations of sexual prestige and even of class in the cause of population growth: the unmarried are allowed their subsistence but virtually excluded from civil and public life; indeed, so constricted is the individual's lot that the procreative totalitarianism of Diderot's Tahiti seems abroad already.

Not surprisingly, the axiom, 'Toute la république sera distribuée en familles', embodies the political nub of the scheme, and, by logical progression, his demonstration in the *Lois* of the supreme influence of political factors in social history reveals an intense concentration on the laws of succession (XXVII, on the Roman laws of inheritance). Here above all the desire to prove a constant relationship between the distribution of patrimony and the political constitution is balanced by repeated protestations of the true impartiality of the legislation in question. In XXVI, 6, Montesquieu enunciates the general principle that the frequent exclusion of females from succession is authorized not by natural law, but by civil and political law, subsequently capping this in his discussion of the Roman Republic's most glaringly anti-feminist statute, the *lex Voconia*, with an eloquent and utterly sincere lament on the necessary sacrifice of human values to *raison d'état* (XXVII; Pl. II 786). The striking quality of these ingredients is their gratuitousness, for there would have been no inconsistency and no discredit in supporting the idea of the paramountcy of political interest with a full endorsement of male ascendancy. In fact, the details of the text betray a sustained attempt to disguise the real patriarchal nature of ancient systems of law, with their denial of juridical validity to any relationship other than that between males; an attempt difficult to construe as anything but deliberate in view of Montesquieu's expertise in the field.[18] And whether symptomatic of a bad conscience or of private sympathy, the same process operates on home ground in relation to the Salic Law, once again explicitly dissociated from premeditated repression of women (*L.* XVIII, 22).

But how and when did history consecrate values that nature ignores, for the letter as opposed to the spirit of the laws cannot be neutralized? To a degree, as everywhere else in his work, the scientist in Montesquieu must repudiate the polarized categories invoked by the question, but he did answer it and significantly at much the same time as he was concocting his blueprint for legal reform. Fragments in the *Pensées* of the lost *Histoire de la jalousie*[19] not only indicate extensive research into the anthropological and sociological aspects of sexual relations, but also represent his general theory of causation in an important phase of its gestation. They offer a relativistic but not inauthentic vision, going back to the beginnings of history, of the pattern of marital customs. With the machinery of social transformation geared to large-scale political developments, it can be established that prehistory, dominated by the Egyptians and the Scythians, was characterized by matriarchal structures; if, Montesquieu continues, either race had established world dominion, then female ascendancy would be the norm. But though manners are presented as being essentially malleable, he seems to posit at the same time an archetypal pair-bond, most fundamentally natural and constituted by mutual affection. He speculates that the ancient Massageta, while regarding it as his social duty to offer his wife to guests, never for a moment anticipated thereby destroying the love binding her to him. Here perhaps is the key to the ambiguity of Montesquieu's attitude. The reciprocity of mutual affection establishes for the moralist enamoured of pure justice the measure of a natural right, sometimes celebrated in custom, sometimes contradicted by it; but, disconcertingly, customs too, as the historian must concede, may acquire the force and universality of nature.[20]

So it is that while reflecting on incest, Montesquieu could happily postulate the co-existence of heavily authoritarian patriarchalism and perfect equality in marriage: 'On ne trouve pas que, dans les premiers temps, les hommes exerçassent sur leurs femmes le même empire que sur leurs enfants. Au contraire, les premières alliances nous donnent l'idée d'une parfaite égalité et d'une union aussi douce que naturelle' (P., Bkn. 1928 (MS 205); Pl. I, 1464). It is presumably this natural law which Roxane invokes at the moment of her triumph, drawing the threads of fiction and myth in the work tightly together. One is reminded of Aphéridon's rebuke to his sister Astarté, who epitomizes even more absolutely than Roxane the beauty and virtue of woman now shrouded and shackled by Mohammedan law: 'Votre mère, qui était si chaste, ne donnait à son mari, pour garant de sa vertu, que sa vertu même. Ils vivaient heureux l'un et l'autre, dans une confiance mutuelle, et la simplicité de leurs mœurs était pour eux une richesse plus précieuse mille fois que le faux éclat dont vous semblez jouir dans cette maison somptueuse. En perdant votre religion, vous avez perdu votre liberté, votre bonheur et cette précieuse égalité qui fait l'honneur de votre sexe' (Lp. LXVII, Gar. 142).

The treatment of women in the Lois and the Pensées, rather than contradicting, thus illuminates the meaning of heroic action in the Lettres persanes and defines its scope, limited in practical terms though egalitarian in spirit. This, indeed, is the interpretation that circumstantial evidence recommends. Montesquieu was possibly influenced by Poulain, the radical Cartesian, but if so, it was among the company that frequented Madame de Lambert's salon, and conscientiously as it treated the question of women, one may enquire, with due respect to the verdict of other critics, how radical its commitment was.[21] Claude Buffier fully rehearses the case for the equality of the female intellect in his *Examen des préjugés vulgaires*, but his application of it, in no wise ironical, is that women may find time to acquire 'des connaissances honnêtes' after they have fulfilled the duties of their station, 'le gouvernement du dedans et du détail d'une famille'.[22] Madame de Lambert herself is equally cautious. Both in the *Avis d'une mère à sa fille* (1698) and in the work which Montesquieu actually possessed, the *Réflexions nouvelles sur les femmes* (1730),[23] she argues for a moral regeneration based on the cultivation of 'pudeur', which she, like the President after her, isolates as the archetypal characteristic of feminine nature and as the supreme object of woman's spiritual discipline. At the level of social experience she pleads for intellectual liberation, while condemning the licentiousness, the mindless frivolity of contemporary life.[24] No doubt, she would have heartily endorsed Montesquieu's lamentation in a fragment of the *Devoirs* on women's neglect of their traditional role, particularly its educational aspect, on the contagion of their infidelity and on the unhappy isolation of the virtuous exception (*P.*, Bkn. 621 (MS 1272); Pl. I, 1147). Sensitivity and intelligence were as unlikely to confuse the libertine values of the Regency with true freedom in social as in political life.

The riddle of Roxane is still not quite solved. The compound of lapidary utterance and terminological ambiguity which characterizes the President's style will perhaps in any case preclude a definitive interpretation of his attitude to women. Yet to do full justice to the philosophical stance so far established, one can and should widen the discussion to include a study of her literary counterparts and antecedents. Within Montesquieu's own fiction, Roxane represents a distinctive type of heroine: the woman who combines tenderness and passion with courage and resource; and this type harks back to the *femme forte* of the imaginative literature of the mid-seventeenth century, to a figurehead of the age of the *Frondes*.[25] The possibility thus arises that Montesquieu's choice of literary model carried a subversive charge, even though, in herself, the *femme forte* had not been conceived as a direct challenge to the place of women in the existing legal and political order.[26]

If so, the ideological reverberations attending the renewal of this particular literary tradition—libertarian precisely because of their conservative tonality, their evocation of a pre-absolutist value-system—could be seen to harmonize in their political and historical register with the assumptions underlying the doctrine of right which has been brought to light by the investigation of Montesquieu's theoretical treatment of the status and nature of women. In ways which are far from the obvious, woman is the touchstone of Montesquieu's liberalism, and reveals in it archaic dimensions at odds with the narrowly individualistic premisses of its typical Lockian form.

Politically, the combination of egalitarian principle and reaction against the spurious freedoms of women under the existing régime coincides with a view of Montesquieu as a champion of conservative reform inspired by the model of feudal monarchy. In a sociological context, his conservative posture may be taken to denote scientific intelligence rather than acquiescence in patterns of repression. It is here however, that close scrutiny of detail begins to undermine first impressions of calm objectivity, revealing strands of bias and personal sensitivity. Here one must balance the detachment shading into cynicism, which enabled him, citing the impact of Verginia and Lucretia on the Roman *plebs*, to detect the role of women as vehicles and catalysts of mass feeling, and elsewhere to dismiss their chastity as 'une petite vanité sotte', against his no less sociologically acute, but compassionately ironical dissection of the sexual prejudice which transformed old women into witches.[27] One must contrast his vindication of paternal authority with his championing of a woman's right to privacy and the charge of her own body over the topical issue of public disclosure of pregnancy.[28] Finally, one must set the restricted range of his female characters beside the force of imagination, manifest in his insight into the psycho-sexual roots of behaviour, by which he has some claim to anticipate modern psychology. Speaking politically, Montesquieu habitually equated beauty with power; but this tribute to women's real personal influence was as far from connoting endorsement of the ideology of romantic love with its denial of female sexuality, as it was from complete rejection of the patriarchal family in favour of the tight conjugal unit. Nowhere in his fiction does Montesquieu deny or deride women's sexual appetite. He also appreciated the exorbitant social and psychological cost at which power was bought: 'Une femme est obligée de plaire comme si elle s'était faite elle-même' (*P.*, Bkn. 1247 (MS 1624); Pl. I, 1309). Beyond this, he was capable as one might expect from the *Histoire véritable*, his tale of metempsychosis, of transforming, if only in jest, his own sexual identity: 'Les Grecs disoient: "Il n'est beau de vieillir qu'à Sparte." Moi, je disois: "Il n'est beau de vieillir qu'à Vienne." Les femmes de soixante ans y avoient des amants; les laides y avoient des amants. Enfin, on meurt à Vienne; mais on n'y vieillit jamais' (*P.*, Bkn. 50 (MS 2163); Pl. I, 985). Even in this remote and most cerebral of writers, one glimpses the imponderable burden of Flaubert's famous confession.

4

Women in Marivaux: Journalist to Dramatist

H. T. MASON

'Aucun auteur n'a cru plus fermement à l'éternel féminin', says a recent author, with justice, of Marivaux.[1] Many a critic has laboured to define the 'féminin marivaudien' with all its equivocations; the task is endless. In the plays and novels, we can never be sure how far his self-avowed 'misanthropie' established in his adolescent years[2] is held at bay by benevolence and sympathy. The Journals offer a rather better basis for confidence (though here too we must beware of taking the narrator as simply Marivaux's mouthpiece) because of their more direct approach. It may be useful to consider some of the aspects of the feminine condition upon which the essayist lays emphasis, proceeding thereafter to see how those attitudes are exemplified in his drama.

With the appearance of his *Lettres sur les habitants de Paris* in the pages of the *Mercure* (1717–18), Marivaux may be said to come of age as a prose writer, the sharpness of his observation as he describes the Parisian scene giving promise of what is to come. In this loosely-linked, almost random, series of topics he characteristically devotes an important section to women. There is an amusing vignette of the clever saleswoman overwhelming the raw provincial customer so completely by her courteous attentions that he cannot escape without buying something (p. 16). Marivaux dwells on the moral dangers to which such a woman is exposed, constantly living in the public gaze and acquiring from her environment a boldness which is transmitted from eyes to speech and eventually to actions.

If coquetry were to disappear, says Marivaux, it would be rediscovered amongst women shopkeepers. For the dominant passion of *bourgeoises* is vanity, which is seen in their love of pleasure, finery, good food and in their back-biting. Marivaux has already announced the *leit-motif* of his views on feminine attitudes: *coquetterie*. Equally significant, he does not pursue the theme among bourgeois company but switches to 'femmes de qualité'. For the aristocratic woman is the summit of refinement and therefore of affectation: 'Grâces ridicules aux gens raisonnables . . . inimitables aux bourgeoises . . . peut-être le chef-d'œuvre de l'orgueil' (pp. 26–7). Everything is studiedly artificial: l'habillement, la marche, le geste et le ton' (p. 26)—developed by parental vanity and the examples set by other gracious ladies, and consummated through personal study in this particular domain. Marivaux is struck by the magnificence of the paradox: so much effort and style, all deployed to serve the ends of folly. He sees clearly how fundamental is the play-element to this code of behaviour: 'tout est jeu pour elles; jusqu'à leur réputation' (p. 27). It is a striking observation for the light it throws on a refined class imprisoned by their gratuitousness and irresponsibility (one thinks, for instance, of Mathilde de la Mole in *Le Rouge et le noir*, striving to escape from frivolity into the perils and joys of commitment).

Everything for these women is ritual, courtship above all; and the garment most proudly worn is the slightest, the *négligé*, because it is the equivalent of nakedness, pretending to do without extra charms but pretending falsely. It is 'une abjuration simulée de coquetterie; mais en même temps le chef-d'œuvre de l'envie de plaire' (p. 28). It has the simplicity of modest clothes, but it is itself immodest, the product of the lubricious vanity that invented it. Not that the unchastity is itself deliberate, adds Marivaux, for the motive force is a feeling of complaisance for one's own charms; but the end result is the same. Women dressed in a *négligé* exclaim: 'Laissez-moi . . . je me sauve, je suis faite comme une folle.' But in reality they are thinking the very opposite: 'Regardez-moi, je ne suis point parée comme les femmes doivent l'être . . . tout naît de moi, c'est moi qui donne la forme à mon habit, et non mon habit qui me la donne . . .' (p. 29). The apparent rejection of coquettish aids proves to be the highest form of coquetry; the female form, barely clad and accessible to furtive glances in the boudoir, is at its most erotic. It is the world of Fragonard.

Here then, as Marivaux enters into his true domain, the observation of man in his contemporary reality, and discovers within
himself 'ses dons, ses pouvoirs et ses armes',[3] the basic elements
of his attitude to women are being set down. His fascination with
feminine coquetry will henceforth be constant. The fundamental
marvel of womankind is that it must, out of necessity, set out to
please men. Coquetry is of the essence of being feminine: 'c'est
en un mot le mouvement perpétuel de leur âme, c'est le feu sacré
qui ne s'éteint jamais; de sorte qu'une femme veut toujours plaire,
sans le vouloir par une réflexion expresse. . . . Une femme qui
n'est plus coquette, c'est une femme qui a cessé d'être' (p. 28).
Here Marivaux is manifestly not speaking only of titled ladies.
These latter may represent the crowning glory of feminine charms,
because education and leisure have allowed the opportunity of
perfectibility, but all women possess this motivation, which forms
the ground of their being, as instilled by nature itself. The coquette
is a wearer of masks, instinctively equivocating, and disguising
the dross of reality; she will provide the dramatist with a lifetime's
reservoir of ironic situations.

By the time Marivaux begins editing *Le Spectateur français* a few
years later, these attitudes have been confirmed and augmented.
The *Spectateur* period (1721–4) coincides with the appearance of
some of his most penetrating comedies, including *La Surprise de
l'amour* and *La Double Inconstance*;[4] the dramatist is fully fledged.
Looking at *Le Spectateur*, we find an insistence upon the essen-
tiality of cosmetic devices as an inherent part of the feminine
personality. Marivaux calls upon a beautiful woman and catches
her unprepared. She is indeed wearing a *négligé*, but it is not one
meant for show: 'un négligé des plus négligés, tranchons le mot
. . . un négligé malpropre'. The author goes on to portray most
evocatively the embarrassed actions of the poor woman, and concludes with the shrewd observation: 'une belle femme qui n'a
point encore disposé ses attraits, qui n'a rien de préparé pour
plaire, quand on la surprend alors, on ne peut pas dire que ce soit
véritablement elle' (16e feuille, p. 200). Well might we anticipate
Voltaire's famous paradox of the 1730s on luxury: 'Le superflu,
chose très nécessaire' (*Le Mondain*, v. 22). Marivaux may have
had in mind Dufresny's similar observation in the *Amusemens
sérieux et comiques* (1699): 'telle qui a besoin de toute la matinée

pour perfectionner ses charmes, seroit plus fâchée d'être surprise
à sa toilette, que d'être surprise avec un galant'.[5] But the unsurprising if witty comment by Dufresny has been transformed by
Marivaux into a more universal point: the very selfhood of such
women depends upon external graces.

For, as Marivaux sees it in *Le Spectateur*, women have no choice
but to be *coquettes*. To cite one of the most famous passages in the
essays, given to a female narrator: 'on ne peut être femme sans
être coquette. Il n'y a que dans les romans qu'on en voit d'autres,
mais dans la nature c'est chimère, et les véritables sont toutes
comme j'étais' (p. 209). But there is a darker side to this for
women. They must flirt, but they must also lose. A virtuous
woman resists advances by her lover; 'mais en résistant, elle
entre insensiblement dans un goût d'aventure; elle se complaît
dans les sentiments vertueux qu'elle oppose' (10e feuille, p. 162).
There follows a detailed description of the way in which she con-
nives at her own ineluctable defeat, a passage which, as the editors
of the *Journaux* point out (pp. 595-6, nn. 197, 199), is highly
characteristic of a Marivaux manner that inspired Crébillon fils.
Trivelin puts it with epigrammatic brevity in *Arlequin poli par
l'amour*: 'Femme tentée, et femme vaincue, c'est tout un'.[6] This
sense of fatalism had been implicit in the *Lettres sur les habitants de
Paris*; now Marivaux has given it explicit articulation. There is
scarcely any way of remaining virtuous if one is a young and
attractive woman in society. Marivaux chooses to make the point
with hyperbolic emphasis at the very outset of the second number
of *Le Spectateur*: 'Les austérités des fameux anachorètes de la
Thébaïde, les supplices ingénieux qu'ils inventaient contre eux-
mêmes pour tourmenter la nature; cette mort toujours nouvelle,
toujours douloureuse qu'ils donnaient à leurs sens; tout cela, joint
à l'horreur de leurs déserts, ne composait peut-être pas la valeur
des peines que peut éprouver une femme du monde jeune, aimable,
aimée, et qui veut être vertueuse' (pp. 118-19). For the architect
of a woman's downfall is not simply her seducer; he is aided by
her willingness to believe his false words, she like him has 'le
transport au cerveau' (11e feuille, p. 170). Otherwise, her complaisance is inexplicable, as every rational inclination urges her to
refrain. Women are self-deceived, not just about their beauty (as
for instance the third number of *Le Spectateur* makes clear) but

about all their desires in life. In a striking prefiguration of 'bovarysme' Marivaux has a woman write, as she looks back on her life: 'avec de la passion . . . nous ne voyons plus les objets comme ils sont, ils deviennent ce que nous souhaitons qu'ils soient, ils se moulent sur nos désirs' (19e feuille, p. 219).

Marivaux is also becoming interested in the social circumstances under which women are placed at a disadvantage. In the last two issues of *Le Spectateur* the narrator tells of being left at the age of eighteen a poor orphan with his sister. He can make his way in the world, but she is utterly defenceless, without any honest means of advancement. Only the convent is open to her, and this is where she flees, despite her grief at parting from her brother, after an experience in which her poverty exposes her to moral danger. The incident serves to remind us that social structures work in harmony with a desire to please men and aid in her seduction. To remain chaste, flight is the only answer.

We shall return presently to Marivaux's sociological observations on women in *Le Cabinet du philosophe* (1734). Before that he had published seven numbers of *L'Indigent Philosophe* (1727), where a more provocative, even cynical attitude appears towards life. Women too fall under this mocking gaze. It is fortunate, says the narrator, that nature has made women necessary, for seen from one particular angle 'elles paraîtraient trop risibles pour avoir rien à démêler avec notre coeur, elles cesseraient d'être aimables . . .' (7e feuille, p. 319). Though we should not forget that the 'Indigent Philosophe' is a more colourful personality than the 'Spectateur' and that he himself is one of the characters in the world he is portraying rather than just Marivaux's mouthpiece, it is as well to set passages like the above alongside the more sympathetic views which generally emerge from *Le Spectateur*. Woman for Marivaux is Other in her endlessly fascinating persona.

To this statement a rider must be added which can be clearly exemplified also in *L'Indigent Philosophe*. The narrator's supercilious attitude easily accommodates a story he tells about a young girl married to a very old man. Virtuous and sensible, she was confident of a happy marriage: but 'c'était compter sans son hôte . . .; et cet hôte, c'est le diable, ou nous' (7e feuille, p. 320). The bride's awakening to the truth is melancholy. This tale typifies Marivaux's naturalist materialism about human instincts. But then a still more interesting aspect of Marivaux's thinking emerges. For, having made the point about women, he goes straight on to generalize, not about women but about the whole of human nature: 'C'est que nous sommes des esprits de contradiction: pendant qu'on peut choisir ce qu'on veut, on n'a envie de rien; quand on a fait son choix, on a envie de tout; fût-il bon, on s'en lasse, comment donc faire? Est-on mal, on veut être bien; cela est naturel; mais est-on bien, on veut être mieux; et quand on a ce mieux, est-on content? oh que non! Quel remède à cela? Sauve qui peut (ibid., p. 321). The crucial conclusion is about mankind in general; women serve only as a means to that end.

Woman, then, wears a dual aspect. She has manners and attitudes quite foreign to men, almost enough to make her a race apart. Feminine vanity may be a source of derision; but by her vanity, woman rejoins men: 'Les hommes sont plus vains que méchants; mais je dis mal: ils sont tous méchants, parce qu'ils sont vains' (ibid., p. 323). Women serve Marivaux's purpose admirably, because they are by far the more complex and interesting half of the human race; but their special characteristics are ultimately of interest because they enlighten our understanding of ourselves, whichever our sex.

The *Cabinet du philosophe* retraces much of the same ground, often with new perspectives. Marivaux's fascination with coquettish ways ever finds new objects for its delight, as when he describes a lady removing her gloves, ostensibly to work on embroidery but in reality to show off her pretty hands: 'les femmes, et même les plus sages, ont tant de ces petites industries-là! (8e feuille, p. 403). He returns to the more general question of women's desire to be seduced. In one of the boldest passages in his essays he points out that a suitor who says: 'Je vous aime, madame, vous avez mille charmes à mes yeux' is really saying: 'Madame, je vous désire beaucoup, vous me ferez grand plaisir de m'accorder vos faveurs'. What is more, the lady, far from being deceived by the complaint, fully understands its explicit sexual reference and indeed is delighted by the flattery which it contains, whereas a platonic declaration of love would have been of no interest: 'toute femme entend qu'on la désire, quand on lui dit: Je vous aime; et ne vous sait gré du: *Je vous aime*, qu'à cause qu'il signifie: *Je vous désire* (1ère feuille, p. 337). It is because of passages such as this that Paul Gazagne was right to stress the sensual aspect of love in Marivaux;[7] and though Gazagne goes too far in suggesting that the key to Marivaux's characters is sexual desire,[8] his thesis served a useful contribution in providing a corrective to the view that love in Marivaux was purely cerebral.

So the essayist reiterates his opinion, asserted in *Le Spectateur*, that a lover can hardly fail to win as he presses his suit with a lady, even if 'le tout finit par une banqueroute qui la déshonore' (5e feuille, p. 379). While Marivaux recommends prudence, and suggests that the best way of maintaining a partner's passion is to keep him anxious and uncertain, he is sceptical that reason can dominate the heart to this extent. The cause of such unfortunate human weaknesses lies in natural necessity: 'Si l'amour se menait bien, on n'aurait qu'un amant, ou qu'une maîtresse en dix ans; et il est de l'intérêt de la nature qu'on en ait vingt, et davantage.

'Et voilà, sans doute, pourquoi la nature n'a eu garde de rendre les amants susceptibles de prudence; ils s'aimeraient trop, et cela ne ferait pas son compte' (2e feuille, p. 344). If love is fragile and lovers inconstant, our biological condition provides the *raison d'être*.

As in *Le Spectateur*, we see that social circumstances reinforce the biological in tending to the same end. One of the most compassionate sections in the *Cabinet* deals with the situation of the married woman. If she finds herself with a brutish husband, she has scarcely any choice open to her but patience and resignation unto death.[9] For if she takes a lover, 'Point de quartier pour elle: on l'enferme, on la séquestre, on la réduit à une vie dure et frugale, on la déshonore . . .' (5e feuille, p. 376). Marivaux is not particularly sympathetic to her plight, adding 'et elle la mérite'. But he is exercised by the double standard which prevails concerning conjugal infidelity. A man, far from suffering any punishment, does not even need to conceal his libertinage. Indeed, his *galanterie* makes him a hero: 'on se le montre au spectacle' (ibid., p. 377); one thinks of Prévan at the end of *Les Liaisons dangereuses*.[10]

From this Marivaux moves on to the old theme of coquetry; this time he lays the blame for it squarely upon men. Giving women the right to speak for themselves, he has them assert that they have no other resource than 'le misérable emploi de vous plaire'. Men are their jailers. 'Dans cet état, que nous reste-t-il, que la ruse? . . . Notre coquetterie fait tout notre bien. Nous n'avons point d'autre fortune que de trouver grâce devant vos yeux.' Otherwise, single girls will never escape from the seclusion of their own family: 'nous ne sortons du néant, nous ne saurions vous tenir en respect, faire figure, être quelque chose, qu'en faisant l'affront de substituer une industrie humiliante, et quelquefois des vices, à la place des qualités, des vertus que nous avons, dont vous ne faites rien, et que vous tenez captives' (ibid., p. 378). Nowhere in his essays does Marivaux use more eloquent words in defence of women, sharing the view of his friend Mme de Lambert that the whole of civilized society, through its educational system, customs, laws, is set up to ensure male hegemony.[11]

It is then a particular blend of sympathy, fascination, and condescension regarding women that Marivaux carries over into his plays. An oft-quoted passage in *Le Spectateur*, describing the moment when he had surprised a young girl affecting her apparent naturalness before a mirror, explains, he says, the source of his 'misanthropy': 'c'est de cette aventure que naquit en moi cette misanthropie qui ne m'a point quitté, et qui m'a fait passer ma vie à examiner les hommes, et à m'amuser de mes réflexions' (1ère feuille, p. 118). But the author is over-simplifying; misanthropy unmitigated could not have produced the insights of his *œuvre*. More significant is it perhaps to note that here again he uses woman as the springboard for conclusions about 'les hommes'. The otherness of the female sex is subsumed, in classical manner, beneath the universality of human nature.

It is possible to trace, in Marivaux's plays as in his essays, a steadily growing concern about feminine inequality;[12] in the space of this article, however, one can do no more than touch on some of the more significant plays in this regard. *L'Ile des esclaves* (1725) addresses itself essentially to class differences between masters and servants; but the dramatist does not fail to comment on the caprices of 'femmes de qualité'. On this island, slaves and servants (no clear distinction is made) wish to destroy the barbarism in their masters' hearts and restore them to the ranks of humanity. Candour being one means to this end, Arlequin and Cléanthis recount their masters' faults with great enthusiasm and no small penetration. Cléanthis reminds her mistress Euphrosine

of an evening when the latter had used all the tricks of coquetry
to conquer her *cavalier*. Having damned a rival with faint praise,
Euphrosine had pretended not to notice when her lover 'offrit son
cœur'. 'Continuez, folâtre, continuez, dites-vous, en ôtant vos
gants sous prétexte de m'en demander d'autres. Mais vous avez
la main belle; il la vit, il la prit, il la baisa . . .' (Sc. 3). This picture,
which strikingly resembles one of Sartre's most famous examples
of *mauvaise foi* in *L'Etre et le néant*,[13] anticipates the description we
have already noted above in the *Cabinet du philosophe*. In the same
scene Euphrosine reiterates Marivaux's views on the *négligé*:
'Regardez mes grâces, elles sont à moi, celles-là. . . . Voyez
comme je m'habille, quelle simplicité! il n'y a point de coquetterie
dans mon fait.' But before the play is over Euphrosine, her
pretensions now shattered, wins Arlequin's pity by her heartfelt
cry for mercy. The servants' revolt is not pushed to the point of
total ascendancy. The radicalism of the play is moral and religious
rather than social and political. Once the masters have acquired a
degree of self-knowledge and contrition it is time to call a halt.
The attitude which emerges is that of a Christian moralist.
Feminine vanity, like human vanity in general, can never be
erased but only, at best, abated through the workings of charity
and greater understanding.

L'*Ile de la raison* (1727) dwells too on the marvels of coquetry
(II, 6), but adds a different aspect of the feminine situation: on the
Island of Reason only women may make declarations of love.
Men become the passive element, sought out only when the
women want them, and obliged to play the reluctant role until
the alliance is assumed. Blectrue, one of the islanders, is horrified
at European courtship customs (II, 3: 'Que deviendra la faiblesse
si la force l'attaque') which he argues are the consequence of
men's vicious inclinations. By contrast, on the Island of Reason
men help to save women from themselves. 'L'homme ici, c'est le
garde-fou de la femme' (II, 7). This feminist paradox presumably
owes something to Mme de Lambert's *Réflexions sur les femmes*
(1727), but probably represents too the dramatist's desire to see
what the 'pure' woman is like when the need for coquetry is
removed.[14]

If so, the exploration of woman *in esse* is more arrestingly
carried out in *La Dispute* (1744). Marivaux organises an enquiry

into which of the sexes first proved unfaithful, and in typical
eighteenth-century manner[15] constructs a situation where two
boys and two girls are brought up in isolation from the world.
The first heterosexual encounters are idyllic; each looks on the
other and loves. The first meeting between the two girls is quite
other. The mental universe is Hobbesian; jealousy, suspicion,
hostility are the instinctive reactions on each side. By contrast,
the two men are initially well-disposed towards each other, so long
as no sexual conflict comes between them. Why this essential
difference? Because, in Marivaux's view women, being obliged to
please others, are immediately moved to jealousy in the presence
of another attractive member of their sex. So it is that the girls
take the first step in arranging infidelities; it springs almost
simultaneously from the inclination in each to prove that she can
assert her superiority by winning the other's lover. As Deloffre
points out in his 'Notice' to the play (p. 597), if it were transposed
into a tone less naïve and more libertine, these attitudes would be
appropriate to *Les Liaisons dangereuses*.

Significantly, the dramatist presents the meeting of the two
girls before that of their lovers; their reactions are so much richer
for psychological portraiture. Whereas the men drift along more
amiably, but also duller of sense, the girls' state of mind is complex
to the point of being incomprehensible even to themselves. Eglé,
for instance, is upset with herself, upset with her lover Azor: 'je
ne sais ce qui m'arrive . . . je ne sais à qui j'en ai'. The real reason
for her discontent emerges: she has found Mesrin to be more
attractive than Azor. But Mesrin's only advantage is novelty—
'd'être nouveau venu'. Even so, Eglé is unhappily divided within
herself: 'Je ne suis contente de rien, d'un côté, le changement me
fait peine, de l'autre, il me fait plaisir' (Sc. 15). She is able to
resolve the dilemma only when she learns that Mesrin is the lover
of the other girl, Adine; at that point jealousy impels swift action.

The conclusions of *La Dispute* are therefore sombre ones.
Inconstancy, it would appear, is well-nigh inevitable; woman
designs, man consents. Though one should not interpret a fable
such as this with undue literalism, it seems that for Marivaux the
urge to please is deeply ingrained in womankind. Social conditions
may, as he shows in the essays, confirm this inclination, but in the
uncorrupted environment of *La Dispute* the female sex is just as

bent on ruthless demonstration of its capacity to attract the male.

But the women do not emerge as villains from the play. The judicious conclusion of the Prince, who had arranged the whole experiment, is that virtues and vices are equal between the two sexes. Hermiane protests at this: 'votre sexe est d'une perfidie horrible, il change à propos de rien, sans chercher même de pré-texte'. The Prince agrees: 'Le procédé du vôtre est du moins plus hypocrite, et par là plus décent, il fait plus de façon avec sa conscience que le nôtre' (Sc. 20). This observation, striking in its disillusioned detachment, seems to sum up Marivaux's whole attitude to women. They are more 'civilized'. More complex psychologically, more committed to the desire they feel to attract the opposite sex, they are more alive in their sensibilities, more aware of a moral order; they do not drift into falsity as do men. Paradox though it is, they show greater integrity in coming to terms with the human predicament.

These attitudes are therefore probably more far-reaching than those emerging from the comedy which one immediately thinks of as most involved with the female question, *La Colonie* (1750). In this play Marivaux's views are sharply developed and dramatic-ally rich; but the subject is narrower. Here the dramatist is mainly concerned with the social question. In *La Colonie* the feminist leaders seek for equality with men, and especially within the state of marriage. Men, however, treat women as 'à n'être . . . que la première de toutes les bagatelles' (Sc. 9). As in the 5e feuille of the *Cabinet du philosophe*, coquetry is a response to male domination, in a world where, says Arthénice to the men, 'c'est votre justice et non pas la nôtre' (Sc. 13). Women are brainwashed into sub-mission and self-denigration. Madame Sorbin finds herself unconsciously saying 'je ne suis qu'une femme' until Arthénice points out to her how deep the conditioning has gone (Sc. 9). Coquetry therefore becomes the only answer. But what a waste of talent and energy go into it; 'plus de profondeur d'esprit qu'il n'en faudrait pour gouverner deux mondes comme le nôtre, et tant d'esprit est en pure perte' (ibid.).

The women ask for equality in all realms: finance, judiciary, the army. The claims seem utopian, and besides there is near-revolt in the ranks when the leaders urge their followers to make them-selves ugly; in addition, young lovers like Lina will always follow the spontaneous promptings of the heart. So it is hardly a surprise when the feminist cause collapses at the end. Marivaux's attitude towards the women protagonists appears sympathetic; but it is also equivocal.

In *La Colonie* and elsewhere Marivaux seems concerned about the rights of women. But though he indicts men for their tyrannous ways, he feels that the problem goes to the roots of human nature and is not to be solved by social reform. Improvements are however possible. One of the pleas most eloquently expressed in *La Colonie* harks back to the *Cabinet du philosophe*. Both of the women leaders want equality between husband and wife: 'le mariage qui se fait entre les hommes et nous', says Arthénice, 'devrait aussi se faire entre leurs pensées et les nôtres' (Sc. 13). Here at least is a practical way forward, though it depends more on improving the moral climate than on the institution of new laws.

In Marivaux subsists a deep-rooted pessimism about ever effecting wholesale changes in man's, and therefore woman's, lot. The picture is however not black. The essayist, like the dramatist, is presenting a human comedy. Women suffer many disadvantages, but they have consolations. Not only are they prettier, they are more interesting. Besides, if men rule the earth, women rule men:

> Si les lois des hommes dépendent,
> Ne vous en plaignez pas, trop aimables objets:
> Vous imposez des fers à ceux qui vous commandent,
> Et vos maîtres sont vos sujets.
>
> ('Divertissement', *La Nouvelle Colonie*, I, p, 771)

Marivaux can scarcely be termed a leading feminist of his day. He is alive to feminine inequality, but he deals relatively little with the disabilities facing eighteenth-century women: the economic and legal limitations, the right to divorce, educational reform. Not that he was unaware of these problems. By choosing for instance a widow as heroine of *Les Fausses Confidences* he recognized the greater degree of liberty she enjoyed as compared with a single girl. But these details were of interest to him in serving the ends of psychological enquiry. If Marivaux can be termed a feminist at all, it is surely in his acceptance, as in *La Colonie*, that women are men's equals intellectually. Indeed, as we have seen and as almost any one of his comedies makes clear, women's minds are far more interesting. They are the more colourful part of the species. Ultimately, they are of value for what they tell us about the human race as a whole; for they are the quintessence of humanity. When in *La Dispute* Adine, who has never seen another young girl, meets Eglé she asks ingenuously: 'Etes-vous une personne?' Eglé retorts: 'Oui assurément, et très personne' (Sc. 9). It is the reply that, about womankind, Marivaux himself might have made.

5

Women and Sexuality in the Thought of La Mettrie

JOHN FALVEY

'Il est aussi impossible de donner une seule idée à un homme, privé de tous les sens, que de faire un enfant à une femme, à laquelle la Nature aurait poussé la distraction jusqu'à oublier de faire une Vulve, comme je l'ai vu dans une, qui . . . pour cette raison fut démariée après dix ans de mariage' wrote La Mettrie in one of his arresting asides (*HM* pp. 35–6[1]). Here, as also for example in his accounts of treatment given by certain doctors to selected lady patients (*O. Pen.* passim, e.g. i pp. A102, B208ff, iii p. 94) or of the ingenious Neapolitans who, by driving out their 'femmes de joye' defeated the besieging French army with syphilis (*SMV* p. 11), the effect is whimsical and anecdotal, and a casual reader could believe that La Mettrie saw sex mainly as a subject for humour. Yet within each of these examples lies a core of genuine medical concern, and La Mettrie was quick to present his serious credentials to the public when, in 1735 at the beginning of his practising medical career, he introduced his translation, *Système de . . . Boerhaave sur les maladies vénériennes*, with a 'Dissertation' which attempted to consolidate the reputation of physicians in general as the only possessors of the expertise needed in a difficult and dangerous cure, as opposed to the surgeons who, La Mettrie argued, not required to study Latin, had no access to much of the literature on the disease (*SMV* pp. 109f, cf. pp. 160, 174). At the same time, La Mettrie was attempting to make a name for himself, exploiting Boerhaave's godlike reputation, and including, in well explained and richly informative passages, descriptions in which his command of the relevant practical knowledge is displayed. Thus we find him discussing a dark and tragic side of sexual love, involving pain, despair, revulsion and death, for the clinical passages spare few details of the hazards of the cure, involving 'archets' or sweating-barrels which severely taxed the patient's stamina, and had been known to explode, and doses of mercury, which voided the infected fatty substances of the body through salivation, and would cause loss of teeth, parts of the nose and sometimes an eye (*SMV* pp. 90–106). More directly linked to La Mettrie's later writings on love as the sovereign pleasure are passages where he gives details of the progressive damage caused by the disease and, following Boerhaave, describes the structure and functions of the sexual organs during coitus, using the language of gallantry (*SMV* pp. 45f, 54f, 60, cf. pp. 155f., 190; cf. also *La Vol.* pp. 47–9, 81). La Mettrie was subsequently to use passages of close anatomical description not only to support an argument, but also to impress readers with the authenticity of his medical knowledge. He makes the case against French medical schools where anatomy is taught *ex cathedra* in theory only (*O. Pen.* i p. B196); he gives accounts of the nervous system for convincing effect (*HNA* 45 passim eg. pp. 57ff, 64ff; *APQM* pp. 283–90) and he relates cases of monstrous abnormality, both physical, as that of the woman of Ghent cited at the beginning, and mental, as those of female cannibalism (*HNA* 45 p. 388, *HM* pp. 19, 45).

The overall value of these anatomical aspects of La Mettrie's writing in relation to his views on women, is that he can be seen, even by an unqualified reader, in the first place to be fully and reliably conversant with physical realities of female existence and sexual behaviour, information seldom if ever presented outside medical writings, and in the second place to be compassionately disposed towards women, showing a Hippocratic desire to understand, cure or alleviate their suffering in even the most hideous deviations

Despite some uncompromisingly patronising remarks about the relative delicacy of the female physique, and the consequent lack of mental vigour among women (*HM* p. 20), La Mettrie's work as a whole shows his readiness to accept female intellectual achievement on equal terms. For example, he refers respectfully to, and sometimes quotes from, the poetess Mme Deshoulières

(*HNA* 45 p. 173, *O. Pen.* iii p. 163, *SE* p. 341), and the authoress of a highly successful treatise on midwifery, Louise Bourgeois or Boursier (*O. Pen.* ii pp. 39, 86, 265, 367, iii p. 33²). Most prominent of female influences on La Mettrie's writings is Mme Du Châtelet. The 'Epître' of *La Volupté* (1747) (a work which contains ideas similar to those advanced in 'Discours sur le Bonheur' in 1748) is apparently addressed to her, and the 'Lettre Critique' of 1747 names her as addressee.

In this letter La Mettrie treated Mme Du Châtelet in a manner not unlike that in which he had treated Astruc, and in which he was about to treat Haller in the 'Dédicace' of *L'Homme machine*, that is to say, he made a claim to be an influenced admirer of their published scientific works, at the same time offering re-interpretations of their conclusions. At least part of the purpose of such claims was to draw attention to his own work. Astruc, no doubt perceiving the attempt to achieve cheap publicity, gave a crushing criticism of La Mettrie's *Nouveau Traité des maladies vénériennes* (1739), and refused to be further drawn, despite a volley of taunts. Ultimately, in 1751, La Mettrie realized that continued public hostility to the established Astruc was counter-productive to his desire to re-enter France and to the furtherance of his own medical reputation, and gave him a flattering mention in the 'Preface' of his *Œuvres de médecine*. In the cases of Haller and Mme Du Châtelet, La Mettrie spiced his attack by claiming to be not only a scientific disciple, but an intimate friend. We know that in respect of Haller this latter claim was quite untrue, for Haller allowed himself to be drawn into controversy, effectively killing public and professional interest in La Mettrie's eight-volume translation of Boerhaave's *Institutions*, but giving him a platform for further untruthful retaliatory slanders, which eventually had to be retracted by Maupertuis.[3] Mme Du Châtelet (possibly advised by Voltaire or Maupertuis) seems to have found the best answer to La Mettrie: silence. (Diderot treated La Mettrie's persistent overtures in similar fashion until well after the latter's death.) This extended perhaps even to her correspondence, for so far no mention by her of La Mettrie has come to light. For this reason, however, we cannot say that there was no acquaintance between them, and several remarks by La Mettrie suggest that there might have been.

To judge from La Mettrie's comments, it would appear that her *Institutions de physique* (1740) had a considerable effect upon a crucial area of his thinking, namely the theory of the basic structure of matter. In 'Lettre critique sur l'*Histoire naturelle de l'âme*. A Madame . . . Du Châtelet', he rejects the scholastic theory of matter which he had advanced in the *Histoire naturelle de l'âme* (1745). At the same time, however, he indicates the closeness between, on the one hand his present idea of matter, in which 'force motrice', a Leibnizian term often used by La Mettrie to denote independent self-movement,[4] exists potentially in all elements, and in which sentience and intelligence are believed to derive from it, and on the other hand the system of monads. La Mettrie had explained, two years earlier, his interpretation of the monad as an animated atom: 'Leibnitz fait consister l'essence, l'être, ou la substance . . . dans des monades, c'est à dire dans des corps simples, immuables, indissolubles, solides, individuels, ayant toujours la même figure et la même masse. Tout le monde connaît ces monades, depuis la brillante acquisition que les Leibnitiens ont faite de M. la M. du Châtelet' (*HNA* 45 p. 230). Thus, La Mettrie is suggesting in 'Lettre critique' (p. 6) that the theory of matter he had advanced in 1745 was, when stripped of its scholastic jargon, basically that of Leibniz as interpreted by Mme Du Châtelet. It was in this non-scholastic form that the theory was shortly to re-appear in *L'Homme machine*, as a vitalistic atomism, save that atomism was an insufficiently experimental concept for La Mettrie, who spoke instead of the 'force motrice' of 'fibres'.

At this point we must face a curious problem, common to much of La Mettrie's writing, but raising itself here in concentrated form: it is the difficulty created by his irony. It can be contended, with some plausibility, that the 'Lettre critique' is, beneath a layer of irony, a presentation of La Mettrie's corpuscular vitalism, in which he tries to show that Mme Du Châtelet is really in a position of support for the materialism of the forthcoming *L'Homme machine*. Thus, the objections which he raises to materialism ought to be taken as sarcastically affected arguments, intended to bring out the naivety of orthodoxy, or the folly of metaphysical speculation. According to this interpretation, all these objections in philosophical theory would be swept away by the practical observations and the empirical, scientific method-ology of *L'Homme machine*. However, the irony is not always pointed enough for us to be sure of this intention: the objections raised by La Mettrie are substantial; they do not seem strikingly metaphysical or absurd; and the tone is often—though not always —genuine, as if La Mettrie were conceding points to spiritualism.

A consideration of the objections will illustrate this problem. (1) La Mettrie asks how matter acquires the complexity of organisation needed for it to become sentient. The answer of 1745 (*HNA* 45, pp. 44-7), by 'ether', or 'fire', as 'cause directrice, intelligente' was based on the view of a 'fire soul' advanced by Quesnay in his *Essai de l'économie animale* of 1736.[5] But Quesnay like Mme Du Châtelet, continues La Mettrie, really believed that 'le feu n'agit que comme cause matérielle purement instrumentale'. He leaves unspoken the implication that it is 'instrumental' for some spiritual intelligence—presumably God's—as creator. (2) La Mettrie admits that, in arguing that the soul must occupy spatial extent, because the sensory nerves enter the brain at different points (so that seeing occurs in one part of the brain, hearing in another etc.) his 1745 work clashed with common experience that all senses are united in one individual. (3) He points out that, though the work of 1745 affirmed that the sentient and reasoning souls are material, we have, by common experience, totally different ideas of states of consciousness (such as sentience and reasoning), and of material entities. In a similar connection, why should we identify self-movement in matter with the power to feel and to think? (4) He observes that the anecdotes (*HNA* 45, pp. 344-98) which purported to show that there is no thought where there is no sensation, do not exclude the possibility that the soul has a constant *potential* to think, or that it might think and subsequently forget its thoughts, as in cases of delirium.

Not only are these objections accurately focused on the gaps in La Mettrie's thesis: they are also left largely unresolved in *L'Homme machine* and subsequent writings. On (1), the question of the origin of organization in organisms, La Mettrie (a) asserts our permanent ignorance (*HM* p. 68), (b) nevertheless suggests that each organic structure has pre-existed from eternity as a miniature in the seed (*HM* pp. 72, 75, cf. *HP* pp. 258f.) (c) albeit reverting —intermittently—to the theory of a creative 'fire-soul' as the

instrument of God (*HP* pp. 265f.: '. . . il n'y a point d'autre âme
du monde que Dieu et le mouvement; d'autre âme des plantes
que le chaleur . . .' cf. *O. Pen.* i p. A49 and ii p. 249: 'il y a dans les
corps animés des traces évidentes de la main éternelle et invisible
qui les a formés'). In respect of objection (3), La Mettrie resorts to
simple counter-assertion: the purposive self-movement—'mouvements non déréglés . . . mais réguliers' (*HM* p. 57) which can be
shown (by experiments involving muscular irritability) to exist in
the smallest shreds of organic tissue—'dans des morceaux de
fibres', 'chaque élément fibreux' (*HM* pp. 57, 63) becomes, when
associated with sufficiently advanced levels of organization, both
sentience (for in the experiments described by La Mettrie, the
movement is in response to stimuli such as heat or pin-pricks) and
ultimately, thought. For thought is only purposive self-movement, fed through the complex organization of the human brain:
'L'âme n'est que . . . la partie qui pense en nous', and 'L'âme n'est
qu'un principe de mouvement, ou une partie materielle sensible
du cerveau, qu'on peut regarder comme un ressort principal de
toute la machine' (*HM* pp. 53, 63). Objection (4) is also met with
a simple counter-assertion: 'ceux qui ont avancé que l'âme
n'avait pas moins pensé dans les maladies soporeuses, quoiqu'elle
ne se souvînt pas des idées qu'elle avait eues, ont soutenu une
chose ridicule' (*HM* p. 68). As for objection (2), La Mettrie
employs a mixture of counter-assertion—'[L'âme] . . . a son siège
dans le cerveau à l'origine des nerfs, par lesquels [elle] exerce son
empire sur tout le reste du corps (*HM* p. 59)—and evasion, for he
never returned to a direct explanation of the sense of unity in the
consciousness. From what has already been said, however, it is
clear that the amalgam of self-moving and sentient fibres which
composed La Mettrie's man-machine was in many respects similar
to the image which he had earlier ascribed to Leibniz: 'Ces êtres
qui séparés sont des monades . . . forment par leur assemblage les
corps, ou l'étendue . . . formée par des êtres simples, parmi
lesquels on compte l'âme sensitive et raisonnable', and 'tous les
changements du corps correspondent si parfaitement aux changements de la Monade, appelée *Esprit* ou *Ame*, qu'il n'arrive point
de mouvements dans l'une auxquels ne coexiste quelque idée
dans l'autre . . . Dieu a préétabli cette harmonie.' (*HNA* 45 pp.
233, 234).

Thanks to the 'Lettre critique', and to *Les Animaux plus que machines*, another seemingly self-critical work, we can plot fairly closely the slight differences between the foregoing view, ascribed to Leibniz, and La Mettrie's own position. In the first place, we find La Mettrie supporting the notion that the monads have perceptions: 'Leibnitz a reconnu dans la matière . . . des perceptions et des sensations semblables en petit à celle des corps animés. On ne peut en effet les refuser, du moins à tout ce qui n'est pas inanimé' (*HNA* 45 p. 233). Wolff is taken to task for having 'dépouillé les Monades Leibnitiennes des perceptions' ('Lettre critique', cf. *HNA* 45 p. 238). In the second place, we find him talking readily of 'corpuscules', 'éléments des fibres', 'particules', and 'molécules' (*APQM* pp. 282, 287, 302, 308, 310, 311), as being animated by 'force motrice' or 'force générale de la vie' (*APQM* pp. 307, 308). Thus, when La Mettrie speaks vaguely of the 'Unité matérielle de l'Homme' (*HM* p. 61), we can be sure that he finds it, if not in one ruling monad/corpuscle in the brain (as, in La Mettrie's view, Leibniz had done), at least in an assembly of such corpuscles or fibres, in which the life-force and sentience are somehow fused into a single centre of consciousness and assertive energy.

That such a theory is incomplete philosophically has already been pointed out.[6] And even if one overlooks the lacunae, the picture presented is neither a mechanistic nor (given the 'life-force') even a materialistic view of man. This curious feature of La Mettrie's position is particularly apparent in *Les Animaux plus que machines*. This work opens with an account of the slightness of man's superiority to animals (*APQM* pp. 277–81), and proceeds to the argument, backed by anatomical description, that at no point in its passage does sensation cease to be a physical event occurring in the matter of the nerve and the brain, and become a purely psychical or immaterial happening (*APQM* pp. 281–96). A third section pours ridicule on Wolff for insistence on dualism, and the consequent clumsiness of the theory of 'harmonie préétablie', extending this criticism to Leibnizians in general (*APQM* pp. 296–302).

In all this, however, La Mettrie shows not only the muddles arising for those who insist that the soul is incorporeal, but also the positive strengths of this 'spiritualist' position: quoting

Augustine's arguments against sensualism at length and with apparent approval, he writes 'Saint Augustin objecte . . . plus solidement peut-être que ceux qui ont lu Locke et Condillac ne se l'imaginent . . .' (*APQM* p. 286f.); he speaks of the crude inadequacies of the materialists, 'petits philosophes qui ne jugent que sur l'écorce des choses' (*APQM* p. 300f.); and he reminds readers, gratuitously, that the 'esprits animaux', on which one of his materialistic suggestions depends, have never been seen, any more than has the soul (*APQM* p. 305). Similarly, in the fourth section, dealing with 'la volonté' (which he takes to be the organism's power to choose its conduct, and to accept guidance from either 'la raison' or 'l'instinct'), he accepts that, since it cannot be readily located in the brain or elsewhere, it must be a 'cause métaphysique' of physical contractions of the muscles (*APQM* p. 309), appealing to common experience as proof of this dualism: 'Que voulez-vous que je vous dise? Vous savez déjà tout le mystère. Telle est l'union de l'Ame et du corps et nous sommes ainsi faits.' None of these arguments or phrases sound ironic, nor does the re-statement of the last point, in a form which captures the physician's wondering respect at the resources, mental and vital, of the human organism: 'Rien ne relève tant la dignité et la noblesse de l'Ame, que de voir sa force et sa puissance dans un corps impuissant et perclus. La volonté, la présence d'esprit, le sang froid, la liberté même ne se soutiennent- et ne brillent-elles pas, avec plus ou moins d'éclat, au travers de tous ces nuages que forment les maladies, les passions ou l'adversité?', and La Mettrie cites the case of Scarron, whose good spirits and courageous fortitude in suffering much impressed him (*APQM* p. 314).

In a fifth section La Mettrie's meaning becomes temporarily unambiguous. He argues that, by allowing his 'volonté' to be guided by reason, and by his powers to educate and condition himself, man has achieved his position of intelligence and civilization, rendering himself superior to the other animals, but that nevertheless he might be healthier, and more happy, if he were guided instead by instinct (*APQM* pp. 316–20).

The final section dwells on the total diversity of the corpuscles composing the universe: 'pas une feuille d'arbre, pas un grain de sable qui se ressemblent . . . chaque corps a sa physionomie', and the associated essential diversity of souls: 'il y a dans les âmes, comme dans les corps, une variété essentielle'. The emphasis is on the uniqueness of each element or organism: 'la diversité des âmes dans chaque genre, dans chaque espèce, dans chaque individu', and apart from some mockery of dualism, the picture imparted is a Leibnizian one, in which the word 'âme' means 'force de la vie', or 'conatus', the purposive movements by which each entity preserves itself, grows, fulfils itself and multiplies. Thus Leibniz's monads, taken in the sense of material entelechies (as La Mettrie had claimed that Mme Du Châtelet had understood them) seem indeed to be the basis of his theory of matter and view of Nature, a theory which he began to expound by thinking of it as a dialogue with Mme Du Châtelet, and continued, after her death in 1749, still in the form of a dialogue, partly real, with Tralles, critic of *L'Homme machine*, and partly imagined, with Leibnizians in general.[7]

Although La Mettrie developed sophisticated theories of morality involving 'volupté de l'esprit' (*HM* p. 4f.) and the writer's altruistic commitment to posterity and the truth (*DP* pp. xxxvii–liv), he never moved far from the potentially anarchic position of hedonism and self-fulfilment: 'Chaque homme porte en soi le germe de son propre bonheur, avec celui de la volupté' (*La Vol*. p. 77). The striving for pleasure, happiness, and sex are seen as basically the same thing, and form the fundamental motivation of animals: 'le plaisir, le bien-être, leur propre conservation est le but constant où tendent tous les ressorts de leur machine' (*APQM* p. 320). All human behaviour, however eccentrically diversified is basically sexual energy and self affirmation (*La Vol*. pp. 94–5). For pleasure is Nature's way of ensuring the perpetual renewal of life, and La Mettrie consciously echoes Lucretius's invocation to Venus in *De natura rerum* (*La Vol*. pp. 23, 79–81, 93–4) in eulogizing it.

In such a context, woman has great significance as the object of human desire and endeavour—'le plus beau spectacle du monde, c'est une belle femme' (*La Vol*. pp. 88–9), being linked, through her role as bearer of children, to the reproductive processes common to all organisms.

This theme is given particular prominence in *L'Homme plante*.

The work is simply constructed in three chapters, the first of which shows analogy of structure and functions between plant and human anatomy. A second chapter, dealing with the differences between man and plant, formulates a law: the greater the number of needs of an organism, the higher its degree of mental activity ('sagesse'), which includes instinct and intelligence, but not, apparently, the life force in the lower or vegetable forms: 'Après les végétaux et les minéraux, corps sans âme, viennent les êtres qui commencent à s'animer: tels sont les polypes . . .' (*HP* p. 266). The third chapter explores this law as a form of the admirable uniformity and harmony to be found in the spectacle of Nature, and develops particularly the discussion of instinct (the form of mental activity possessed by animals) as superficially distinct from, but basically identical with, intelligence in Man 'ce superbe Animal, fait de boue comme les autres'.[8]

It seems likely that the work originated in a comically satirical criticism of Linnaeus, first conceived as a part of *Ouvrage de Pénélope*, in which La Mettrie gave vent to his opposition to the botanist (*O. Pen.* i pp. B38–51—see especially p. 50, where *L'Homme plante* is promised—and B68–74). One of these passages, the ironic 'Inutilité de la Botanique' was considered of some importance, for a manuscript copy of it (now in the Bibliothèque nationale) was made for circulation in 1747, before the appearance of either *Ouvrage de Pénélope* or *L'Homme plante*, both of 1748.

This passage is referred to in the rare 1748 version of *L'Homme plante* (p. 34), where some of the comic satire remains in the form of a parody of Linnaeus, 'Description Botanique de l'Homme', in Latin, set out in the manner of the *Systema naturae*. La Mettrie confines his 'extract' to 'Foemina', and dwells on the sexual parts, describing the breasts ('Nectareum duplex, rotundo globosum . . .') and contrasting young with old; and describing in similar fashion the reproductive organs as the pistil, in which are included the vulva (as the stigma) and the vagina (as the style). He also pointedly makes much of inessential features: the calyx (i.e. the whorl of protective sepals) is the skirt—'campaniform'—and 'deciduum omni nocte'. In both these features, La Mettrie was expressing his objection to what is technically known as 'artificial' classification, that is, classing according to the most convenient and readily identifiable distinctive features, rather than according to more intrinsic similarities. To La Mettrie, with his leaning towards functional comparative anatomy, this seemed wrong because superficial, and Diderot among others shared this disapproval of Linnaeus.[9]

The parody of Linnaeus was dropped from the 1751 edition of *L'Homme plante*—possibly because La Mettrie thought it too frivolous—but he retained the serious (though not entirely accurate) study of common factors of the reproductive process in man and in plant, in the course of which he presents in some detail his theory of pre-existence in the *germe*: 'la plante humaine en miniature' is contained in each of the spermatic animalcules of the 'semence de l'Homme', and is implanted 'dans l'ovaire de la femme' (*HP* pp. 257–8, 260).

The seriousness of La Mettrie's concern, both with the analogies between man and plant, and with the importance of woman, is demonstrated by the extensive list of learned works referred to in the notes of the 1748 edition of *L'Homme plante*, dropped for no obvious reason in 1751.[10]

Outspokenness in discussing the orgasm is one of the distinctive qualities of *La Volupté*. La Mettrie saw the five senses as culminating in a 'sixième sens', which is not the *sensorium commun*, but a faculty more exclusively related to the orgasm, and he dwells on the medical necessity of these moments of human experience —'le souverain plaisir'—for a full and healthy existence (*La Vol.* pp. 56, 79–82, 88–93, 106–7).

Despite a torrent of practical vulgarized information in French on the neighbouring field of pregnancy, child-birth and infant-rearing, little authoritative advice was available on techniques of lovemaking or psychological difficulties (e.g. fears, inhibitions, impotence, frigidity). The orgasm, especially in women, seems to have been regarded as an unmentionable mystery or as a frivolous, even sinful matter, appropriate only to more or less erotic fiction. La Mettrie's evaluative survey of such literature in this connection, his requests to lady-readers not to be affronted but to recognize the importance of his advice, his cloaking in would-be delicate circumlocutions of quite detailed descriptions of the sexual organs and their functions (*La Vol.* pp. 7ff., 19, 45–7) might seem to us today as no more than titillating in an impish mode, but they should be recognized also as attempts to navigate through the accepted channels of communication of his age. *La Volupté* offered medical advice to women as well as to men, and La Mettrie was taking stylistic measures to reach both sections of his readers.

In his defence of feminine rights in this respect we find La Mettrie once again advocating control of mind over body, and thus engaging in an apparently non-materialistic thesis. A major cause of female dissatisfaction is over-eagerness in the male. La Mettrie condemns the 'débauché', who seeks pleasure selfishly, and whose performance, though enviable in its animal energy, resembles rape insofar as he is indifferent to the arousing of his partner. In contrast, 'le voluptueux' is a satisfying partner: his imagination retains, scrutinises, savours and thus augments the pleasure of each sensation, and he can offer the insight, 'cœur', 'tendresse' and self-control needed to overcome the reticences and fears of his partner. La Mettrie develops a portrait of 'le voluptueux' not only as an unselfish lover, but as an ideal member of society (*La Vol.* pp. 49–50, 55–8, 62–3, 68–74).[11]

Exemplifying this idea, La Mettrie notes, among factors which can mar female 'jouissance', the limits of physical stamina in the male. One solution is offered by understanding and inventive auto-suggestion, through which the male can overcome the exhaustion and 'dégoût' following orgasm, and thus help his partner to achieve hers; another is to be found in genuine affection: where it exists, the female, though not physically satisfied, may nevertheless find emotional fulfilment: 'J'ai vu des moments où ma Céphise, éperdument livrée à la douce sympathie des cœurs . . . méprisait dans mes bras des faveurs qu'elle prétendait que l'amour, en pareil cas, eût dédaignée lui-même' (*La Vol.* pp. 55, 61–3, 66). Frigidity in women also attracted La Mettrie's sympathetic concern, for he recognized the damage to mental stability caused by sexual deprivation, and suggested the need for medical care (*La Vol.* p. 53, cf *HM* p. 20, *O. Pen.* iii pp. 116f., 129ff., 154f.). It is the role of the male, thinks La Mettrie, to undo, by gentle persuasion, the lifetime of conditioning through which shame (e.g. fear of pregnancy as a disgrace) of a social, not natural, sort binds a woman to 'la raison' (i.e. convention), and prevents her from happily following her instincts (*La Vol.* pp. 5, 27–8,

47–8). 'Combien peu se respectent eux-mêmes dans les bras de la volupté?' asks La Mettrie, pinpointing the problem, and the persuasion by which such respect is restored involved 'sentiment', 'instinct', 'cœur', 'tendresse', 'sympathie', 'humanité' (*La Vol* e.g. pp. 18, 20, 25, 27). One notices that these are key words in the current vogue for 'sensibilité', and in arguing for their psychological and medical importance, La Mettrie brings a realistic dimension to the usually more anodine forms of that mode.

Consideration of women and sexuality in La Mettrie's thought has led us, by several different paths, and no doubt fortuitously, to confront a possibly non-materialistic La Mettrie. In the 'dialogue' with Mme Du Châtelet, with its complex ironies, we meet him as a vitalist, falling into the trap of which he had warned the Leibnizians, that of spiritualizing matter, rather than materializing the soul (*HM* p. 10). Elsewhere, the nature of the soul, while not made totally clear, seems to be more spiritual— in the discussion of 'volonté' (*APQM*) and 'sagesse' (*HP*)—than the life-force in the lower vegetable forms. We find him asserting the importance of psychology and self-controlling attitudes—in the discussion of 'le voluptueux'—as opposed to an instinctive, animal-like pursuit of bodily pleasure (*La Vol.* p. 81). Of course, such features are reconcileable with La Mettrie's unusual form of materialism, in which each organism is immutably unique, being determined in its behaviour by its structure, which has pre-existed 'de toute éternité dans le germe' (*HM* p. 77), but a fatalism which is individualistic to this degree is hardly a materialism at all for any practical purpose: nothing can be controlled, and little can be explained, since one is blocked at every turn by unique and unknowable causes, not open to scientific investigation, as the recurrent Pyrrhonism shows (e.g. *HM* p. 51: 'ignorance absolument invincible'; p. 68).

The presence of attitudes more usually associated with spiritual beliefs than with hedonism, is also apparent in the little we know of La Mettrie's personal relationships with women. The liaison with Mlle Leconte, his companion at the time of his death, was apparently of long standing, and approved of by his family at St Malo (she was perhaps the 'Céphise' of *La Volupté* (1747), and the 'Thémire' of *Système d'Epicure* and *l'Art de jouir*, 1751). His wife, from whom he separated after three years in 1742, remained sufficiently high in his esteem for him to write to console her at the death of their son aged five in the spring of 1748; and a letter to his sister Jacquette on the same occasion (when insincerity seems unlikely) suggests that he retained a strong religious conviction.[12] Taken with the apparently unironic references to 'Dieu' already noticed (in 'Lettre critique', *O. Pen.*, *HP* and *APQM*), this indication leads us to wonder how far the much-vaunted 'materialism' and 'atheism' were played up for the benefit of Frederick II. They also indicate the existence of unexplored dimensions and possibly irreconcilable ambivalences in his thought, and the need for further investigation of his less familiar writings.

6

Diderot and Women

ROBERT NIKLAUS

Woman's lot in the eighteenth century was unenviable. A woman had no status of her own according to Salic laws and was offered little protection in the courts.[1] *Contrats de mariage* provided scant protection as Diderot discovered when drawing up one for his beloved daughter Angélique. A widow had often to request a *lettre de cachet* to secure minimal inheritance rights and a modest *rente*. In law a woman was treated as a chattel and was powerless against masculine tyranny in the home.[2] 'L'empire que nous avons sur elles [les femmes] est une véritable tyrannie', wrote Montesquieu who was in possession of the facts. It is, therefore, surprising that in the age of enlightenment more was not done to ensure for her a higher status. The *philosophes* failed to mount a crusade urging the emancipation of women. As other writers in this volume have noted, they put forward reforms, especially in regard to the education of women,[3] but these were for the most part subordinated to the overall programme they were promoting. Other factors besides male chauvinism can be adduced to account for this fact. Living conditions for 90 per cent of the population that formed *le peuple* were so appalling for men and women alike that there was little point in differentiating between their respective plights, and both sexes would benefit equally from any improvement in living standards. Sheer survival was often the main problem for the mass of the people. In the bourgeoisie women played a distinctive role and their importance rested not on their legal rights but on their position in the home as mother and as housekeeper. They were confined to a life of domesticity, but this contributed to their adoption of a moral code of virtue and fidelity which served to enhance their status. A wife was not ashamed to live with her husband, and home life brought couples closer together.[4] Among the bourgeoisie the stern parent gave

way to the doting father who would even indulge the vagaries of
a scapegrace as is recorded in Voltaire's *L'Enfant prodigue* (1736),
a practice which eventually extended to the nobility and is still
found in the early nineteenth century as shown for example in the
attitude of Oncle Van Buck towards his ward, the rakish Valentin,
in Musset's *proverbe* entitled *Il ne faut jurer de rien*. It may well be
that the bourgeois conception of home life which developed
earlier in England than in France, and is so clearly manifested in
countless *drames*, disguised the very real lack of independence of
women. Among the aristocracy conditions appeared to be better.
At the top of the social tree were there not monarchs like Christina
of Sweden and Catherine of Russia who held power which they
wielded with intelligence and political acumen? Were not
mistresses of kings to be found exercising a determining influence
on public affairs? And if the policies of Mme de Pompadour
might be challenged, her ability was not put in question. Among
the nobility marriages were certainly being arranged for family
reasons and young girls without dowry, or illegitimate, were
obliged to take vows and enter convents which Voltaire's Huron
defined as 'une espèce de prison où l'on tenait les filles enfermées'.[5]
Cloistered life rendered women petty-minded, sadistic or maso-
chistic and gave rise to physiological disturbance, as Diderot
brought out in *La Religieuse*. Moreover, convent education which
was hopelessly inadequate, as R. Pomeau has recently reminded us
in his book on Laclos,[6] led to the subjection of women. It could
be of short duration since a girl might be married at twelve years
of age to a man whom she had never even seen. These *mariages de
convenance* were commonly unhappy and helped to discredit
marriage as an institution. Husband and wife commonly lived
apart in 'société distincte', and their relationship became meaningless. Love itself was belittled and turned into a mere pastime, a fact
which outraged women's deepest feelings, as became apparent
when they quickened in response to the presentation of true,
romantic love in *La Nouvelle Héloïse*. Their enforced idleness and
craving for greater freedom led to the excesses of the Regency and
the prevalence of a mode of life dominated by pleasure. Women
took to drinking and pipe-smoking, to wearing those fantastic
headdresses which so shocked Lady Montague when in Paris, and
to painting blue veins on their hands.[7] They became arbiters of

taste and elegance, but their vanity and the relaxed code of behaviour engendered a sense of decadence rather than a spirit of freedom. The development of the *salons*, as Voltaire was one of the first to recognize,[8] contributed greatly to raising the status of woman in society. She could now become a hostess of distinction whose natural intelligence and conversational powers could successfully mask her inadequate education and even enable her to cut a figure in intellectual circles. But in fact only the married woman enjoyed consideration and had social importance. If she stepped beyond the bounds of conventional behaviour she soon found herself ostracized by society and any public scandal would force her to leave the capital, witness Mme de Merteuil in *Les Liaisons dangereuses* after her exposure.

It remains surprising that more works were not written to vindicate the rights of women. Legrand, Destouches, La Chaussée drew attention to their plight, but did not urge political or economic independence, nor request that they be given access to jobs. It should, however, be remembered that it is only in 1788 that the 'question préalable' was abolished and that civil rights were extended to non-Catholics. At this date a *Société des amis des noirs* was founded in Paris shortly after that founded in London, but the time had not yet come for a *société des amis de la femme*. Women were, nevertheless, increasingly depicted as slaves, and as from 1770, as L. Versini has pointed out, the apologia of women becomes standard.[9] Slowly the realization came that the radical principles of the *Discours sur l'inégalité* should be applied to women. For woman, too, is born free although her lot could be compared to that of the Negroes in the colonies, and Laclos in his 'Discours sur l'origine de l'inégalité féminine' writes of *colonialisme masculin*. His suggestion, however, that women should read *Clarissa Harlowe* for their education provides a very limited solution to the problem.

It is against this background, briefly outlined, that we must judge Diderot's views on the feminine universe and woman's place in society. The subject is an important one, for women certainly played a great role in his life and in the elaboration of his thought. Two theses deal with it which arrive at very different conclusions. Susanna Marchiewicz[10] has provided an impartial and fairly complete inventory of his ideas, concluding that

Diderot had marked a step, albeit halting, towards securing for women a juster place in society. Pamela H. Smith,[11] on the other hand, is evidently dismayed at Diderot's hesitations, qualifications, even contradictions when it comes to writing about women, and cannot hide her disappointment that Diderot failed to formulate a feminist doctrine or initiate comprehensive, yet specific, reforms.

Certainly Diderot was well-placed to speak sensibly on the subject of women. He had a wide range of feminine friends and acquaintances which ranged from royalty and high society to the middle and the lower classes. Like Voltaire he was without social prejudice in his personal relations. He was greatly attached to his family, his father whom he respected, his sister Denise, Angélique, another sister who was to die as an Ursuline nun at the age of twenty-eight. He loved for a time his wife Tonton and for many long years Sophie Volland, not to speak of dubious women like Mme de Puisieux and other 'femmes de petite vertu'. There was his beloved daughter Angélique, and the many friends and acquaintances: the women in the society of Grimm such as Mme d'Epinay, Mme d'Houdetot; those in the circle of the Baron d'Holbach, Mme le Baronne, Mme d'Aine; and so many others from Mme Helvétius and Mlle de Lespinasse to Mme de Prémont-val, Mme Riccoboni and the Volland family. He knew not only Mélanie de Sallignac, the blind girl who inspired some of his additions to *Lettre sur les aveugles*, but also courtesans, prostitutes, cheap actresses, servant girls, artists and peasant girls whose beauty he could appreciate on a canvas by Greuze. The long gallery of women to be seen in his fiction and his philosophical writings reveals that he knew both angelic and demonic women, reasonable and irrational ones, the coldly calculating and the hysterical or insane, the strong-willed and the weak, the proud and the humble, the libertine and the devout, the earthy and the mystic. Like Voltaire he praises women for virtues such as fidelity which he denies them in another context. He does not look upon queens as he does upon the lowly-born, upon the old as he does upon the young. In his later works more especially he looks beyond mere femininity and considers woman as an individual. Hence no doubt his great success in fiction and in dialogue gained by casting aside sweeping generalizations about women as a sex. In his early works we see for the most part stereotypes which are in keeping with some notional and traditional view of women, partly because he introduces them as elements in an argument of broad philosophical significance. He is concerned with their special significance in a sensationalist philosophy and already in *Lettre sur les aveugles* he noted the influence of the body over the mind, so strong in the case of women. For them even more than for men 'Nos idées les plus intellectuelles . . . tiennent de fort près à la conformation de notre corps',[12] and his preoccupation with physiology and pathology finds expression in *Les Bijoux indiscrets*. The style of the latter may be frivolous, but it cannot disguise the fact that women's peculiarities are in his eyes the result of their physical condition. 'Telle qui croyait suivre sa tête, obéissait à son bijou', he writes. Mlle de Lespinasse in *Le Rêve de d'Alembert* warrants a close study. At one level she is the intelligent and sensitive friend of d'Alembert, at another a conventional woman who professes to be shocked at the boldness of her own observations as befits the traditional prudery of her sex. Diderot exploits the situation dramatically for the purposes of his dialogue, but it would be difficult to draw inferences as to Diderot's true views on women from an exercise such as this in which characterization plays a lively role but is invariably subordinated to the furtherance of his ideas. In this work is to be found Diderot's oft-quoted aphorism: 'L'homme est le monstre de la femme et la femme le monstre de l'homme', which prompts P. H. Smith to comment that for Diderot the latter part of the sentence was the more significant, but, at the time, Diderot was thinking in terms of physiology, and she surely misses the main point which is that, however different men and women may be, they belong to the same species. Again it is a mistake to believe that Diderot is ignoring womenfolk when he does not specifically mention them. His pleas for freedom, civil rights and a better society are for the benefit of all mankind which includes women. It is also unwise to generalize too freely about Diderot's views on women on the strength of their presentation in his fiction or in his plays. The necessities of the literary form adopted often determine the portrayal and can explain many inconsistencies. Understandably, Diderot is overwhelmed by the diversity with which he is confronted, the good and the bad women, the sincere and the deceitful, the faithful and the fickle. When, however, it comes to accounting for their peculiarities, in particular their vices, he never fails to fall back on physiological and environmental factors that seem to him basic. Woman is frail and weak and more impressionable owing to the delicacy of her organs and her greater social dependence; this can account for her coquetry, her vanity, her deceitfulness, her curiosity and waywardness, perhaps the mystery with which she is commonly enshrouded. His concern with the processes of generation leads him to stress maternity as woman's chief function in life. He recognizes that woman can dominate society through her charm, her insight and her wit, and the study of women around him as well as of Marivaux's Marianne enables him to substitute dissimulation for deceitfulness. With Diderot, as with Challes and Marivaux, the place of woman depends largely on a conception of the masculine role. Woman can help a philosopher to understand the world, and her uncanny power of expression is for him a source of wonder and admiration. Although Diderot was highly sensitive to female beauty as we can judge from his *Salons*, he could also appreciate a delicacy of feeling unknown to nature, and at times he waxed lyrical over woman's saintliness or maudlin over 'la jeune fille qui pleure un oiseau mort'. There is pity and compassion for her in *Entretien d'un père avec ses enfants* and in *Jacques le fataliste* (as for example for the woman who shelters Jacques after the battle of Fontenoy), and he indulges in emotion whenever a woman appears on stage in his *drames*.

It was only in the 1770s that Diderot thought of systematizing his ideas on women. He was prompted to do so by the reading of Antoine-Léonard Thomas's treatise, *Essai sur le caractère, les mœurs et l'esprit des femmes dans les différens siècles*, which he reviewed for the *Correspondance littéraire* of 1 April 1772. He annotated the work freely and entitled his own composition *Essai sur les femmes*. On 1 July 1772 he gave an expanded version of this essay which included some emendations by Grimm to which his attention was not drawn. He returned to his text subsequently, sketching in sociological and ethnological considerations taken from the *Histoire des Deux Indes*. Roger Lewinter[13] believes that, quite understandably, Diderot sought to recover in his original article some of the fragments he had drafted on the same subject for the abbé de Raynal. It is this fourth version of the essay which

R. Lewinter has reproduced in his edition of Diderot's works in addition to the text of the first. But even this fourth version can hardly be called definitive, for the *Essai sur les femmes* is one of the many works Diderot subjected to constant minor revision. Something can be made of these re-workings to show the importance Diderot attributed to the subject, but one needs to bear in mind that the essay which started as an annotation of Thomas's treatise follows naturally Thomas's *exposé* and has precisely the gaps in portrayal of women which we find in Thomas's work. His general style when indulging in lyrical enthusiasm for the specifically feminine and the 'pythie de Delphes' was also inspired by the writing of *Les Eleuthéromanes* which he had just completed.

Characteristically Diderot begins his essay by praising Thomas as a worthy man whose eloquent eulogies, as well as his position as Director of the Académie française, had won him some notoriety, but he soon proceeds to castigate him for a pedestrian approach to a wonderful subject. Interestingly one of Diderot's fundamental ideas, that of the importance of physiological and environmental factors in determining the nature of women, is already to be found in Thomas. Diderot's strictures on a type of woman he claims can never have existed fail to impress P. H. Smith who points out that this is precisely the woman he admired so much on many canvasses by Greuze. With some justification he reproaches Thomas for his lack of verve. He himself writes in a personal manner, brimming with enthusiasm when generalizing about womankind. His style is vivid, showing imagination, and carries conviction. He writes: 'C'est surtout dans la passion de l'amour, les accès de la jalousie, les transports de la tendresse maternelle, les instants de la superstition, la manière dont elles partagent les émotions épidémiques et populaires que les femmes étonnent; belles comme les séraphins de Klopstock, terribles comme les diables de Milton. J'ai vu l'amour, la jalousie, la colère, la superstition portés dans les femmes à un point que l'homme n'éprouve jamais . . . Les distractions d'une vie occupée et contentieuse rompent nos passions. La femme couve les siennes; c'est un point fixe sur lequel son oisiveté ou la frivolité de ses fonctions tient son regard sans cesse attaché. Ce point s'étend sans mesure, et pour devenir folle il ne manquerait à la femme passionnée que l'entière solitude qu'elle recherche.'[14] He then dwells on female sexuality and passes on to the psychological characteristics which it engenders: 'Impénétrables dans la dissimulation, cruelles dans la vengeance, constantes dans leurs projets, sans scrupule sur les moyens de réussir, armées d'une haine profonde et secrète contre le despotisme de l'homme, il semble qu'il y ait entre elles un complot tacite de domination, une sorte de ligue telle que celle qui subsiste entre les prêtres de toutes les nations; elles en connaissent les articles sans se les être communiqués'.[15] Very quickly he returns to physiological data: 'La femme porte au-dedans d'elle-même un organe susceptible de spasmes terribles, disposant d'elle et suscitant dans son imagination des fantômes de toute espèce. C'est dans le délire hystérique qu'elle revient sur le passé, qu'elle s'élance dans l'avenir, que tous les temps lui sont présents. C'est de l'organe propre à son sexe que partent toutes ses idées extraordinaires.[16]

He believes that he holds the key that can explain the saintliness of Saint Theresa as well as common female hysteria: 'La femme dominée par l'hystérisme éprouve je ne sais quoi d'infernal ou de céleste.'[17] and he adds comments which find their illustration in La Religieuse: 'Les femmes sont sujettes à une férocité épidémique; l'exemple d'une seule en entraîne une multitude; il n'y a que la première qui soit criminelle, les autres sont malades. O femmes! vous êtes des enfants bien extraordinaires!'[18] She may be a child, but there is within her the 'bête féroce' which society has fostered. He notes the sad lot of woman in childhood, at puberty, in marriage and in old age, in the complex societies we have evolved, but also in the primitive society of the American Indian. Everywhere woman is subservient to man, so that 'L'homme commande à la femme, même dans les pays où la femme commande à la nation.'[19] She is oppressed and unhappy, over-preoccupied with sex and often corrupt, though a distinction must be made between sexual freedom and immorality as the Supplément au voyage de Bougainville clearly shows. Diderot does not fail, however, to recognize that social progress, the development of art, commerce and luxury enhanced woman's importance without making her any happier. When she is endowed with genius, she is often more original than man. Women remain a mystery, yet there is much to be gained by frequenting them because of their intuition, quick perception and the polish of their manners. By studying them the philosopher can probe the secrets underlying society, and their ability to communicate outside and beyond language enables him to fathom the very nature of artifice. He is not clear, however, on the extent to which women's vices and virtues are innate or acquired. By being at once natural and artificial woman finds herself driven to duplicity. She becomes the perfect actress and mirrors a society of which she is not truly a part. In practice his sympathy for women, his understanding of the female heart, his sensitivity to female beauty, his very vulnerability, coupled with his humanism, led him at times to exalt women and, more significantly, to urge greater freedom for them. He could not bear to see their suffering and their frustration, and his traditional view of the good, moral, home-loving woman which recurs constantly in his work, and which strikes us today as superficial and out-dated, served to idealize woman and place her on a new pedestal.

It is to his fiction and not to his theatre that one must turn for the elaboration of his ideas, remembering, however, that in his novels only individual cases which allow for examination in depth are presented. Already in *La Religieuse*, Suzanne, the unfortunate nun cloistered without vocation, comes to life as an individual although she is undoubtedly the mouthpiece of Diderot to the extent that the author might well have exclaimed: 'Suzanne, c'est moi', as Flaubert did of Emma Bovary. Even so Suzanne herself has the value of a symbol created to further a philosophical purpose. From being a particular woman she acquires the dimension of a representative figure. The Mother Superiors, too, so well delineated, have been carefully chosen as types to bring home a general point. Thus Diderot transcends common realism to provide a hallucinatory vision which holds the truth he wishes to convey, and his portraits have a depth that art enables us to perceive. This serves to further his total rejection of a uni-sexual society, and his empathy for his female protagonists leads him to make an impassioned plea for freedom and a life fully in accord with the laws of nature. Suzanne, the hapless victim of society, deprived of the freedom which is her birthright, enslaved by convention and superstition, touches to the quick the average sensitive reader who is led to adopt Diderot's point of view without becoming aware that he is yielding to a subtle propaganda. The realistic depiction of hysteria in nunneries which provides an effective

backcloth to the tale has the truth of fiction and has been carefully
subordinated to the message the author has successfully conveyed
to us. In his preface to *Zaïre*, Voltaire, who had already bitingly
expressed his disgust that the daughter of 'la divine Emilie'
should be shut up in a convent, wrote: 'La société dépend des
femmes. Tous les peuples qui ont le malheur de les enfermer sont
insociables.' Likewise, Diderot's condemnation is in the light of
moral and utilitarian considerations which he integrated into a
general philosophy of nature.

Diderot's two *drames* offer a very conventional and superficial
view of woman. Just as the moralizing sounded unconvincing so
does his apologia of marriage. How else could it be, for Diderot
had good personal reasons for doubting the eternity of vows
taken in good faith. This fact did not, however, prevent him from
being highly critical of divorce, then urged by Helvétius, on
account of an overriding need to protect the children. *Le Fils
naturel*, more clearly concerned with the rights of women, contains statements which may be sincere but have a hollow ring such
as 'perdre le plus grand bien: un époux vertueux'. In his later
fiction the part of rhetoric and with it the tendency to broad
generalizations decreases. The very cynicism of Rameau's nephew
in acting as a pimp and exploiting the charms of his consort brings
out forcefully an indictment of a society that fosters such a state
of affairs. The nephew's ideas on the education of women are
certainly not precisely those of Diderot, but they show how point-
less it is to provide a conventional, moral education in an immoral
society and lead to recognition of woman's right to sexual grati-
fication as well as man's. In his *Contes* Diderot resolutely turns to
individual cases. As a result his women become more convincing.
He brings out their dignity, their tenderness and great sensitivity,
and even such secondary characters as Olivier's widow or the
coachman's wife in *Les Deux Amis de Bourbonne* stand out as good
women in their own right. More important are the two stories
which form *Ceci n'est pas un conte*, which appeared for the first time
in the *Correspondance littéraire* of April 1773. Their theme is the
same, but the role of the man and the woman has been reversed
in the second *conte*. In the first the loving Tanié is victimized by
the cruel and treacherous Mme Reymer, in the second a very real
and passionately loving Mlle de la Chaux is ruthlessly abandoned

overnight by her lover, the doctor Gardeil. Diderot says at the end of the first tale: 'S'il y a des femmes très méchantes et des hommes très bons, il y a aussi des femmes très bonnes et des hommes très méchants.'[20]—a point illustrated in the second tale. Diderot is apparently unwilling to discriminate between men and women. Throughout he insists on the veracity of his story which had in fact an historical basis, and he refrains from pointing any moral, arguing by way of conclusion that social reasons should lead one to decide against the unfaithful lover even if the latter cannot help his change of heart: 'Mettez la main sur la conscience et dites-moi, vous, monsieur l'apologiste des trompeurs et des infidèles si vous prendriez le docteur de Toulouse pour votre ami? Vous hésitez? Tout est dit.'[21] In practice the juxtaposition of these two stories serves to make it abundantly clear that there is something wrong with a society that allows such misfortunes. *Madame de La Carlière* also appeared first in the *Correspondance littéraire*, this time in two instalments, in May 1773. Its title there is *Second Conte*, which underlines its connection with *Ceci n'est pas un conte*. The Assézat-Tourneux manuscript calls it *Madame de La Carlière, conte*, but recalling the title Naigeon gave to the work H. Dieckmann argues that the true, full title seems to be: *Madame de La Carlière ou Sur l'inconséquence du jugement public de nos actions particulières*, thereby underlying its relationship with the *Supplément au Voyage de Bougainville ou Dialogue entre A et B sur l'inconvénient d'attacher des idées morales à certaines actions physiques qui n'en comportent aucune*, which was also published in the *Correspondance littéraire* in 1773.[22] Mme de La Carlière, an inflexible, devout if not truly Christian woman, cannot forgive her husband the chevalier Desroches for having broken his promise to her and been unfaithful. His life becomes one long misery and his wife comes to an early death through grief, actually passing away in the church of Saint-Eustache where she had gone in the hope of receiving the sacrament. As in the other cases the story has a basis in fact and Diderot has taken much trouble to give it an atmosphere of truth. H. Dieckmann[23] rightly stresses the role of public opinion as a main actor in the presentation of the conflict between the two individuals. 'Not the sacrament of marriage, he writes, not the promise given before God's representative, not faith constitute for her [Mme de La Carlière] the binding force, but society's judgement.' Public opinion acquires an absolute value and she acts against the law of nature. One may conclude that society is held to blame for the final catastrophe as in the earlier *conte*. Thus historical veracity and a realistic presentation, exclusively personal characterization merely serve to bring out more tellingly the social indictment. It is made clear that no form of legislation can remedy the human misery inherent in the social order Diderot knew. Here is how Diderot concludes his tale: '. . . sans approuver les maris infidèles, je ne prise pas autrement les femmes qui mettent tant d'importance à cette rare qualité. Et puis, j'ai mes idées, peut-être justes, à coup sûr bizarres, sur certaines actions que je regarde moins comme des vices de l'homme que comme des conséquences de nos législations absurdes, source de mœurs aussi absurdes qu'elles et d'une dépravation que j'appellerais volontiers artificielle.[24] These ideas found fuller expression and elaboration in the *Supplément au Voyage de Bougainville*, which can be considered as the third panel of a triptych and which embodies Diderot's personal ethics. The introductory remarks by Grimm or Meister in the *Correspondance littéraire* of April 1773 make the link between the three works explicit: 'Le Conte que l'on va lire [*Ceci n'est pas un conte*] est de M. Diderot, il sera suivi de plusieurs autres du même auteur. On ne verra qu'à la fin du dernier la morale et le but secret qu'il s'est proposé.' Having established that society is the culprit Diderot now offers us an ideal society based on freedom which challenges our conventions and preaches free love as an answer to the frustrations and unnatural mode of life of his contemporaries. Moreover this ideal society, new to us, is not unknown in the newly discovered world. It is to be found in Tahiti where women do not suffer from hysterics and vapours, and Diderot can once again base himself on sufficient authenticated fact to carry conviction whilst embroidering somewhat the truth and leading the unwary reader to espouse his attitude through the art of his dialogue. We can now understand his insistence on portraying female characters in his tales and also how, in the final analysis, he transcends the particular instances he has presented in order to reach a general truth which embraces the whole of mankind. In Tahiti at least 'la femme n'est pas le chien de l'homme'.

The story of Mme de La Pommeraye in *Jacques le fataliste*, written at the same time, provides a further instance of the damage done by the conventions we have established and which are the cause of a war between the sexes exacerbated by the current *libertinage* which finds its literary culmination in Laclos's *Les Liaisons dangereuses*. J.-L. Leutrat[25] has brought out the connection between the story of Mme de La Pommeraye and Mme de La Carlière, to which he might well have added Mme Reymer, showing that the plot in both stories unfolds according to a 'schéma rigoureusement identique';[26] and, quoting from the *Essai sur les femmes*, he sees how aptly Diderot's general statement fits the character of Mme de La Pommeraye, and concludes: 'Quant à la 'haine profonde' et 'secrète' qu'elles (les femmes) nourrissent à l'égard des hommes, rien ne l'illustre mieux que les commentaires suggérés à l'Hôtesse du Grand Cerf au cours de son récit. Ces commentaires soulignent d'ailleurs que l'histoire de Mme de La Pommeraye s'inscrit dans la perspective d'une revendication féministe.'[27] This last fact is what establishes an essential difference between Diderot's tales of around 1772 and the long list of works which offer us examples of feminine revenge.[28] The vindictiveness of woman, already brought out in the article *femme* of the *Encyclopédie*, which is not by Diderot, is a social phenomenon and vengeance for her is a form of self-defence, on the part of a creature who feels herself to be weak. In our view J.-L. Leutrat in his excellent article just fails to make the significant point that Diderot did in fact provide a moral and physiological answer to human needs, albeit in an ideal society and in a wholly unpractical way. This of course he knew full well. His pragmatism leads him to caution: *Entretien d'un père avec ses enfants* has a subtitle: *Du danger de se mettre au-dessus des lois*. There can be no conclusion to the dialogue of natural and social man, nor can we turn the clock back. But Diderot had a *but secret* in presenting his true tales of human suffering in an impossible social system. It was to unfold a vision of a free society that would solve at least one problem of behaviour in a way satisfactory to men and women alike and lay the foundation of a revolution that would upset the prevailing social system. It is therefore a mistake to believe that only on the subject of women Diderot failed to show insight and a prophetic vision. At one level he went undoubtedly further than the most ardent feminist would countenance, whilst at another he acknowledged the impracticability of his proposals in the Western world of his day. He was more concerned with the general moral and social problem than with any specific reforms of immediate advantage to women, and he wrote little on the rights of women largely because he was more concerned with those of mankind as a whole.

7

Diderot and the
Education of Girls

EVA JACOBS

Diderot had already lost three children when a daughter, Marie-Angélique, was born on 2 September 1753. The precariousness of babyhood and early childhood, which the three deaths in his own family had underlined, meant that with the birth of this daughter the whole attention of both parents was concentrated on keeping her alive. Projections into the future, concern about how she would be brought up, were meaningless when the balance of life and death was so delicate. Diderot's wife insisted on dressing the baby in white and consecrating her to the Virgin and Saint Francis.[1] Even if Diderot was horrified by such a show of superstition, at the time he could not really protest. His emotional state, if not his intellectual assessment, was no doubt close to his wife's feeling that anything and everything should be done to ensure the child's survival. Later, when Mme Diderot regularly pronounced that God had allowed Angélique to live as a reward for her religious vow, Diderot was irritated at being trapped by his wife's illogical, but irrefutable, proof.[2] At all events, the child did live, and the upbringing and education of his only daughter was to become one of the central concerns of her father's life.

He appears to have taken little enough part in her early years. Perhaps his capitulation to her mother's superstitious practices at her birth prevented him from reasserting his authority as the child began to develop. But it is more likely that he did not consider intervention appropriate. Balanced against his total disapproval of his wife's values and his contempt for her intellect, there was the whole weight of contemporary opinion, which stated that a child's early upbringing should be the responsibility of the mother. In the mid-eighteenth century, this was a progressive view, that of the new theorists of education who pointed out the deleterious effects of handing children over to a succession of wet-nurses, servants and tutors, claiming that the mother was the repository of the young child's physical and moral welfare. While far from feeling that his wife fitted the role assigned to the mother as an ideal, Diderot could hardly fail to be influenced by progressive thinking on this point. A less respectable reason for his lack of involvement in Angélique's early upbringing he gives himself in a significant passage in *Le Neveu de Rameau*. Whether *Moi* is simply the author has been the subject of much debate, but it is undeniable that the work contains many straightforwardly autobiographical elements, among them a short discussion between *Moi* and *Lui* on the subject of Angélique's education. It seems certain that the passage in question was written in 1761–2 and that Diderot's reluctant answer to Rameau's question about the age of his daughter, 'Supposez-lui huit ans', can be taken as precise information. Rameau's expectation that Diderot, now a 'gros monsieur', is already hiring tutors in the various disciplines to instruct his daughter, is denied by her father, who admits: 'Pas encore. C'est sa mere qui se mêle de son education; car il faut avoir la paix chez soi.'[3]

That Diderot was dismayed by the education Angélique was receiving from her mother is evident from many remarks made in his correspondence. The results of Mme Diderot's influence, which he had avoided describing to Rameau, he reveals in a letter to Sophie Volland written just after his daughter's eighth birthday: 'Elle grasseye; elle minaude; elle grimace; elle connoît tout le pouvoir de son humeur et de ses larmes; et elle boude et pleure pour rien. Elle a la mémoire pleine de sots rébus . . . le goût du travail et de la lecture, qui lui étoit naturel, se perd . . . sa mère, qui s'en est emparée, ne souffrira jamais que j'en fasse quelque chose.'[4] But in spite of his gloomy prediction that Mme Diderot would never allow him to participate in Angélique's upbringing, exactly a year later he was able to announce to Sophie Volland that he had at last obtained his wife's permission to take over her education.[5] It was an opportunity that he had long desired, if not expected. That he had meditated on the problem of the education to give his daughter is evident from the continuation of the discussion with Rameau. Again, although it is possible that at times in

the dialogue Diderot is satirizing *Moi*, here the tone is too sober
to allow for such an interpretation. *Moi*'s plans for the education
of his eight-year-old daughter are certainly those of Diderot. To
Rameau's outrageous, but he believes practical, suggestion that
the only things that a girl of good family needs to be taught are
to play the harpsichord, sing, dance and be 'jolie, amusante et
coquette', *Moi* solemnly replies with a programme that will teach
his daughter 'à raisonner juste'.[6] This programme consists of 'de
la grammaire, de la fable, de l'histoire, de la geographie, un peu
de dessein, et beaucoup de morale.'[7] So that when, just after
Angélique's ninth birthday, he was allowed by his wife to under-
take her education, he had a clear idea of his objectives and the
means by which to fulfil them. There is no evidence that he
changed his mind about either, although he at first despaired of
progress. Only four days after his announcement to Sophie
Volland, he was already claiming that he was getting nowhere
with Angélique's education because 'on [presumably her mother]
étouffe en un instant tout ce que je sème en un mois.'[8] But he
loved his daughter, almost obsessively, and he persevered.
Paradoxically, it was precisely in the studies that Rameau had
advocated that Angélique showed unusual talent. Was Diderot
teasing Rameau when he claimed to have no intention of including
harpsichord lessons in his 'plan de son [Angélique's] education'?[9]
Certainly, as early as July 1762 we find him involved in her
harpsichord practice and ecstatic over her gifts. Soon after he is
teaching her history,[10] and there are frequent echoes in his letters
of 'beaucoup de morale'.

It is to be supposed that Diderot obtained tutors for Angélique
in some of the subjects that he believed she should study, for to
Rameau's question 'ne lui faudra-t-il pas un ou deux maitres?'
Moi replies 'Sans doute'.[11] Even though this exchange is followed
by a criticism of the inadequacy of tutors, in which *Moi* and *Lui*
find themselves in perfect agreement, practical necessity probably
led Diderot to hire the 'un ou deux maitres', unsatisfactory though
he may have felt them to be. Angélique certainly needed a music
teacher. In 1769, this was Antoine Bemetzrieder, with whom
Diderot reports a conversation that echoes curiously *Moi*'s
discussion with *Lui*, written many years earlier. Here, however,
Diderot offers Rameau's views as his own. Had he become even

more cynical as the years passed? Bemetzrieder, who hopes to be engaged as a tutor, claims to be qualified in mathematics and law, but Diderot rejects these subjects for Angélique. He is more enthusiastic about history and geography as being solid and useful, thus repeating the view expressed in *Le Neveu de Rameau*, but it is Bemetzrieder's offer of harpsichord and harmony lessons that leads to the young man's appointment, made in terms that would have given Rameau's nephew enormous satisfaction: 'Chez un peuple frivole comme celui-ci, les bonnes études ne mènent à rien; avec les arts d'agrément on arrive à tout.' The verbal contract is drawn up: 'Monsieur, vous viendrez tous les soirs à six heures et demie; vous montrerez à ma fille un peu de géographie et d'histoire; le reste du temps sera employé au clavecin et à l'harmonie. Vous trouverez votre couvert mis tous les jours et à tous les repas; et comme il ne suffit pas d'être nourri, qu'il faut encore être logé et vêtu, je vous donnerai cinq cents livres par an.'[12] This generous offer was accepted with alacrity by the applicant, and Angélique continued to make excellent progress as a musician, while presumably also extending her knowledge of history and geography. It seems that Diderot himself taught her English.[13] It is clear, at all events, from Angélique's own correspondence, that she was far from ill-educated,[14] and that the mixture of private tutoring and parental guidance and teaching organized by her father provided a satisfactory general upbringing. There had been alternatives open to Diderot. Daughters of the middle classes were commonly boarded at convents, and there did exist some lay girls' schools, staffed by schoolmistresses.[15] But Diderot was firmly against sending his daughter to a convent,[16] and he probably preferred to keep her education directly under his supervision rather than send her to a lay school, even supposing that a convenient one were available. He took a constantly active part in her lessons, even when they were given by tutors, and in particular he sat in on her music lessons and frequently supervised her practice. As far as her general education was concerned, therefore, Angélique made up in parental involvement what she may have lacked in formal instruction, and her lasting devotion to her father shows that she certainly felt no deprivation.

Nevertheless, one cannot fail to be struck by the very limited nature of the education that Diderot considered it appropriate to give to his only child. His early acquiescence in his wife taking over the girl completely may be explained by a mixture of concern and pusillanimity on his part. As late as 1767, he had not lived down the opprobrium directed by his fellow-*philosophes* against what they felt to be a betrayal of principle and a contradiction of deeply-held convictions. Voltaire, in his preface to *Les Scythes*, had paid public tribute to Diderot, a tribute that could not but please him, in spite of his secret reservations about Voltaire. But in a private letter to a close mutual friend, Voltaire, too, expressed reservations. Speaking of his tribute he adds: 'Ce n'est pas que je sois content de lui [Diderot]. On dit qu'il laisse élever sa fille dans des principes qu'il déteste. C'est Orosmade qui livre ses enfants à Arimane. Ce péché contre nature est horrible. Je me flatte qu'il sèvrera enfin un enfant qu'il a laissé nourrir du lait des furies.'[17] At this time Angélique was thirteen years old, but it seems to have been believed among members of the philosophic fraternity that Diderot continued in his own household to sacrifice principle to peace. We know that as Angélique's understanding developed, Diderot, in his moral lessons, tried to counteract the influence of his wife's narrow religious outlook. But the *philosophes* were less concerned about private actions than about public stances in their battle against the Church, and Voltaire's dismay at Diderot's unwillingness to use his daughter's education as a weapon reveals his annoyance at an opportunity missed. One need not, however, be a participant in the philosophic battles of the time to be conscious of serious deficiencies in Angélique's education. While Diderot's desire to obtain peace by compromise in an often stormy domestic environment can be understood by any sympathetic and uninvolved outsider, less easily acceptable is the content of his educational programme. Here, the sense of an opportunity missed depends on no firm position in a set battle, but on a knowledge both of Diderot and of contemporary discussions on the education of girls.

There is almost no area of human activity to which Diderot did not at some stage in his long career address himself. On most subjects, he had something new and exciting to say. But on the subject of Angélique's education, setting aside any kind of partisanship, one has to admit that he said nothing that was not both dull and conservative. A little history and geography, 'beaucoup de morale', and music, described, belittlingly enough, as one of the 'arts d'agrément'. In what does this differ from what the convents offered? Apart from the absence of religious instruction, apparently supplied in any case by Mme Diderot and her familiar priests? Even if the 'morale' Diderot himself preached was not exactly that of the convents? But was it in fact so very different? He recounts a conversation with Angélique on one of their walks: 'Je me proposai dans la dernière [promenade] de lui faire concevoir qu'il n'y avoit aucune vertu qui n'eût deux récompenses: le plaisir de bien faire, et celui d'obtenir la bien-veillance des autres; aucun vice qui n'eût deux châtimens: l'un au fond de notre cœur, un autre dans le sentiment d'aversion que nous ne manquons jamais d'inspirer aux autres. Le texte n'étoit pas stérile.' There follows an almost mediæval-morality descrip-tion of the effects of sin: 'Nous parcourûmes la pluspart des vertus; ensuite, je lui montrai l'envieux avec ses yeux creux et son visage pâle et maigre; l'intempérant avec son estomac délabré et ses jambes goutteuses; le luxurieux avec sa poitrine asthmatique et les restes de plusieurs maladies qu'on ne guérit point . . .'[18] Supernatural sanctions are admittedly absent from this lurid account, but the moral teaching could be that of any sin-conscious priest. Certainly, one might conclude from looking at Diderot's educational plans for his daughter and their implementation, that his determination to keep her away from the convent did not stem from any desire to give her a radically different education, but rather from the general human and social dislike of conventual life that was to find such powerful expression in *La Religieuse*.

Meanwhile, the debate on the education of girls went on around him. This, of course, was not a new phenomenon in France. The *Précieuses* of a century earlier had called for the emancipation of women, and had already seen clearly that social progress had to be accompanied by, or even preceded by, educa-tional reform. The vicious circle of a girl's upbringing leading to intellectual and social inferiority which in turn justifies inferior education had to be broken. A determined feminist apologist of the late seventeenth century, François Poulain de la Barre, whose book *De l'égalité des deux sexes* (1673) ran to several editions, had argued strongly that 'les femmes considérées selon les principes de la saine Philosophie, sont autant capables que les hommes de toutes sortes de connoissances.'[19] Nevertheless, although his ideas found echo in several other writers, although the cause of women's education had been espoused by figures as famous as Fénelon, Mme de Maintenon, the abbé Fleury and Rollin, and although educated women were by no means rare, among the aristocracy at least, a hundred years later the same arguments were being put forward in very much the same terms by men such as Fromageot,[20] Le More,[21] and Riballier.[22] The conclusion seems inescapable that very little progress had been made in the area of the education of girls during the many years that had passed since the stormy *querelle des femmes* at the end of the seventeenth century.[23] But the debate was still very much alive. Discussions on education were given renewed impetus with the publication in 1762 of *Emile*. Although Rousseau was not primarily concerned with the education of girls, his description of the education of Sophie certainly aroused the anger of some proponents of women's education. Riballier, for instance, though a disciple, not to say a plagiarist, of Rousseau, nonetheless attacked his master's 'maximes Asiatiques' relating to the place of women in society and the inferior education offered by Rousseau as being suitable to their station.[24] But in all this, Diderot remained strangely silent. Apart from his concern for the education of Angélique, he seems to have taken little interest in the subject of the education of girls as such. Before his marriage, he had had experience as a tutor, but both his charges had been boys. He was twice to take the opportunity of offering advice on the education of children. In each case, although the recipients of his advice were the parents of children of both sexes, Diderot limited his advice to the education of sons rather than daughters, by implication at least.[25]

In view of Diderot's general sympathy for radical ideas as well as the contact we may presume he had with contemporary discussion on the education of girls, it is interesting to speculate on how he came to offer his own daughter so conservative an education. He never seems to have felt it necessary to justify his views, but there are indications here and there of his thinking. Like all parents, Diderot gave Angélique the education that reflected his desires and ambitions for her. She was less than one and a half years old when he wrote, 'J'ai une petite fille à qui je veux laisser le plus d'éducation et de bien que je pourrai, afin qu'elle soit digne de son petit prétendu.'[26] The 'petit prétendu' in question was Abel-François, son of the addressee, Nicolas Caroillon, and Diderot refers to him in the same letter as 'ce petit mari'. Angélique did in fact marry him, but not before her father had also offered her to two or three very unsuitable other potential husbands. Clearly, from her earliest childhood Diderot's one obsessive desire for his daughter was that she should get married. Everything was to be subordinated to that purpose, including her education, here coupled with a dowry as making her worthy of a husband. The fact that he disapproved of marriage as an institution, that his own marriage was disastrous for both himself and his wife, that he knew many gifted unmarried women who managed to earn their livings, none of all this seems to have influenced his conviction that Angélique's sole purpose in life was to obtain a husband. With a limited aim in view, a limited education was appropriate. From her very birth, Diderot thought of her not as a child to be educated, but as a girl to be educated. If he solemnly rejected Rameau's belittling 'Pourvu qu'elle soit jolie, amusante et coquette' so that she might please men, in fact his own programme of education for his daughter was scarcely less designed to ensure her attractiveness to a future husband. Of course, it was her happiness he had in mind, but he believed that a woman could achieve happiness only by submission to her spouse. The letter he wrote to Angélique four days after her wedding set firmly the limited horizons she should accept: 'Ayez pour votre époux toute la condescendance imaginable. Conformez vous à ses goûts raisonnables. Tâchez de ne rien penser que vous ne puissiez lui dire; qu'il soit sans cesse comme au fond de votre âme. Ne faites rien dont il ne puisse être témoin. Soyez en tout et toujours comme sous ses yeux.'[27] One can almost hear Arnolphe applauding every word. Diderot hopes that his daughter will spend most of her time at home, employed in running the household, or, in her hours of leisure, reading and further developing her musical talent. The education he had given her fitted her exactly for the role in life that he had planned for her from babyhood. She was not frivolous or empty-headed, for she had always had contact with books and ideas. She had a talent for music that was both a social advantage and a personal resource in a narrow life. But she was trained for nothing, was certainly not a *femme savante*, and could have no personal ambition. Her father bought her a husband, at enormous personal as well as financial cost to himself, and he sincerely believed that he had done his very best by her.

It would nevertheless be unjust to ascribe Diderot's upbringing of his daughter merely to a residual bourgeois conservatism. He is frequently criticized for the apparent gap in his life between his radical ideas and his cautious money-conscious and family-centred practical concerns, and his attitude towards his daughter is often taken as an example to show that Diderot was radical only in the abstract. But such an interpretation of his conduct fails to take into account important aspects of his thought. His rejection of the case for equality in girls' education was conscious: he simply could not accept the intellectual basis of the reformers' arguments. In the mid-seventeenth century in France, arguments for the identity of men's and women's intellectual capacities began to be presented in strictly logical terms. Previously, the method had been to select examples of clever women to show that the inferiority of females was a wicked or convenient myth. Now, with the growing acceptance throughout society of the Cartesian theory of man, postulating the dualism of matter and mind in the formation of the human being, reformers were able to argue that although men and women obviously differed to some extent in their biology, mind, as a single, immaterial substance, was necessarily identical in both sexes. Since education was concerned only with the mind, the same education must be appropriate to both.[28] It is an attractive argument, but it depends for its persuasive power on an acceptance of Descartes' cosmology, with its rigorous separation of mind and matter. If Diderot was ever attracted to Cartesian dualism, and this is highly doubtful, by the time he had to consider Angélique's education he was far from accepting its premises. His developing materialism, from the *Lettre sur les aveugles* (1749) up till *Le Rêve de d'Alembert* (1769), led him to the interpretation of the whole human being as a purely biological entity, in which mind is a function of the brain, and the brain a specialized area of the body. Unlike the Cartesians, he could not separate, conceptually, the mind, as an educable entity, from the material body. He did not believe that women could be abstracted from their biological reality as women. His adoption of Locke's sensationalist epistemology meant that for him knowledge reached the brain filtered by the senses, through the body. This was not a pure process, but one that could be interfered with, and was indeed necessarily interfered with, by all kinds of material agencies, both outside and inside the individual. A girl's biological femininity was part of her inescapable material wholeness, and in Diderot's view the weakness of the neo-Cartesian case for equality lay in that it tried to bypass reality.

Angélique was already married and pregnant when an important work appeared making a radical case for reform in women's education. This was Helvétius's *De l'homme*, published posthumously in 1773. Diderot and Helvétius shared many ideas, including their fundamental materialist cosmology and sensationalist epistemology. In *De l'homme*, Helvetius took sensationalist epistemology to its logical conclusion and argued that since men were born without ideas, the contents of all minds could only be ascribed to education, in the broadest sense. This was as true for females as for males. Education could be controlled and society could therefore choose the input it fed into the individual. A woman's mind, like a man's, was purely the result of this process. Men and women could, if the decision were made, have a rigorously equal education, with absolutely identical results. There is no doubt that Diderot was shaken by Helvétius's systematic development of sensationalism. While there is no evidence that it was the implications of Helvétius's argument for the education of women that particularly moved him to meditate a reply, was there perhaps some feeling on his part that if Helvétius were right, his own upbringing of his daughter had been wrong? Had he needlessly deprived Angélique of all the knowledge that he himself enjoyed and could have given her? At all events, his *Réfutation suivie de l'ouvrage d'Helvétius intitulé l'Homme*, written between 1773 and 1775 and unpublished during his lifetime, is a wide criticism of Helvétius's ideas, which deals with the education of women only as part of the general problem. Diderot attacked the conclusion Helvétius drew from his sensationalist epistemology that 'l'éducation fait tout', replacing it with his own 'l'éducation fait beaucoup'. He denied the view that 'L'organisation [that is, the physical make-up of the individual] ne fait rien', and suggested instead 'L'organisation fait moins qu'on ne pense'.[29] For in answer to Helvétius's totally abstract sensationalism, in its own way as rationalistic as Cartesian dualism, Diderot offered a tentative pragmatic interpretation of the process of learning and thinking, based upon the observation of reality. While agreeing with Helvétius that the mind was a function of the brain, he could not envisage the brain as a passive receptacle, the same in all normal individuals, only receiving and organizing what was put into it. Its biological links with the rest of the body precluded such independence. It was affected by everything taking place in the individual, and in turn influenced the body at the biological as well as the behavioural level. Regarding the implications for women's education, Diderot answered Helvétius's radical 'Les femmes sont susceptibles de la même éducation que les hommes' with his old conservative 'On pourrait les élever mieux qu'on ne fait'.[30] To Helvétius's argument that the fact that women of genius exist proves that their physical constitution is irrelevant to their intellectual abilities, and its obvious corollary 'Si les femmes sont en général inférieures, c'est qu'en général elles reçoivent encore une plus mauvaise éducation,'[31] Diderot replies: 'Mais leur organisation délicate, mais leur assujettissement à une maladie périodique, à des grossesses, à des couches, leur permettent-ils cette force et cette continuité de méditation que vous appelez la créatrice du génie et à laquelle vous attribuez toute importante découverte? Elles font les premiers pas plus vite, mais elles sont plutôt lasses et s'arrêtent plus promptement.'[32]

As regards the education of girls, therefore, Diderot had not moved at all from the position that justified Angélique's upbringing. His opinion of women had not long previously been defined in his essay *Sur les femmes*, where, along with some understanding and some sentimentality, there is expressed his profound feeling about the biological irreducibility of women to the same model as men. In the end, a girl's biological nature rendered all discussion about her education in the same terms as a boy's, a totally meaningless exercise. Her essential being was as a female of the human species. Her condition as a woman was inescapable. In his *Réfutation*, Diderot, quite unconvinced by Helvétius's logical system, reaffirms long-held and recently re-examined opinions.[33] Certainly, he has no regrets about the education he had given

Angélique. Its conservatism had been justified by nature. In one area, he had in fact offered her an unconventional and radical programme. If a relatively poor intellectual education was necessitated by a girl's biological condition, so her biological condition demanded an advanced sexual education. Here, Diderot had not hesitated. He spoke to Angélique freely about the realities of sex and child-bearing, and paid for her to attend lessons in sexual anatomy given by Mlle Biheron with the aid of realistic wax anatomical models.[34] But his radicalism in this area only served to corroborate his conservatism in the rest.

When, after Angélique's marriage, Diderot finally made the long-projected voyage to Russia at the invitation of Catherine the Great, he took with him something of a reputation as an educator. No doubt he was able to speak as brilliantly on the subject of education as on any other, and the Empress sought his advice on educational matters. She had founded in St Petersburg in 1764 the first state educational establishment for girls in Europe, the Smol'nyi Institute, attended by daughters of the nobility. A year later, a second girls' school, for daughters of the bourgeoisie, was attached to it. Catherine was greatly committed to the education of girls, and her visits to her protégées afforded her the deepest satisfaction. Expecting Diderot to share her enthusiasm for girls' education, she took him to visit the school and asked his opinion about the curriculum. It was only on the subject of sexual education that he showed any creative concern. As enchanted as ever with Mlle Biheron's anatomical models, he tried to persuade Catherine to invite the elderly spinster to Russia to give demonstrations at the school and to instruct some Russian disciple in the art of making the models.[35] Catherine bought the models, but Mlle Biheron stayed at home.[36] On his return to France, Diderot wrote at the Empress's request a *Plan d'une Université pour le Gouvernement de Russie*,[37] a document concerned with both secondary schooling and University education. But, in spite of Catherine's particular interest in the education of girls, Diderot's *Plan* appears to relate only to boys.

Diderot's ideas on the education of girls serve to demonstrate once more the underlying consistency of his thought. To label him as a radical, and then to feel surprise at the conservatism of his theory and practice on this subject, is to do him less than justice. His preoccupation, as always, was with the happiness of the individual. The legitimacy of happiness he never doubted. Of the difficulty of achieving it he was often conscious. He wanted happiness for his daughter, as he wanted it for himself. He was convinced that for a woman to be happy, she had to accept her biological condition as a female. She was a prisoner of her physiology. The proper education for girls had to be directed towards making the prison as comfortable and fulfilling as possible. Diderot never regretted the education he gave his daughter. Its limitations, he believed, were those imposed by nature, and conformity with nature was a central tenet of the philosophic world view. It is sobering to reflect that in the case of a leading *philosophe*, pragmatism and the empirical consideration of reality only served to confirm the general belief in the otherness, and implied inferiority, of women. Empiricism, modern as it is as an approach to reality, does indeed militate against the equality of women. There are too many facts against it. Only rationalists, who, like those of the seventeenth and eighteenth centuries, are unencumbered by facts, can hope to provide a radical case for women's emancipation. The rest of us, like Diderot, must be content with lesser reforms.

8

Restif de la Bretonne and Woman's Estate

DENNIS FLETCHER

Restif de la Bretonne's obsessive interest in the opposite sex is reflected in the exceptional amount of attention which is devoted to women in an exceptionally voluminous *œuvre*. The luridly aberrant aspects of this obsession—incestuous inclinations, irrepressible foot-fetishism—have, predictably, escaped neglect. The same cannot be said for Restif's superficially eccentric but basically orthodox views on the nature of woman and her place in contemporary society, a subject which has attracted but little scholarly interest to date.[1]

The main justification which can be offered for this attempt to rescue from semi-oblivion the hardened prejudices of as conservative and traditionalist an upholder of a male-dominated society as could well be found in the eighteenth century is that it may provide a corrective to the quite different picture of Restif which is suggested by a number of recent studies. Among these, Gérard Guillot's represents the most extreme position with its view of Restif as 'un des plus généreux féministes du XVIIIe siècle'.[2] Guy Bruit, from evidence which excludes all the author's theoretical works, reaches a more balanced conclusion: whilst making due allowance for the emergence, under the impact of the revelation of Parisian manners, of feminist elements in Restif's thought, he sees him as still bound to the immemorial rural customs of Sacy in his native Burgundy, 'oscillant de droite à gauche, de sa conception traditionnelle de la femme soumise à une conception nouvelle de la femme libre et divine'.[3] The basis upon which Mme D. Brahimi's discussion of the question rests is even more slender: a selection of 18 out of the 261 *nouvelles* which make up *Les Contemporaines*. In her 'Restif feministe?'[4] she offers a justifiably tentative response in the affirmative to the question which she poses. That it is possible to offer a different answer after wider sampling of Restif's many explicit formulations of opinion on 'the woman question', this essay attempts to show.

In the general perspective of the history of the manners and morals of men and women considered primarily as human beings rather than males and females, the two poles of *nature* and *culture* (or *nurture*) usefully situate and delimit the field of discussion. They can be seen even more clearly to define the spectrum of attitudes towards the question of the relations between the sexes, whether in the discussions generated by the activity of the women's liberation movement of today or in those centred upon earlier struggles for female emancipation. Indeed, the radical feminists of the twentieth century are as ardent in their allegiance to the ideal of transcending nature and in their espousal of the cause of a truly universal and humanizing culture as were their ideological ancestors, the *salonnières* of the seventeenth century. The male chauvinists of the present generation are, for their part, no more nor less benighted than those anti-feminist *philosophes* of the Enlightenment who would have liked to immure their women-folk in the biological prison of female sexuality from which no escape to a more civilized environment was possible. It is with this frame of reference in mind that Restif's view of woman's estate will be considered.

Professions of attachment to the natural order were common enough in the eighteenth century, but few were as strident as Restif's. In his *Philosophie de Monsieur Nicolas*[5] (1796) Nature is enthroned and the consequences of this dominion are shown reaching into all areas of human life. Responding to imperious and infallible inner promptings, Restif, 'le prêtre et le docteur de la Nature animalisée' (*PMN*, 292), unfolds his vision of a vitalist cosmogony invested with all the authority of divine inspiration: 'Je proteste que j'ai écrit toute cette PHYSIQUE sous la dictée de la Nature...' (*PMN*, 424). What are offered as the profound truths of 'la haute physique' provide the basis of a view of life which would nowadays be characterized as blatantly sexist. In the new materialist religion which is put in the place of the Jansenist faith which he had abandoned, certain misogynist elements endemic in Christianity survive. For Restif, God is nothing other than the whole of the material universe ('le grand Tout') but this monism is tempered by the fundamental dualism of sex which colours all his thinking. All forms of life spring from the interaction of the two opposite, but complementary, principles: male and female. This interaction, from the macrocosmic to the microcosmic level, has a decided lop-sided air, however: the male principle is always dominant and the female consistently devalued. For example, of the elements of the Aristotelean quartet which go to make up matter, fire and water are categorized as male and have the lion's share of the work of creation, whilst earth and air are female and play secondary roles. The description of the physical properties of air provides a good example of the way in which Restif's pervasively analogical thinking demeans the second sex, whatever the area of discussion: 'C'est l'air porteur du son . . . ceci prouve encore sa femelléïté; il ne résonne, que parce qu'il est élastique; que parce qu'il est creux, comme toutes les femelles: au lieu que le feu, l'eau sont pénétrans comme les mâles . . . L'origine de l'air est le feu dont l'air est une scorie' (PMN, 232–3).

Earth shares with air the female character of mere dross ('scorie') and the quality of receptivity vis-à-vis the fiery penetrative force of the male principle (PMN, 241). In Restif's cosmogony God is initially hermaphrodite, equated with matter in its primal undifferentiated state, but the compulsive need for an order based on hierarchy ensures subsequent emphasis upon a gradation of substances from the unalloyed purity of the infinitely subtle divine 'intellectual fluid' down to the diverse grosser manifestations of matter. Male superiority is firmly established. The God of the Restivian universe is the lord of creation by virtue of his generative function: 'la vie est le produit de la copulation ineffable de Dieu, premier et essentiellement mâle, avec la nature, première et essentiellement femelle'.[6] The superabundant energy generated by the sun of suns produces sparks, or offshoots, in the form of lesser suns which resemble their progenitor in their intense activity and the similarity of its effects. The waste matter ('scories') which accumulates as a by-product of this process is expelled and this defecation explains the origin of the planets (which go through a preliminary phase of their existence as comets). The planets are female and, compared with the male suns, inert. Their gross matter contains 'moules' or 'matrices', however, which can, in cosmic copulation, receive the solar emissions which bring life.

Mother Earth (whose humble origins in Restif's cosmogony recall Eve's derivation from Adam's spare rib) can be seen already providing the model for the essentially passive child-bearing role which Restif assigns to women: 'l'homme est l'image parfaite du Soleil; la femme, l'image parfaite de la Terre; et tous deux réunis sont l'image parfaite de l'Univers, de Dieu même: le Soleil étant l'image parfaite de Dieu, premier mâle, et la Terre, de la Nature, ou matière palpable, première femelle' (*PMN*, 275). The superior status of 'le mâle, auquel la nature a départi la faculté de communiquer l'étincelle de la vie' (*PMN*, 227) is never left in doubt. Restif's personal priapic fantasies, which led him to claim the paternity of an incredibly large number of children and which are generalized as the male 'tendance insurmontable à multiplier son existence' (*PMN*, 258), are reflected in his image of the male animal as 'une bougie, qui en allume cent, mille autres' and the female as 'la bougie qu'il allume, le sujet sur lequel il opère en allumant la mèche' (*PMN*, 381). A woman's sexual identity, physiologically based upon the natural functions in the procreative process which are specific to her, is altogether different from that of a man. Her role in life, biologically determined, is necessarily in marked contrast to his. For her, as much as for him, anatomy is destiny: she is meant to serve as the grateful and submissive recipient of his thrusting sexuality, a privileged instrument of his capacity for creating new life: 'L'Être animé . . . a, pour se reproduire, une double faculté: l'active et la passive. L'active est le lot du mâle. Il a en lui-même, outre la vie, la divine, l'inconcevable, faculté de la donner, par un membre qui lui est propre' (*PMN*, 179). It is by this faculty that Man (i.e.man) is God-like: 'la nature . . . a divinisé les mâles en leur donnant, bornée, une qualité, une faculté sans bornes en Dieu (*PMN*, 270); tout mâle a en lui-même, comme Dieu, dont il est la plus parfaite image, . . . le *sperme*' (*PMN*, 254). As the torch-bearer of Humanity engaged in the sacred mission of perpetuating his species, he is superior to woman. In Restif's materialist 'système de la nature', the Christian conception of the immortality of the soul (of men *and* women) is replaced by the concept of exclusively male immortality in the form of the transmission of generative power to male posterity. Cartesian notions of spiritual substance and *l'automatisme des bêtes* are derided; man is presented as the paragon of animals but it is his kinship with the male part of the brute creation, through his possession of a material *âme communicative*, denied to the second sex, which is heavily emphasized: 'Il est des choses essentielles dans la différence des sexes; ces choses sont telles, qu'il y a plus de différence entre un homme et une femme, qu'entre un homme et un singe mâle, un chien mâle, un taureau, un cheval, un cochon etc. . . . Ainsi, je la répète à ce siècle rempli d'erreurs et de folie, qui cherche, malgré la nature, à confondre les deux sexes, de toutes manières, l'homme ressemble plus au cochon mâle, qu'à la femme qui l'a porté dans son flanc, et à celle dans le flanc de laquelle il dépose son fils' (*PMN*, 529–30).

If there were any doubt as to whether Restif deserved to be regarded as a male chauvinist pig, such testimony would surely place him squarely in the sty!

Restif's overriding concern with sexual identity contrasts strongly with feminist insistence upon the importance of the social identity of individuals as the most important line dividing humanity. His exultant assertion of the ineradicable physiological distinction between the sexes may be compared with the question posed by the seventeenth-century feminist writer Marie de Gournay: 'Se trouve til plus de différence des hommes à elles [les dames] que d'elles à elles mesmes, selon l'institution qu'elles ont prinse, selon qu'elles sont eslevées en ville ou village, ou selon les Nations?'[7] The idea of the arbitrariness of sexual roles in society which stem from the mental conditioning wrought by custom, tradition and education continues to give feminism its radical cutting edge. The anti-feminist, on the other hand, is deeply conservative in his veneration of the age-old principle of male superiority, regarded as sacrosanct since it consecrates a natural state of affairs. Restif's cosmology is founded on this principle, but its author may well have felt that it would appear a trifle insecure when 'la voix de la nature' was constantly being equated by him with something as flimsy as his own intuition. Certainly, he takes pains to buttress his system with evidence from the myths and religions of antiquity which support his view of the relationship between the sexes. The ancient Chaldeans and Egyptians are, *inter alios*, pressed into service to illustrate the universality, in allegorical form, of the basis of his 'système de la nature' in the interaction of the male and female principles. In the 'magnifique théogonie' of the Chaldeans one finds the sun, the active principle of 'intellectualité', the 'ange-de-lumière', in conjunction with the passive, female earth, the 'ange-de-ténèbres', characterized by 'corporéïté' (*PMN*, 124). 'La superbe religion physique des Egyptiens' (*PMN*, 315) reproduces the same opposition in the forms of Osiris and Isis, and this pattern of male dominance is perpetuated in the mythical elements of both Greek and Roman religion and Christianity.

Appeal to the distilled experience of the wisest peoples of ancient times, however, is not meant to be regarded as an essential prop of Restif's system. The truths which lie hidden behind the veil of myth, symbol and allegory are easily discoverable at any time by recourse to analogy, the keystone of the entire structure, expressed in the wearisomely reiterated formula 'tout est image et type dans la nature'. For Restif, analogy is 'le raisonnement par lequel je monte du connu à l'inconnu'; with unconscious irony, he exposes the naked subjectivism of his philosophy: 'Le connu, c'est moi; je juge de tout l'Univers par moi' (*PMN*, 461). Applying the principle of correspondance between macrocosm and microcosm, he can affirm that 'les petits êtres sont l'image des grands' (*PMN*, 293), and is able to tell himself: 'Tu es un petit dieu, image du Dieu universel' (*PMN*, 153). Being in God's image, he has the dominant role, by virtue of his superior intellectual endowments and native dynamism, in all his relations with the opposite sex: as lover, husband, father. Women, not being in God's image, are born underlings. Wedlock is the social form of their natural subjection to the male of the species, upon whom they are destined to dance attendance as a satellite orbits the sun: 'Tout est subordonné dans la Nature . . . . . .; il est sans exemple qu'il y ait à-côté l'un de l'autre deux Soleils, on deux Terres de la même grosseur; le Soleil est le chef unique, et les Planètes lui sont subordonnés: c'est la plus belle image qu'on puisse donner de la *Gamarchie*, ou subordination matrimoniale.'[8] The inferior status of the female partner in the orderly coupling of heavenly bodies is clearly mirrored in matrimony. Similarly, procreation, the aim and *raison d'être* of marriage, reinforces the principle of subordination by bringing into existence the family, with its *paterfamilias* playing the role of Supreme Being, 'le Père universel'. This was the way of the world, and ever more should be so in Restif's opinion; it was the lot of woman to accept gracefully (ingratiatingly even) the inevitability of patriarchy.

Convinced that contemporary French society was sick, Restif never tired of offering prescriptions for its restoration to a state of rude natural (i.e. patriarchal) health. The various 'projets de règlement' which he put forward in his *Idées singulières* series and the innumerable suggestions he made less systematically elsewhere aim at regulating the mechanism of society by, quite simply, putting the clock back. *Les Gynographes* (1777), third of the *Idées singulières* group, explicitly designed 'pour mettre les Femmes à leur place, et opérer le bonheur des deux sexes', lives up to its epigraph, taken from Molière's *Ecole des Femmes* ('A d'austères devoirs le rang de femme engage, . . .'); Restif vies with Arnolphe in his rejection of the rights of woman and his insistence upon her duties. Molière's Agnès is called to mind again by the reactionary temper of Restif's remarks on wifely conduct in *L'Andrographe* (1782), the pendant to *Les Gynographes*: 'La Femme doit presque tout ignorer; c'est-à-dire, toutes les choses qui peuvent la distraire ou la degoûter de ses occupations sédentaires: elle doit toujours être dans le cas d'écouter avec admiration ce que dit son mari; le bonheur des deux sexes en dépend . . . Enfin l'âme de la Femme est si peu ressemblante à celle de son Chef, qu'elle est substanciellement dépendante; une Femme ne peut être solidement heureuse, que par sa liaison avec l'Homme, et sa dépendance de ses volontés: En dépit d'une prétendue expérience contraire, toute Femme maîtresse est très-malheureuse; toute Femme soumise par goût, se trouve à sa place, vit contente, et goûte des satisfactions inconnues à toutes Celles de son sexe qui ne suivent pas la même route.'[9] His man's-eye view of a woman's happiness, unclouded by any considerations more noble than male self-interest, was that there could be no higher form of satisfaction for her than to be a dutiful daughter, spouse and mother. Such was the message of his *La Femme dans les trois états* (1773), based on the same smug assumption that one can call no woman happy unless her happiness comes from making a man happy. The way to fulfilment for the second sex lies in developing an inborn capacity to please: 'Les Femmes . . . ne doivent rien se permettre qui change à leur égard la destination de la Nature, plaire'.[10] 'Plaire est le lot des Femmes: une Femme qui ne plaît pas, est un être nul', if we are to believe the eponymous and articulate Gynographes,[11] whose strenuous anti-feminism, whilst dissipating any suspicion of nullity, would not endear them to their more militant sisters, who are left in no doubt as to the submissiveness and constant sense of inferiority necessary for pleasing the first sex: 'Vous serez donc heureuses par la soumission; et les Hommes par le commandement: considérez s'il convient que votre Mari vous soit subordonné; examinez, si en vous saisissant de l'empire, vous aurez tout ce qu'il faut pour le conserver; la force dans le physic; les lumières, la fermeté dans le moral, et non seulement vous personnellement, mais tout votre sexe; si vous n'avez point ces qualités au même degré que les Hommes, cédez donc, car, le terme de la vraie sagesse, c'est de connaître notre place, et d'être assés sages, pour nous y tenir sans orgueil et sans bassesse. Quittez la chimère de l'égalité; elle est contraire à l'ordre, et par conséquent il serait préjudiciable de la réaliser. Dès que nous devons être soumises, il est aisé de déduire de ce principe toutes nos obligations: La première (qui les renferme toutes) est la nécessité de plaire; c'est-à-dire de se rendre agréable à celui dont nous dépendons.'[12]

In the inevitable 'projet de règlement' in *Les Gynographes*, Restif's incorrigibly bureaucratic tendency to formalize human relations is apparent in a 'modèle d'un règlement de maison', a document setting out the duties of husband (briefly) and wife (at great length) and intended, in his totalitarian utopia, to have the force of law. The following pledge shows Restif's conception of marital relations: 'Et moi Marie-Anne N. je voue à mon Mari obéissance et soumission entières; promettant de faire en toutes choses ce qui pourra lui plaire, absent comme présent: Je me propose de me conduire de manière à mériter qu'il me confie le gouvernement intérieur de notre maison, par mon économie, mon aplication et ma vigilance. . . . Je promets et m'oblige de n'employer toutes les qualités que je puis avoir reçues du Ciel, et mes talens acquis, qu'à plaire à mon Mari: de m'interdire ce qu'on apelle tenir-maison, donner des concerts, présider à des assemblées de Beaux-esprits, et autres choses pareilles. Je mettrai mon bonheur à faire celui de mon Mari; je respecterai ses occupations, et ne me rendrai jamais importune, ni par mes demandes, ni par mes caresses, dans des moments d'occupation. Si mon Mari a des torts, je les dissimulerai, persuadée que les plaintes aigrissent, que la patience ramène tôt ou tard, et qu'une Femme douce et vertueuse, si elle n'est pas toujours l'Amante de son Mari, est toujours le premier de ses Amis. Je tâcherai de me faire au caractère de mon épous, et d'y plier le mien, de-manière que ses volontés soient mes volontés, ses désirs mes désirs, en-un-mot, de n'être qu'un avec lui; de partager même ses haines, s'il en a, convaincue, que la première vertu d'une Femme, est d'être identifiée à son Chef.'[13]

Restif's essentially backward-looking utopian vision leaves the reader who is acquainted with his better-known works—*Monsieur Nicolas*, *La Vie de mon père*, the *Paysan/Paysanne perverti(es)* trilogy —with a sense of *déjà vu*. The faceless 'André N. et Marie-Anne N.' of the model contract are pale reflections of his own father and mother, those twin pillars of the patriarchal family, bastion of the traditional values of *la vieille France*, memories of which determined all Restif's thinking about the future.

'L'Etat est une grande Famille; chaque Famille est un petit Etat; il faut que tout se gouverne par les mêmes principes':[14] the paternalism of Restif's social and political thought blends naturally with the cosmological vision of his 'religion physique', and the stuff of which M. Nicolas's dream universe is made is his experience of life in the society of his native Sacy. In this society, woman's status is assured by the importance attached to motherhood. Only as a mother can a woman realize her supreme and peculiar potentialities as a human being, as the 'dépôt sacré, où l'Homme, principe générateur, dépose une existence nouvelle' (*GYN*, 178), and thereafter as the chief formative influence upon the children in their earliest years. The overriding authority is always that of the *paterfamilias*, as powerful in his own little world as the divine-right monarch in the macrocosm of the state, but through the responsibility delegated to her and the moral support she provides, his wife comes into her own. Since the family is the most important school of citizenship, a mother's role in the home is of pre-eminent *social* importance. As far as Restif was concerned, the feminist notion that women were impeded from exercising a valuable influence in society through their relegation to exclusively domestic affairs was fundamentally wrong-headed. If man was the actor on the public stage, woman, as the producer, did not need the limelight to direct the action effectively. The very quality of the action depended on her: 'les Femmes font les mœurs publiques' (*GYN*, 12). The principles upon which the male based his conduct were imbibed with his mother's milk (breast-feeding was an important part of Restif's materialist philosophy of life and wet-nursing was anathema to him). From personal experience (abundantly reflected in his work), Restif was able to appreciate the lengths of devotion and self-sacrifice to which a mother could go. Mme Parangon, a privileged member of Restif's restricted gallery of ideal women, writing to congratulate Ursule, heroine of *La Paysanne pervertie*, on the birth of her son, illustrates the author's conviction of a mother's importance in a man's world: 'un fils est tout pour sa mère. Elle doit lui tout immoler, hors l'honneur, mais la vie et le bonheur sont au nombre des sacrifices à lui faire; sans cela, elle n'est pas mère, elle est marâtre.'[15]

Matrimony, for a woman, was but the preliminary to maternity which, in Restif's eyes, constituted her crowning glory. Celibacy was unnatural for both sexes, and, if voluntary, should be regarded as 'le plus grand des crimes' (*PMN*, 177). Restif's sneaking attraction to polygamy was more than counterbalanced by a deep concern for social stability, which led him to regard compulsory monogamy as the ideal system for perpetuating the species in an orderly fashion. Childless marriages were abhorrent and Restif's utopian legislation enforced the annulment of a marriage after three years if the wife had proved to be barren (the possibility of male infertility not even being considered).[16] Feminists would applaud Restif's advocacy of the secularization of marriage, his condemnation of the dowry system as being contrary to natural law (*GYN*, 190), and his approval of quick and easy divorce as a means of resolving antagonism which was making a union unproductive. They would find less admirable, however, certain aspects of the rigorous control of relations between the sexes in his utopia: *mariages de raison* organized by the state in which the mates are, in the interests of eugenics, matched according to their moral compatibility as revealed by carefully-kept dossiers; the severest punishments (including the death penalty in certain cases) for adultery and harsh treatment for those guilty of more minor breaches of the oath of marital fidelity. The following extract from article XLIII of Restif's 'Projet de règlement proposé à toute l'Europe pour remettre les Femmes à leur place' (GYN, 94), shows what the luckless married woman might expect if found straying from the narrow path of good wifely conduct: 'Une Femme qui aurait souffert des libertés, comme des baisers, autres que ceux du salut, sera ajournée, et entendra à genous la sentence qui la condamnera à ne sortir qu'avec l'habit des Vieilles, ou à rester chés elle. La Femme mariée coupable de la faute entière, ou qui en sera véhémentement soupçonnée, sera battue de verges par deux Femmes qui auront cette commission, condamnée à l'habit des Vieilles comme la précédente, rasée, et si son Mari le veut enfermée au pain et à l'eau. S'il s'agissait de punir la Coupable à l'insu de son Mari, on supposerait une cause pour la faire enlever, on la mettrait au secret pendant huit jours, durant lesquels elle serait torturée avec son Complice.' The bitterness generated by Restif's unsuccessful marriage to Agnès Lebègue probably had much to do, as Mark Poster suggests, with his creation of this 'world so anti-feminist that "the most severe penalties" would be meted out to girls who "abandoned themselves to indecent bursts of laughter" '.[17]

Agnès, a would-be bluestocking and 'femme autrice' dissatisfied with her husband's idealization of dreary domesticity, must have accentuated his distaste for emancipated women and his particular animus against learned ladies with a penchant for socializing. His impatience with the aggressive egalitarianism of such creatures and with their wilful renunciation of their own most precious gift, their femininity, can be felt in the exclamation of Mme Parangon's aunt in La Paysanne pervertie: 'Fi! des femmes qui font les hommasses! Il n'y a rien au monde de si vilain, de si messéant! Ça conduit à perdre toute pudeur.' Her niece's endorsement of the opinion sums up Restif's standpoint: 'il faut que les femmes soient femmes' (Ppe, 139). Gaudet d'Arras, in the same work, takes up the theme and enlarges upon it: 'Nos Gynomanes . . . veulent qu'il n'y ait plus qu'un sexe; que tout soit homme. Mais la femme est la plus belle fleur de la nature. Cet Etre charmant, en le laissant ce que l'a fait cette bonne nature, est le puissant lénitif qui adoucit les hommes: l'attrait qui les réunit, les attache les uns

aux autres: d'où vient donc le détruire? Car c'est le détruire que
de lui donner l'éducation des hommes; que de lui ôter son aimable
ignorance, sa naïveté enchanteresse, sa délicieuse timidité; que
d'empêcher qu'il ne soit le parfait opposé de l'homme courageux.
Maudit soit celui qui ravira pour jamais à l'homme l'inexprimable
plaisir d'être le protecteur, le défenseur, le *rassureur* de la femme
contre ces craintes enfantines, qu'il est si ravissant de calmer! ...
Il faut donc laisser femmes les femmes; comme il ne faut pas
efféminer les hommes' (*Ppe*, 346–7).

'La plus belle fleur de la nature' is sometimes represented by
Restif as clinging ivy or woodbine—misleadingly, since the
amount of honest toil which he believes should be woman's lot
makes her anything but a parasite. The austere work-ethic which
was a familiar feature of Restif's Jansenist background is reflected
in comments like the following, which typifies his contempt for
the drones and butterflies of social life: 'Voilà donc ce que
produisent la science et l'instruction données aux femmes! La
fainéantise, les comédies, les bals, la délicatesse, la braverie, la
flatteuserie, les dévergondent! Eh! qu'elles travaillent comme ma
bonne mère, elles seront sages comme elle!' (*Ppe*, 367 n. 1). The
influence of Barbe Ferlet, epitome of 'natural' womanhood can
be felt here, but it is not always the dominant one in Restif's
writings. The beguiling image of the sophisticated Parisienne
sometimes eclipses that of the matron of Sacy: the charms of
urban civilization could not be denied altogether. Restif's Parisian
experience confirmed what he had already begun to learn: that
'la parure devenant l'effet des goûts factices, il arrive que lorsque
ces derniers sont satisfaits à un certain point, la parure excite plus
que les appâts naturels' (*Ppe*, 268). 'Parure et luxe' were essential
subjects for the legislator of utopia; if, as a housekeeper, the feck-
less society-woman of the city compared unfavourably with her
frugal country cousin, she nevertheless showed exemplary initia-
tive in improving nature by art and enhancing her beauty in a way
that could only bring pleasure to her husband and strengthen the
bonds of their marriage. In this matter, as in all others, the man of
the house must be the judge of what the woman should wear, but
the superlative judgement of the fashion-conscious Parisienne is
acknowledged: 'Je ne sais si l'homme peut prescrire aux femmes
leur costume! Leur instinct de plaire ne vaudrait-il pas mieux que

nos leçons? Non, non; c'est à nous qu'elles doivent plaire, c'est
nous qui sentons ce qui nous charme. Cependant, qu'au fond, ce
soient toujours les femmes qui soient les législatrices du goût,
pour leur sexe. Qui n'a pas rencontré dans Paris, de ces déesses
du goût, que tout le monde admire, et qui font s'écrier: "Que de
goût! que de grâces! comme tout lui va!" . . . Voilà celles qui
seraient les types, les modèles, pour tout leur sexe' (*PMN*,
580–1). In these 'goddesses' nature and culture are reconciled,
since they offer man a source of refined enjoyment, and 'la
jouissance modérée est le plus bel apanage que la nature nous ait
donnée: c'est la baume de la vie' (*Ppe*, 269). This dictum of
Gaudet's echoes Restif's own profession of moderate hedonism,
just as his abundant advice to Ursule, whilst conducing powerfully to her corruption, reflects the genuine appeal which social
grace and urbanity held for his creator. Ursule, urged to cultivate
her dress-sense, so as to appear 'toujours neuve, toujours piquante,
toujours originale' (*Ppe*, 327), responds by creating out of her
own person a 'chef d'œuvre de goût, d'élégance, de coquetterie'
(*Ppe*, 383), an object calculated to give maximum pleasure to the
opposite sex. The art of the courtesan should not be spurned by
the country wife; boredom, the mortal enemy of any marriage,
could be dispelled with the help of a little imagination.

The common prostitute met with Restif's disapproval not
because she was a professional purveyor of pleasure but because
her mercenary attitude usually led her to ply her trade in a heart-
less way which denied her customer satisfaction. The exception,
the whore with the heart of gold, like Zéphire, epitome of 'la
vertu dans le vice', who recurs in his fiction with revelatory
frequency is but one side of a coin. On the other side is the
titillating image of the respectable lady like Mme Parangon,
superficially sedate but capable of plumbing the depths of passion.
Each of these figures, like countless other denizens of Restif's
fantasy-world, serves the same function he assigned to all women:
pleasuring the male of the species. Whether he really had the
happiness of women at heart in giving them this role, as he
claimed, is doubtful. The patent selfishness of the following *cri de
cœur* makes it seem unlikely: 'les femmes sont toujours des enfants;
mais en cela même, elles sont encore ce qu'elles doivent être. Eh!
que deviendrions nous, si elles avaient une âme d'homme! Elles

seraient bien malheureuses, et nous le serions avec elles et par elles!' (*Ppe*, 170). Woman's estate, reduced to such petty proportions by an overweening male ego, would not find a place in any sort of feminism, however loosely defined.

9

Women in Mercier's
Tableau de Paris

JOHN LOUGH

Since the twelve volumes of the *Tableau de Paris* which Mercier published between 1781 and 1788 offer an amazing variety of pictures of life in the capital at the approach of the Revolution, it is inevitable that approximately half its population should figure fairly prominently in its pages. It is true that unlike another *Conventionnel*, Condorcet, Mercier was no feminist; he would never have insisted, as did Condorcet, on equal rights for women, including the right to the same education as men. Yet despite his admiration for Rousseau Mercier did not altogether share the violent anti-feminism of *Émile* which ruthlessly subordinates women and their education to the needs of men: 'Toute l'éducation des femmes doit être relative aux hommes. Leur plaire, leur être utiles, se faire aimer et honorer d'eux, les élever jeunes, les soigner grands, les conseiller, les consoler, leur rendre la vie agréable et douce, voilà les devoirs des femmes dans tous les tems, et ce qu'on doit leur apprendre dès leur enfance.'[1] However, while his attitude to the sex had superficially certain 'progressive' features, he certainly stood closer to Jean-Jacques than to Condorcet.[2]

Of his dealings with women in his childhood virtually nothing is known. He lost his mother when he was only three; he then acquired a step-mother and in due course a step-sister, but his relations with both of these are lost in an impenetrable fog. During his stays in Neuchâtel in the 1780s he appears to have inspired a violent passion in one of the daughters of his publisher, Osterwald, but without reciprocating it.[3] Marriage came to him in the fullness of time, but long after he had written the *Tableau de Paris*, indeed about as late as marriage can come to anyone. In

1792 he had acquired a daughter, appropriately named Héloïse; another, Sébastienne, followed early in 1794 while he was imprisoned during the Terror; a third, Pauline-Sébastienne, was born two years later by which time, more fortunate than many other members of the Convention, he was sitting in the Conseil des Cinq-Cents. It was not, however, until 9 February 1814 that he repaired to the *mairie* of the XIe *arrondissement* and was joined in matrimony with the forty-five-year-old Louise-Marie-Anne Machard and so legitimized his daughters. Less than three months later, on 25 April, he died. His numerous comments on marriage as it was practised in the Paris of the 1780s arose thus not out of personal experience, but only out of what he had observed going on around him.

It would, of course, be possible to produce a fair-sized book by bringing together and commenting on the very varied observations in the *Tableau de Paris* on the activities and morals of the women of the capital, high and low. Some of these have their amusing side, and certain of his remarks on women's fashions even have relevance to those of the present day. For instance, noting that women as well as men had taken to walking with a stick, he adds: 'Ce n'est pas pour elles un vain ornement; elles en ont besoin plus que les hommes, vu la bisarrerie de leurs hauts talons, qui ne les exhaussent que pour leur ôter la faculté de marcher.' (i, 172)[4] Again, he strongly disapproves of women imitating men's dress: 'Le vêtement des femmes doit avoir un sexe; et cet habillement doit contraster avec le nôtre. Une femme doit être femme des pieds à la tête; plus une femme ressemblera à un homme, plus elle perdra à coup sûr. Mais les femmes se rapprochent le plus qu'elles peuvent de nos usages. Elles portent actuellement les habits d'hommes, une redingote à trois collets, des cheveux liés en catogan, une badine à la main, des souliers à talons plats, deux montres, et un gilet coupé' (xi, 11).

A great many of his short chapters are given up to accounts, often extremely lurid, of one section of the female population ranging from the courtesans, flaunting their new-found wealth, to the lowest types of prostitutes who ended up in the Hôpital Général. Considerable attention is given to the poverty and hard lives of women of the poorer classes whom Mercier encountered in the streets. There is, for instance, a striking passage in the chapter

'Porte-faix': 'Mais ce qui fait peine à voir, ce sont de malheureuses femmes, qui, la hotte pesante sur le dos, le visage rouge, l'œil presque sanglant, devancent l'aurore dans des rues fangeuses, ou sur un pavé dont la glace crie sous les premiers pas qui la pressent; c'est un verglas qui met leur vie en danger: on souffre pour elles, quoique leur sexe soit étrangement défiguré. L'on ne voit point le travail de leurs muscles comme chez les hommes, il est plus caché; mais on le devine à leur gorge enflée, à leur respiration pénible; et la compassion vous pénètre jusqu'au fond de l'ame, lorsque vous les entendez, dans leur marche fatigante, proférer un jurement d'une voix altérée et glapissante.' Mercier was certainly well aware of the extremes of wealth and poverty around him. He continues: 'Quel contraste! L'une succombe en nage sous une double charge de citrouilles, de potirons, en criant, *gare*, *place*! L'autre, dans un leste équipage, dont la roue volante rase la hotte large et comblée, sous son rouge et l'éventail à la main, périt de mollesse. Ces deux femmes sont-elles du même sexe? Oui' (iv, 19–20).

More than once Mercier takes up the point made by Beau-marchais in the singularly uncomic scene in *Le Mariage de Figaro* (III, 16), in which Marceline inveighs against the way men have usurped jobs which rightfully belong to women. In the volumes of the *Tableau de Paris* which appeared in 1788 the same theme is introduced and in strong terms: 'N'est-il pas ridicule de voir des coëffeurs de femmes, des hommes qui tirent l'aiguille, manient la navette, qui sont marchands de linge et de modes, et qui usurpent la vie sédentaire des femmes; tandis que celles-ci dépossédées des arts qu'elles pourroient exercer, faute de pouvoir soutenir leur vie, sont obligées de se livrer à des travaux pénibles, ou de s'abandonner à la prostitution? C'est un vice impardonnable dans tout Gouvernement, de permettre que tant d'hommes deviennent femmes par état, et tant de femmes, rien' (ix, 107). In the chapter 'Filles publiques à l'Hôpital' this loss of employment to men is once more given as one of the causes of the spread of prostitution: 'Voulez-vous diminuer les progrès de la prostitution? restituez aux femmes tous les métiers qui leur appartiennent; frappez de mépris les hommes qui se dégradent en maniant l'aiguille, en se consacrant au service des femmes; ces lâches usurpateurs de la propriété du sexe, privent les femmes de leur industrie, et sont leurs plus grands ennemis.' (xi, 53) Although these same demands were to be voiced by women in pamphlets which appeared during the Revolution,[5] neither Beaumarchais nor Mercier could expect gratitude from latter-day feminists for giving expression to them.

Another point of contact with the drama of the period is furnished by the chapter 'Les Demoiselles'. Here Mercier argues that authors of comedies give a totally false impression of contemporary life when they portray on the stage upper-class girls courted by their lovers: 'Rien de plus faux dans le tableau de nos mœurs, que *notre Comédie*, où l'on fait l'amour à des *Demoiselles*. Notre théâtre ment en ce point. Que l'étranger ne s'y trompe pas: on ne fait point l'amour aux *Demoiselles*; elles sont enfermées dans des Couvents jusqu'au jour de leurs noces. Il est moralement impossible de leur faire une déclaration. On ne les voit jamais seules, et il est contre les mœurs d'employer tout ce qui ressembleroit à la séduction. Les filles de la haute bourgeoisie sont aussi dans des Couvents; celles du second étage ne quittent point leur mere, et les filles en général n'ont aucune espèce de liberté et de communication familiere avant le mariage.' Girls lower down the social scale, in particular *grisettes*, did enjoy a much greater freedom and therefore, in accordance with his general principles on drama, Mercier suggests that the playwright would do better to depict them: 'Un Auteur comique . . . devroit savoir qu'une déclaration d'amour ne se fait jamais à une Demoiselle que lorsqu'on y est autorisé par le vœu des parents, et le mariage est alors ordinairement arrêté' (iii, 86–7). This criticism of contemporary comedies might well be applied to many novels of the period; the reader of *Les Liaisons dangereuses* cannot help wondering whether, given this state of affairs, the way in which Laclos has Cécile Volanges brought out of a convent in preparation for marriage with one man and then has her pursued by two others is not somewhat contrived.

Marriage is one topic to which Mercier constantly returns. He notes the fact that, while many women could not marry for lack of a dowry, it was not uncommon for others to remain unmarried by choice. In the chapter 'Filles nubiles' he writes: 'La fille célibataire par choix, n'est point rare aujourd'hui dans l'ordre mitoyen. Des sœurs ou des amies s'arrangent pour vivre ensemble, et doubler leurs revenus en les plaçant en rentes viageres. Ce renoncement volontaire à un lien constamment chéri des femmes, ce système anti-conjugal, n'est-il point remarquable dans nos mœurs?' (iv, 24). He also observes a similar retreat from marriage on the part of men, some of whom prefer to have a *gouvernante*, a housekeeper-mistress, rather than a wife. 'Rien de plus commun à Paris que cet arrangement, depuis que les femmes ont contracté le goût effréné de la parure et de la dissipation. On en voit dans l'ordre de la bourgeoisie dédaigner les soins de l'intérieur de la maison, l'abandonner à des valets, frémir au seul nom de cuisine, et dire à leurs maris qu'elles ne leur ont pas apporté *quarante mille francs* pour avoir soin du linge' (vi, 5). Mercier blames the law on marriage settlements and the absence of divorce for this state of affairs and defends the character of such women, arguing that a *gouvernante* may well be worthy of esteem: 'Celle de Jean-Jacques Rousseau, devenue ensuite la femme de ce grand homme, avoit acheté le singulier ascendant qu'elle avoit sur lui par des soins infatigables, et une patience à toute épreuve' (vi, 8).

Mercier repeatedly blames the *coutume de Paris* for the haughty attitude adopted by wives towards their husbands and for the break-up of marriages as well as for men's unwillingness to assume such bonds. Thus in the chapter 'Des Femmes' he declares: 'La coutume de Paris a trop accordé aux femmes; ce qui les rend impérieuses et exigeantes. Un mari est ruiné s'il perd sa femme. Elle aura été malade pendant dix années, elle lui aura coûté infiniment; il faut qu'il restitue tout à son décès. De-là la tristesse avec laquelle on serre des nœuds qui ailleurs sont si doux' (iii, 93). He returns to the same theme in the chapter 'Enfants devant leur pere' where the lack of respect shown by children to their father is put down to the same cause: 'Ce singulier et déplorable abus vient de la coutume de Paris. Elle a ôté aux hommes ce que le droit Romain leur attribuoit. Les femmes, en vertu de la loi, deviennent presque maîtresses. La source de tout le mal, si l'on y prend garde, est donc nos loix civiles, et dans notre coutume qui accorde trop aux femmes.' If a man loses his wife, Mercier declares, he is ruined: 'Les enfants viendront demander le bien de leur mere, poursuivront leur pere en justice, le réduiront à la mendicité.' Thus the life of the unfortunate *père de famille* 'se passe à être tyrannisé par sa femme, dédaigné par ses filles, bafoué par son fils, désobéi par ses domestiques, nul dans sa maison' (iv, 62).

The chapter 'Maris' which describes how in many households husband and wife go their separate ways while keeping up appearances, once again stresses the power which the law gives to the women of Paris: 'La coutume de Paris donne aux femmes des droits très-étendus qu'elles n'ont point ailleurs: aussi sont-elles consultées sur toutes les affaires, qui ne se font que par leur entremise. Sans les femmes, aucune affaire ne se conclut' (vi, 190).[6]

In the absence of divorce the only way out after the breakdown of a marriage was a judicial separation. Mercier seems to take it for granted that the reason behind such a breakdown must be the extravagance of women: 'Le lendemain des noces bourgeoises, ou tout au plus huit jours après, quel changement dans l'esprit de l'amoureux mari! De quelle hauteur tombent les espérances de tel honnête artisan! Il croyoit avoir épousé une femme économe, rangée, attentive à ses devoirs. Il lui trouve tout-à-coup l'humeur dissipatrice; elle ne peut plus rester à la maison; elle joint la dépense à la paresse. L'inconséquence, la légèreté, la folie rem-placent les occupations utiles, où elle avoit été élevée dès l'enfance. Loin de fixer dans son ménage l'aisance et la paix par un sage travail, elle se livre à la frénésie des parures' (iv, 43). Adultery, Mercier goes on, is no longer punished by death: 'Aujourd'hui, celui qui parleroit de ces loix austeres et antiques, seroit prodig-ieusement sifflé.' In both comedy and poetry marriage is made fun of: 'Ces gentillesses ne sont que l'apologie perpétuelle de l'adul-tere: on diroit qu'on a peur que les femmes ne comprennent assez tôt que leurs charmes ne sont pas faits pour n'appartenir qu'à un seul' (iv, 44). Divorce, instituted in 1792 by the Legislative Assembly and made much easier by the Convention of which Mercier was a member, is already advocated in the *Tableau de Paris* for marriages which had clearly broken down. The indissolubility of marriage is attacked: 'Le mariage offre une foule d'hommes [there is no mention of women!] que ces liens sacrés meurtrissent et déchirent. Ils frémissent contre l'indissolubilité d'un nœud que tous les efforts ne sauroient rompre.' Judicial separation, Mercier argues, is no substitute for divorce: 'La séparation isole deux êtres, et les laisse dans une espèce de néant.'

In practice, in the absence of a divorce law recourse is quite commonly had to a voluntary separation: 'On demanderoit

vainement aux loix la rupture d'un nœud devenu insupportable:
on le délie de soi-même; et ni les loix civiles, ni les loix ecclésias-
tiques, ne vous interrogent sur cette désunion, pourvu qu'aucun
des contractans ne se plaigne. Voilà comme les loix irréfragables
perdent tout-à-coup leur force et leur vertu' (iii, 94–5). The attack
on the indissolubility of marriage is sharper in the volumes published by Mercier in 1788. There he adopts an even more sarcastic
tone: 'Le mariage est indissoluble; le divorce est défendu par les
loix divines et humaines: mais si deux époux veulent se séparer,
ils n'ont qu'à se donner des chiquenaudes devant deux témoins, la
justice les sépare à l'instant; ils ne peuvent cependant pas se
marier à d'autres, mais ils vivent librement, en attendant que la
mort leur ait l'amitié de limer cette chaîne maudite que la déraison
leur a rendue si pesante. Admirez la sagesse et la profondeur de
cette législation, qui défend le divorce et admet la séparation;
c'est-à-dire, qui rend deux êtres inutiles à l'Etat, et qui les dévoue
au libertinage' (xii, 103). This attitude certainly accords with
Mercier's own extreme reluctance to embark upon matrimony.

Women of all classes of society and all ages are portrayed in the
pages of the *Tableau de Paris*. There is the illiterate servant girl
who makes her appearance in the chapter 'Les Ecrivains des
Charniers-Innocents'. These scriveners, we are told, 'sont les
dépositaires des tendres secrets des servantes. C'est là qu'elles
font écrire leurs déclarations ou leurs réponses amoureuses. Elles
parlent à l'oreille du Secretaire public, comme à un Confesseur;
et la boîte où est l'Ecrivain discret, ressemble à un confessionnal
tronqué' (i, 155).

In contrast to this glimpse of the illiteracy which remained the
lot of the majority of French women until well into the nineteenth
century we find in the *Tableau de Paris* several references to the
convent education received by girls of the upper classes. Given
Mercier's views on monasticism, that picture could scarcely be
expected to be favourable. The chapter, 'Petites filles. Marmots',
after describing how in their early childhood girls are thoroughly
spoilt, goes on to deal with the convent education which followed
from the age of seven or eight: 'Aux premieres impressions des
leçons de coquetterie et de vanité, succedent celles que peuvent
faire la bégueulerie, le pédantisme femelle, la morale rendue
ridicule à force n'être mince et superstitieuse. C'est à travers ces

sentiers qu'une femme destinée à être épouse et mère marche jusqu'à l'âge de nubilité. Pendant tout ce temps, pas un mot des devoirs dont elle devra s'occuper au sein de sa famille' (viii, 29). Elsewhere Mercier speaks of the illogical behaviour of women who have undergone this type of education and yet submit their daughters to it: '. . . Les Demoiselles y restent jusqu'à ce qu'on les marie; et quand elles sont femmes, elles racontent à voix basse les histoires secretes que tout le monde sait, et les singulieres passions qui y regnent. Ce qu'il y a d'étrange et d'inconcevable, c'est que cette même mere ne manquera pas d'y mettre un jour sa fille, quoique bien instruite du danger que l'innocence y court' (vii, 57).

In this same chapter Mercier maintains that thanks to the numerous attacks on the forced vocations of girls this practice has now died out: 'Autrefois de jeunes Sœurs étoient sacrifiées à l'avancement d'un frère au service; et plus d'une mere coquette voyoit avec déplaisir auprès d'elle une fille qui grandissoit.

'On a tant écrit sur cet abus, que les meres les plus ambitieuses et les plus dénaturées n'osent plus parler de Couvent à leurs filles. Celles qui peuplent les Monasteres sont des filles pauvres et sans dot' (vii, 56). It would be interesting to know how reliable a witness Mercier was on this question.

Despite many disparaging remarks on the sex Mercier does accept that thanks to the salons and to contact with enlightened men there are some extremely intelligent women. In the chapter 'Ton du grand Monde' he writes: 'Plusieurs femmes ayant perfectionné leur esprit par le commerce d'hommes éclairés, réunissent en elles les avantages des deux sexes, valent mieux à la lettre que les hommes célebres dont elles ont emprunté une partie des connoissances qui les distinguent. Ce n'est point un savoir pédantesque, capable de décréditer toute connoissance; c'est une maniere propre d'oser penser et parler juste, fondé sur-tout sur l'étude des hommes.' He rebukes Molière for his satire of blue-stockings: 'Molière, qui, dans ses *Femmes savantes*, en voulant frapper la pédanterie, a frappé le désir de s'instruire, Molière regretteroit d'avoir retardé les progrès des connoissances, s'il voyoit aujourd'hui les femmes qui ornent et parent la raison des graces du sentiment.' He does none the less make it plain that such women are only to be found in 'le grand monde' (iv, 66).

He also devotes a rather long chapter to a eulogy of women writers. In 'Femmes-Auteurs' he argues that it was natural that women should pass from being the ornaments of salons to writing books themselves: 'Les conversations roulant sur les livres et sur les ouvrages de théâtre, les femmes qui n'ont point à remplir les états pénibles de la vie civile, au sein de leur doux loisir, ont dit: *faisons des livres*' (x, 200). For once Mercier can see no objection to women assuming such a role: 'Ce seroit dans l'homme une jalousie honteuse que de repousser la femme dans l'ignorance, qui est un défaut avilissant'. All the same he sees a danger for women in such an undertaking: 'L'homme redoute toujours dans la femme une supériorité quelconque; il veut qu'elle ne jouisse que de la moitié de son être. Il chérit la modestie de la femme; disons mieux, son humilité, comme le plus beau de tous ses traits; et comme la femme a plus d'esprit naturel que l'homme, celui-ci n'aime point cette facilité de voir, cette pénétration. Il craint qu'elle n'apperçoive en lui tous ses vices et sur-tout ses défauts' (x, 201).

While masculine hostility remains out of sight, it is clearly revealed when a mass of men are brought together in the theatre with the result that the works of women playwrights are judged with excessive severity. Men, Mercier concedes, are afraid of success in a woman: 'L'homme veut subjuguer la femme tout entiere, et ne lui permet une célébrité particuliere, que quand c'est lui qui l'annonce et qui la confirmé' (x, 202). Naturally, given the extremely limited educational opportunities open to them at the time, it is not by their knowledge that women shine: 'Elles prennent les légèretés, les finesses, le sentiment, les graces originales de l'imagination, la peinture de nos défauts, et elles font tout cela sans études, sans colleges, et sans académie' (x, 203). Such women, says Mercier, 'devinent le pédant à la troisieme phrase, et trouvent de l'esprit à celui qui a placé à propos un silence. Voilà ce que ne pardonne pas la tourbe médiocre des esprits, qui voudroit exiger des femmes un perpétuel aveu d'infériorité'. Mercier ends the chapter with a long catalogue of women writers, ranging from Héloïse to the feminist Olympe de Gouges who, unlike him, was not to survive the Terror.

If Mercier has a low opinion of the women of Paris as wives and even as mistresses, he is full of praise for their attachment to friendship. The chapter 'Amitié des Femmes' opens with generous praise for this virtue in them: 'C'est à Paris qu'un homme sensé doit chercher une amie dans une femme; c'est là qu'on en trouve un grand nombre, qui, accoutumées de bonne heure à réfléchir, libres, plus libres, éclairées qu'ailleurs, se mettent au-dessus des préjugés, et ont l'ame forte d'un homme, avec la sensibilité de leur sexe' (viii, 194). He even enlists in support of this view the testimony of Rousseau, 'qui a parlé des femmes avec sévérité, parce qu'il les aimoit' (viii, 195). This notion that one must treat women severely to show one's affection for them is given its most literal form in an extraordinary chapter entitled 'Abus de la Société'.

At a first reading these pages appear to be just a joke, but in the end after they have been perused several times it would really seem as if Mercier were in deadly earnest. The starting point of the chapter is summed up in the sentence: '*La société tue la société*.' The mingling of the two sexes, he declares, has meant that the impression they should make on one another has been lost: 'On n'est plus *amoureux*; on n'a que des *fantaisies*. Rien de plus rare qu'une vraie passion.' So far all this is pretty banal; what follows is rather less so: 'Or, du temps qu'en France l'amant battoit sa maîtresse, et que le pere de famille battoit sa femme, sa fille, sa servante, l'amour régnoit encore: car, battre ce qu'on aime, lui donner quelques soufflets, voilà le secret du cœur vivement épris, et les preuves d'un grand amour. Ces petites injures, on les répare avec usure par des larmes brûlantes et par des flots de tendresse. Quiconque n'est ni jaloux ni colere, ne mérite pas le titre d'amant; il n'y a point d'amour sans ces fureurs momentanées, qui se transforment en plaisirs vifs et en voluptés nouvelles' (ix, 172). He goes on to argue, apparently in all earnestness, that in rejecting such signs of affection, women are the losers: 'Les femmes de nos jours sont indépendantes; elles ne veulent pas même être grondées, encore moins battues. Les infortunées! elles ne connoissent pas tout le prix d'un soufflet qu'applique l'amoureuse colere, l'avantage inappréciable d'une robe déchirée. Elles perdent les inconcevables baisers de l'amour. Combien elles sont ennemies d'elles-mêmes! A la moindre réprimande elles crient *séparation*; et faute d'être battues, elles sont réduites aux langueurs de cette froide galanterie, qui ne remplace jamais les transports véhéments de la passion. Oui, il vaudroit mieux, pour leurs attraits, qu'on leur arrachât quelques cheveux, que de leur parler trop librement. Elles seroient alors et plus célestes et plus respectées.' No woman, he declares, will ever know what true love is if she does not accept this fact. In support of his argument he goes back to the ancient world, first quoting from the recent French version of the English translation from the Persian of *A Code of Gentoo Laws* (London 1776), and then following this up with: 'Les Grecs et les Romains qui nous valoient bien, battoient leurs femmes et leurs maîtresses; car le grand vice de l'amour, c'est la langueur, la tiédeur' (ix, 173). Nowadays by rejecting such treatment women no longer receive, even at court, allegedly 'le centre de la politesse', the attentions which men once paid to them: 'Aujourd'hui on se sépare lestement des femmes, même dans un bal.' And all this, Mercier suggests, women have brought about by their stupidity in not realizing where their true interests lay.

Although on a number of occasions Mercier is willing to concede that some of the women in the Paris of the 1780s possessed intellectual or moral qualities which placed them on a par with men or even above them, on the whole there is no doubt that he regarded them as inferior beings. They are all too often depicted as frivolous creatures wasting their time and their husband's money on futilities. The chapter 'Les Marchandes de Modes' is typical: 'La dépense des modes excede aujourd'hui celle de la table et celle des équipages. L'infortuné mari ne peut jamais calculer à quel prix monteront ces fantaisies changeantes; et il a besoin de ressources promptes pour parer à ces caprices inattendus. Il seroit montré au doigt, s'il ne payoit pas ces futilités aussi exactement que le boucher et le boulanger' (ii, 125). Moreover Mercier goes on to describe how this taste of the women of Paris imposes itself on women in all countries, far and near, thanks to the famous 'poupée de la rue Saint-Honoré': 'C'est de Paris que les profondes inventrices en ce genre donnent des loix à l'univers. La fameuse poupée, le mannequin précieux, affublée des modes les plus nouvelles, enfin le *prototype inspirateur* passe de Paris à Londres tous les mois, et va de-là répandre ses graces dans toute l'Europe. Il va au Nord et au Midi: il pénetre à Constantinople et à Pétersbourg; et le pli qu'a donné une main françoise, se répete chez toutes les nations, humbles observatrices du goût de la rue

Saint-Honoré.' Although Mercier does not conceal his pride at this triumph of the taste of the women of Paris, and even quotes a passage from the *Lettres persanes*[7] on the economic advantages of women's addiction to fashion, he none the less returns again to the dire consequences for the family when women of more modest rank try to keep up with the aristocracy.

An interesting passage on this subject is furnished by the chapter 'Loix Somptuaires'. Though Mercier begins and ends the chapter with attacks on the extravagance of the women of Paris in their pursuit of fashion, he does recognize that it could be said to have its cause in their exclusion from so many of the professions and honours monopolized by men. After recalling that Paris lacks anything resembling the Oppian law (215 B.C.) which forbade all manner of luxuries to the women of ancient Rome, he continues: 'Le Sénat de Berne défend aussi les rubans, la gaze, les *bouffantes*, les petits cerceaux de baleines. Mais à Paris, tout le monde ressemble au tribun Valérius, qui plaida contre cette loi Oppienne en faveur des Dames. Elles ne peuvent figurer, ni dans la robe, ni au pied des autels, ni dans les armées. Elles ne portent point les cordons, les croix, les décorations extérieures, qui rehaussent les hommes; elles ne peuvent étaler aux yeux des citoyens ces marques honoraires qui satisfont l'orgueil, ou récompensent les services. Que leur reste-t-il donc? La parure, les ajustements. Voilà ce qui fait leur joie et leur gloire. Pourquoi leur envier ce moment d'éclat et de bonheur, ce petit regne domestique?' (ii, 195). While he goes on to reject this argument, Mercier does show here some glimmerings of an understanding of the frustration felt by women of the upper and middle classes at their exclusion from any role outside the home and the social round.

Outside the aristocracy and the really wealthy classes of the capital Mercier finds the happiest women of Paris in the wives of artisans and small shopkeepers who are actively engaged in their husbands' business. In the chapter 'Femmes d'Artisans et de petits Marchands' he maintains that they are 'plus heureuses que les femmes d'huissiers, de procureurs, de greffiers, de commis de bureaux, etc. qui ne touchent point d'argent, et qui conséquemment n'en peuvent mettre à part pour satisfaire leurs fantaisies.' In contrast 'l'épouse d'un marchand d'étoffes, d'un épicier détaillant, d'un mercier, a plus d'écus à sa disposition, pour ses menus plaisirs, que l'épouse d'un notaire n'a de pieces de douze sous' (ix, 105). Such women, he declares, lead much happier lives than those who look down on them and spend their days aping their social betters: 'Les boutiques de Paris recelent donc les femmes les plus gaies, les mieux portantes et le moins bégueules' (ix, 106).

Mercier well deserves his reputation for being muddle-headed and illogical both as a thinker and as an observer. What he has to tell the twentieth-century reader about the different sections of the inhabitants of Paris on the eve of the Revolution has to be treated with some caution. Writing in relatively brief snippets and hopping from one subject to another, he was not the man to stop and ask himself whether what he said one day did not directly contradict what he had written a few pages or a few volumes earlier. Yet with all his quirks and prejudices Mercier does provide two centuries later many valuable insights into social conditions in the Paris of his day, and although his observations on its women are scarcely calculated to appeal to today's feminists, he also has some things of interest to say on this difficult subject.

10

The *Bibliothèque Universelle des Dames* (1785–97)

VIVIENNE MYLNE

The *Mercure de France* of 27 November 1784 carried an *annonce* which began:

> *Bibliothèque Universelle des Dames.* Cet Ouvrage, qu'on propose par souscription, ne pouvoit trouver un plus heureux à-propos. Les femmes, pour plaire aujourd'hui dans le monde, ont besoin d'être plus instruites qu'autrefois; d'un autre côté, les devoirs de la société, les plaisirs mêmes s'étant multipliés autour d'elles, combien n'est-il pas nécessaire qu'elles soient dirigées sur le choix des Livres qui doivent former leur Bibliothèque. Sans ce choix, on sait qu'on peut employer beaucoup de temps à la lecture pour en retirer fort peu de profit. C'est le motif qui a fait entreprendre à une Société de Gens de Lettres l'Ouvrage que nous annonçons, et qui, regardant la plus belle moitié de la Société, doit par-là même intéresser la Société entière.

This *Bibliothèque* can be seen as a logical extension of the widespread interest, during the latter years of the century, in the question of feminine education. After the books on educational theory, the manuals on practice, and the extended reading-lists, it was logical enough to publish a collection of works which would enable women to pursue their education at home.

The editors of this collection may have been motivated to some extent by an altruistic desire to help women enrich their minds and widen their interests. But the *Bibliothèque* was also a commercial proposition, designed to make a profit for its sponsors. The terms of the *annonce* reveal certain limitations of the editors' wish to benefit the fair sex.

The title, for instance, shows this to be a library for Ladies— not for women in general. The presentation and price of the merchandise also make it clear that the editors are aiming at the carriage trade: 'Quant à la forme des Volumes, on s'est décidé pour celle qui est la plus portative: on a adopté le format *in*-18.' These convenient little books, which a lady can slip into her reticule, may be obtained, 'reliés en veau écaillé ou fauve, au choix des Souscripteurs, et dorés sur tranche'. The annual subscription for twenty-four bound volumes is 72 *livres*; and for volumes sent by post, unbound, the charge is 54 *livres* plus postage. As a further touch of personalized elegance, a subscriber may have her own name printed on the title-page. Thus the Bibliothèque Nationale possesses various volumes in which the title-page carries not *Bibliothèque Universelle des Dames*, but *Bibliothèque de madame la comtesse Alexandre de Sparre,* or *Bibliothèque de la vicomtesse de Vintimille.*

We may note, finally, that the description in the *Mercure* does not suggest that self-instruction is an end in itself; if ladies need nowadays to be well-read, it is 'pour plaire dans le monde'. The artfully phrased advertisement thus appeals both to a desire for social success and also to the pleasure of acquiring a prestige product.

The editors stated from the beginning that they would not fix the specific number of volumes to be published. This left them free to continue the *Bibliothèque* for as long as the market would support it. In the event, about 150 volumes came out during the period 1785-91; and a handful of further volumes appeared in 1792, 1793 and 1797, to complete various subject-sets which had been started in earlier years. In all, 156 volumes were published.

The subjects covered by the *Bibliothèque* were to be grouped into *Classes*, which are listed and described in the *Avant-propos* of the first volume, *Voyages I* (the figures in brackets indicate the number of volumes which actually appeared in each category):

Classe	I	*Voyages* (22, including a 2-volume *Atlas*)
	II	*Histoire* (30)
	III	*Mélanges* (= *Belles-Lettres,* 15)
	IV	*Théâtre* (13)
	V	*Romans* (24)
	VI	*Morale* (17)
	VII	*Mathématiques* (9)
	VIII	*Physique et Astronomie* (6)

IX *Histoire naturelle* (15)
X *Arts* (2)

This plan was later amended: a new *Classe X*, consisting of three volumes of *Médicine domestique*, was inserted; and the only work which was published in the *Arts* category, Lacépède's *Poétique de la Musique*, became *Classe XI*.

As for the order of publication, the *annonce* indicated that 'pour répandre plus de variété dans les différentes Livraisons, et pour mettre un plus grand nombre de Lecteurs à portée de s'instruire et de s'amuser, on fera paroître dans le même mois des Volumes de classes différentes'. So the issues for 1785, for instance, included the first volume of *Voyages*, eight volumes of *Histoire* and five of *Romans*. (The publication-dates of some volumes vary from set to set; it would appear that a few volumes were reprinted, presumably for the benefit of subscribers who had joined the scheme some time after its inception, and who wanted to fill the gaps in their collection.)

The *Mercure* continued to carry advertisements for the *Bibliothèque*, as well as reviews of successive volumes. A *Second Prospectus*, dated 30 September 1786, introduced a new approach. It pointed out the usefulness of the collection not only for ladies, but for young men, foreigners, travellers, military men and *les Gens du Monde*, with particular stress on the conveniently portable form of these books. In spite of this attempt to widen its possible readership, the *Bibliothèque* was still addressed primarily to women. This emerges from various comments of the editors, as we shall see shortly. First however, we should consider briefly some further details about the publication of the *Bibliothèque* and those who founded it.

Several of the subject-sets were eventually completed—*Histoire*, *Mathématiques*, etc.—but some of the categories remain unfinished. The twenty volumes of *Voyages*, for instance, deal with Asia and Africa, but do not provide the studies of America and Europe which had been promised. Similarly the fiction category, which was organized chronologically, consists only of eight volumes of translations from Greek and Latin works, a further twelve of medieval French works, and a single eighteenth-century novel.

We cannot of course be sure of all the reasons which brought publication to a halt, but some of them can be deduced. Firstly, although the *Bibliothèque* weathered the early stages of the Revolution, the notion of publishing elegant little tomes destined for the education of society ladies must have appeared less and less acceptable in the early 1790s. Secondly, it is likely that a number of the regular subscribers were either amongst the *émigrés* or else, if they were still in France, no longer had money to spare for such minor luxuries. Finally, the editors themselves had other preoccupations.

According to Antoine Guillois, the moving spirit of the enterprise was Jean-Antoine Roucher (b. 1745), who in 1779 had published a long poem entitled *Les Mois*. Guillois gives a list of Roucher's activities in the 1780s: 'En prose, il recherchait l'honneur d'être utile à la littérature et à l'instruction générale de ses contemporains. Si pour vulgariser dans les hautes classes les doctrines économiques, Roucher songeait déjà à traduire l'ouvrage de Smith sur la *Richesse des Nations*, il n'oubliait pas non plus les femmes, pour lesquelles, avec Lacépède, Lalande et Imbert, il créait cette *Bibliothèque Universelle des Dames*, où il s'était réservé un petit cours de philosophie à l'usage de ses belles lectrices.'[1]

In Barbier's *Dictionnaire des ouvrages anonymes*, Roucher is named as the editor of the *Voyages* and *Histoire* sections of the *Bibliothèque*. This seems all the more plausible in that he was one of the editors of the *Collection Universelle des Mémoires particuliers relatifs à l'Histoire de France* (1785–91, 67 vols.); and he was involved, together with Condorcet, in a project to publish a *Voyage Universel ou Encyclopédie des Voyages*. The 1780s seem to have produced an unusually large crop of such compilations—a phenomenon of social and printing history which merits closer study—and Roucher made quite a good income from his various activities of *haute vulgarisation*. His career came to a sad end, however: he was one of the victims of the Terror, being guillotined on the same day as André Chénier.

The literary progress of Barthélemy Imbert (b. 1747) was somewhat similar, though he was less successful financially and died in poverty in 1790. Imbert too published poetry, and he also wrote fiction and plays, but most of his earnings doubtless came from journalism and hack-work: he provided the articles on *Spectacles* in the *Mercure* for several years, was a co-editor of the *Annales poétiques*, and contributed to the *Bibliothèque Universelle des Romans*.

As for Lalande and Lacépède, the former was by 1785 already famous for his work in astronomy, while the latter still had ahead of him his major studies on fish and cetaceans. For the time being it was as a music-lover that Lacépède figured in the *Bibliothèque*.

A fifth name must be added to those supplied by Guillois: the *Privilège* of the collection, dated 6 July 1784, was granted to 'le Sieur Perrin' for 'un ouvrage de sa composition'.[2] (This phrase was the regular way of indicating that the *Privilège* in question had been issued to an author, editor, or translator rather than to a printer or bookseller.) At this period several men named Perrin were involved in literary pursuits. As regards the *Bibliothèque*, the most likely candidate would appear to be Antoine Perrin, since he too was an editor of the *Collection Universelle des Mémoires particuliers*, and would therefore, in all probability, be acquainted with Roucher.

What these men all seem to have had in common was some sympathy with the ideals of the *philosophes*. Roucher in particular, while endorsing the humanitarian views of Voltaire, was even more fervent in his admiration of Rousseau. The four long letters to Malesherbes, in which Rousseau outlines his autobiography, were first published by Roucher in the notes to *Les Mois*, and he insisted on the inclusion of these letters in spite of opposition from the Académie française.

Jean-Jacques even figures in the *Bibliothèque*, though not by the complete text of any of his major works. His *Lettres sur la botanique* are reproduced at the end of the two volumes on botany; and the last three volumes of the *Morale* section consist of *Pensées de J. J. Rousseau*, which are assorted extracts from his writings.

In the light of Rousseau's importance to Roucher, one might perhaps expect that the *Bibliothèque* would reflect Jean-Jacques' doctrine on the education of women. If one examines the individual works in the collection, however, one finds that both the contents and the editorial comments reveal divergent and contrasting ideas rather than a single consistent educational philosophy. It seems clear that there was no effective editorial policy or supervision of the kind that would have ensured coherence of approach and presentation.

To begin with, there are problems about the suitability of the subject matter for potential readers. The *Avant-propos* suggests that mothers may draw on the *Bibliothèque* when teaching their daughters, and says reassuringly: 'La mère la plus scrupuleuse n'en pourra craindre la lecture pour sa fille.' But any conscientious mothers who took Rousseau's word about the dangers of reading novels would not wish the section of *Romans* to fall into their daughters' hands, and might have similar doubts about some of the Greek and Latin poetry presented in the *Mélanges*.

Incidentally, it would appear that the *Bibliothèque* was indeed used for the home education of some girls. The *Mélanges* section of the British Library copy has title-pages with the heading: *Bibliothèque de mesdemoiselles Eulalie, Félicité, Sophie, Emilie de Marcilly*—a list that evokes the vision of a bevy of daughters pursuing their studies *en famille*. Evidence of a different kind comes in one of the few items of consumer feed-back to appear in the *Bibliothèque*. The second volume of *Voyages* is preceded by an explanation: 'Nous avions cru pouvoir exclure de cette Bibliothèque les formes élémentaires d'un Traité de Géographie, persuadés que nous les suppléerions d'une manière plus intéressante, et non moins instructive, par des discours sur le globe et sur chacune de ses quatre parties. Mail il est plus d'une mère, qui nous a demandé pour ses filles, et pour elle-même, un abrégé de Géographie, semblable au Traité de Chronologie que nous avons placé à la tête de l'*Histoire*. Nous nous empressons de répondre à ce désir.'

Leaving aside the question of what might be proper reading for *jeunes filles*, we may wonder exactly what kind of adult the *Bibliothèque* was meant to cater for. The initial advertisements, as we have seen, say that women now need to be well-informed 'pour plaire dans le monde'. The *Second Prospectus* elaborates on this point: 'Aujourd'hui que l'on parle de tout, que rien de ce qui appartient aux Sciences et aux Arts n'est, pour ainsi dire, étranger à une éducation soignée, un pareil Ouvrage ne pouvoit manquer d'être favorablement accueilli.' The readers here indicated would seem to be members of Parisian society and those ladies in the provinces who were trying to pursue the same kind of social life. What they need, above all, is food for talk; they must be able to keep the conversation flowing, and avoid appearing ignorant.

We can find support for this notion in the first volumes of the

Mélanges, which deal with grammar and spelling (I), pronunciation and versification (II), and logic and rhetoric (III). The reasons which are supplied for studying pronunciation and versification not only confirm the importance of conversation, but also illustrate the whimsical tone adopted by some of the contributors: 'Les Femmes ne sont point destinées par la Nature, et moins encore par nos institutions sociales, à faire de l'Éloquence un exercice public, à parler dans nos tribunes, dans nos chaires, dans nos barreaux. Mais la conversation, parmi nous, est le lycée de leur esprit, comme de leur cœur; c'est là que se développe la délicatesse de leurs pensées et le charme de leur sensibilité; or on ne sauroit nier qu'une prononciation correcte et facile n'ajoute à l'intérêt de la conversation. C'est prêter une nouvelle grace au langage; et tout ce qui tient aux graces, appartient au Sèxe qui en est le modèle et l'arbitre tout à la fois' (*Mélanges*, ii, 113–14). As for the rules of versification, women need to be familiar with them for the purpose of knowledgeable criticism rather than for active use: 'Les Femmes quelquefois ont occasion de dire leur avis sur des vers de société; et il est bon de leur épargner la petite contradiction de ne savoir pas les lire, et de prétendre à les juger. Elles inspirent si souvent la Poésie; il est juste qu'elles s'y connoissent assez pour que leur suffrage devienne le digne récompense du poete' (*Mélanges,* ii, 146).

Now literature, history and travel are acceptable enough as likely subjects of conversation in high society. Given the intellectual interests of the 1780s, we may even allow that botany, physics, chemistry and astronomy are potential topics, too. But it seems less plausible to suppose that trigonometry may come up in such social exchanges, and wholly unlikely that an elegant *cercle* should spend its time discussing the best way of making bread or the running of a *basse-cour*. Once the *Bibliothèque* begins to offer practical material of this kind, it would appear to have acquired fresh aims and to be addressed to a different range of readers.

As regards the question of aims, Parmentier, who produced the eight volumes of *Économie rurale et domestique* (*Classe* IX), explicitly rejects the notion, which we saw expressed in the *annonce*, that women should strive to be attractive: 'Femmes aimables, qui lirez cet ouvrage, persuadez de bonne heure à vos filles, qu'il n'y a point d'occupations plus humiliantes aux yeux de la saine raison, de moins conformes aux bonnes mœurs et à la prospérité de la famille, que celles que leur suggère un vain désir de plaire. . . . Apprenez-leur à conduire leur ménage selon les règles d'une sage et prudente économie, si vous voulez qu'elles réunissent toutes les vertus qui caractérisent les épouses chastes, les mères tendres, les maîtresses compatissantes; en un mot, les bonnes fermières' (*Économie*, i, 73). This is very much in the spirit of *Émile*—though Rousseau did believe that Nature intended women to please men.

The first volume of Parmentier's *Économie* is dated 1788, but already by 1787 another practical subject, the *Médecine domestique*, must have been envisaged: Lacépède's *Poétique de la Musique*, which came out in 1787, is labelled *Onzième classe* to allow for the insertion of this new *Classe X*, which did not begin to appear until 1790. Taking into account the dates and contents of the various sets, we have some grounds for inferring that from 1787 onwards, the practical, technical and scientific elements of the collection became increasingly important.

The range of subjects initially mentioned in advertisements had been: 'Les Voyages, l'Histoire, la Philosophie, les Belles-Lettres, les Sciences et les Arts'. The *Voyages* are largely human geography, more concerned with customs, religious practices and political institutions than with the physical characteristics of the terrain. And we have already seen that some readers asked for a more technical *Traité de géographie*.

As for sciences, the *Avant-propos* does mention mathematics, physics and astronomy, and—under *Histoire naturelle*—chemistry, botany and *l'économie animale*. But the description of what *Classe VII* was to offer suggests a not very serious approach to mathematics: 'On y trouvera les principes qui doivent servir d'introduction aux classes subséquentes. Les *Récréations mathématiques* d'Ozanam et tout ce qui, depuis Géomètre, a été découvert à cet égard, entreront dans cette classe.' (Ozanam's book, first published in 1694, contains a series of mathematical puzzles; the first one involves a blind abbess and the distribution of various nuns and their men visitors in a given number of cells.)

The question of mathematics was raised again in Lalande's volume of astronomy, dated 1786. Lalande begins his preface

with a rather plaintive explanation: in order to grasp the workings
of astronomy, one needs a basic knowledge of geometry and
arithmetic; but the majority of the fair sex cannot be expected to
possess these 'premières notions', and would be put off by an
array of figures and diagrams. He will therefore limit his book to
a general view of the science and its phenomena, an account of
some of the strange discoveries made by astronomers, and an
outline of their methods. When he wrote this preface, Lalande
and the other editors can surely not have foreseen what *Classe* VII
was to become. Published over the period 1790-2, it eventually
consisted of nine volumes: two each of arithmetic, geometry and
trigonometry, and three of algebra. Logarithm tables are included.
And there are problems—rather than puzzles—to exercise the
student's grasp of the material. Therefore any reader who had
worked through these volumes would have had quite enough
mathematical training to cope with the more technical approach
to astronomy which Lalande himself would have preferred.

There is a further indication of the value attached to the more
practical and technical parts of the *Bibliothèque*. The sections of
Romans and *Théâtre* petered out in 1788 (apart from one novel
which I shall discuss shortly), and the *Mélanges* do not go beyond
1789. However, if we consider those sections which did continue
to appear, we find that a list of the issues during the years 1791-7
speaks for itself:

1791	*Voyages*, XIX, XX
	Histoire, XXX
	Romans, XXIII, XXIV
	Trigonométrie, I, II
	Économie rurale et domestique, V
	Médicine domestique, II
1792	*Physique*, V
	Médecine domestique, III
1793	*Économie rurale et domestique*, VI
1797	*Économie rurale et domestique*, VII, VIII

Whether it was Parmentier's own efforts which led to his set of
volumes being completed, or the requests of subscribers, we must
suppose that the printer and bookseller in question were convinced that there was a worthwhile market for these final volumes.

The last work to appear in the *Romans* category deserves special attention, as it is something of an oddity. The author was a doctor of medicine, Antoine Le Camus, and the full title of the novel is: *Abdeker ou l'art de conserver la beauté*. It had first appeared in 1754. The *Bibliothèque Universelle des Romans*, which in its issue of June 1777 gave a résumé of the work, describes it as a 'roman de médecine'. What the novel does is to combine an exotic story with recipes and practical hints about health and beauty. The hero, Abdeker, is a doctor living in Constantinople in the reign of Mahomet II, and he is called upon to attend the ladies of the Sultan's harem. Interspersed throughout the narrative are directions for making various lotions, unguents and creams, as well as advice on matters such as the care of the skin after smallpox. So *Abdeker*, the last item in the category of *Romans* (1790–1), is also one of the practical handbooks which became so prominent in the last stages of the *Bibliothèque*.

There remains one further group of inter-related problems on which the *Bibliothèque* provides divergent views—the whole business of what is possible and desirable in the domain of feminine education. What are girls and women capable of learning? What subjects ought they to study? How should they be taught?

Rousseau's answers to these questions, as set out in Book V of *Émile*, are well known. Women have some intellectual powers, but are incapable of the highest levels of abstract reasoning. Their first duty is to learn all the skills involved in running the home and caring for the family. Beyond that, 'Toutes les réflexions des femmes, en ce qui ne tient pas immédiatement à leurs devoirs, doivent tendre à l'étude des hommes ou aux connoissances agréables qui n'ont que le goût pour objet.'[3] And all their formal studies should be made enjoyable.

Of the various authors and editors working for the *Bibliothèque*, it is of course Parmentier who comes closest to Rousseau's precepts, since the *Économie* is meant to help a woman carry out her prime duties. As for making the study enjoyable, Parmentier adopts the device of incorporating his lessons into a narrative: madame la marquise de * * * discovers, on the death of her husband, that his estates have been neglected; so she takes control and reorganizes the running of the farm. The aims and methods of the Marquise, set out systematically and in detail, constitute the

reader's guide to the successful management of household and
farm. Parmentier offers Rousseau's Julie as the ideal to be imi-
tated, and his first volume closes with an apostrophe to Jean-
Jacques: 'O homme éloquent de qui j'emprunte dans ce moment
le pinceau vigoureux pour achever d'esquisser le portrait de la
bonne Fermière, que ne puis-je présenter les détails de ses travaux,
l'objet de cet ouvrage, avec l'intérêt et le charme qui règnent dans
les avis salutaires que tu as donné (*sic*) aux femmes pour leur
bonheur, qui influe tant sur le nôtre!' (*Economie*, i, 253–4).

The men who dealt with the Humanities subjects for the
Bibliothèque are in general agreement with Rousseau's ideas. They
seek to make their subject-matter both entertaining and easy, so
that the readers need not strain to understand. Geography, for
instance, consists chiefly of 'les relations de différens Voyageurs
. . . fondues ensemble', and Roucher presents these as a series of
letters—the familiar form of the epistolary novel.

The editors of the *Mélanges* section reveal their attitude towards
their readers by undertaking to leave out, where possible, any
tedious or technical elements: 'Persuadés qu'on nous pardonneroit
plutôt des omissions qu'une surabondance laborieuse, nous avons
évité, autant que nous l'avons pu, la forme scientifique. Nous
avons cru que les choses, ou pénibles à comprendre, ou difficiles à
retenir, n'entroient dans notre plan qu'autant que leur nécessité
étoit absolue' (*Mélanges*, i, 3). In due course, when the use of some
grammatical terms becomes unavoidable, these are introduced
with apologies: 'La phrase ou le discours embrasse les *objets*, les
qualités et les *actions*; il faut qu'on retienne et qu'on nous pardonne
ces trois mots métaphysiques' (*Mélanges*, i, 13).

When it comes to presenting the *Traité de logique*, the editors'
tone is playful: 'Enfin nous voilà chargés de l'emploi très délicat
de guider nos Dames dans la carrière du raisonnement.Quelque
agréable pourra bien parier ici contre notre succès; mais il n'aura
fait qu'un misérable épigramme. Pour nous, nous pensons que
c'est au moins de notre part un acte de générosité que de donner
des soins à la raison d'un sexe qui ménage si peu la nôtre' (*Mélanges*,
iii, 4). And of course women should never allow such learning as
they have acquired to become too obvious: 'C'est un objet
intéressant qu'une femme instruite sans affiche et sans prétention;
mais c'est un être dégénéré qu'une femme Docteur' (*Mélanges*, iii, 43).

Much the same line is taken in the volumes by Pierre Roussel. In 1775 he had published his *Système physique et moral de la femme, ou tableau philosophique de la Constitution, de l'État organique, du Tempéramant, des Mœurs et des Fonctions propres au Sexe*. In the *Bibliothèque* this work appears, with some slight revisions, under the less imposing title: *Physique de la Femme* (*Classe* IX, 2 vols.). Roussel maintains that if women go in for any systematic study, they will suffer a 'détérioration de leur tempérament et de leurs charmes'; and he supplies 'scientific' reasons for this deterioration: 'Une forte contention d'esprit, en dirigeant vers la tête la plus grande partie des forces vitales, fait de cet organe un centre d'activité, qui ralentit d'autant l'action de tous les autres organes. . . . Toutes les autres fonctions se suspendent ou se troublent plus ou moins; la digestion en souffre surtout' (i, 142–3). He then proceeds to argue that anyone—man or woman—who either pursues study for its own sake or undertakes 'la fonction pénible et ingrate d'éclairer ses semblables' is likely to pay for it by the loss of bodily health and peace of mind; and scholars make a poor figure in Society. By contrast, 'l'esprit des femmes, inculte mais pétillant, brille d'autant plus qu'il n'est point étouffé par un savoir injuste' (I, 149). (In the original text of 1775, this last adjective was, less flatteringly, 'indigeste'.) In any case, Roussel concludes, 'les études d'agrément sont les seules qui leur conviennent'.

One is tempted of course to ask how Roussel, holding such convictions, could agree to publish his treatise as a part of the *Bibliothèque des Dames*. The answer may lie in the fact that, despite the resounding title of the first edition, this work does not call for much intellectual effort. It abounds in generalities about how women should behave, and a comment by La Harpe conveys the effect which the book created at the time: 'Quoique le fond soit naturellement un peu scientifique, il se fait lire partout avec agrément.'[4]

In general the other writers on scientific subjects, including mathematics, take a different view of women's capabilities. The volumes on mathematics were prepared by Antoine Mongez, whose ideas are diametrically opposed to those of Roussel. The *Avertissement* of the arithmetic volumes starts, almost aggressively: 'Les Mathématiques sont du ressort de tous les sexes. Elles fortifient le jugement et le rectifient même, jusqu'à un

certain point; elles n'exigent aucune connoissance préliminaire;
et elles devraient à ce titre être le commencement de l'éducation.
. . . Le plaisir que l'on goûte en les cultivant fait oublier les maux
et les chagrins; de toutes les sciences, elles seules ne demandent
ni machines dispendieuses, ni de grandes bibliothèques. Tous ces
avantages réunis doivent intéresser les Dames en faveur des
Mathématiques' (*Arithmétique,* i, v–vi). Mongez then cites various
women who have distinguished themselves in mathematics, and
hopes that courageous readers of the *Bibliothèque* will pursue this
subject without being daunted by occasional difficulties.

The algebra volumes display the same attitude. In spite of the
common view that algebra is complex and confusing, 'il est
cependant certain qu'elle ne demande qu'une attention ordinaire,
et qu'elle récompense par des plaisirs réels ceux qui, bravant le
préjugé vulgaire, lui consacrent leurs loisirs' (*Algèbre,* i, vi).

Mongez makes no concessions. He explains firmly that certain
technical terms are necessary, and having defined these terms,
proceeds to use them freely. He undertakes to give full and
detailed explanations of mathematical procedures for the benefit
of beginners, but he does not attempt to sweeten his subject-
matter with arch or whimsical *obiter dicta.*

Lalande, although persuaded (by his editorial colleagues?) to
avoid the more technical aspects of his subject, has no doubts that
women *can* understand them. He dedicates his *Astronomie des
Dames* to Mme de Piery, the woman with the best command of
this science, and gives a list of more than a dozen other women
who have achieved distinction in this field. He then affirms: 'Je
crois qu'il ne manque aux femmes que les occasions de s'instruire
et de prendre de l'émulation; on en voit assez qui se distinguent,
malgré les obstacles de l'éducation et du préjugé, pour croire
qu'elles ont autant d'esprit que la plupart des hommes qui
acquierent de la célébrité dans les Sciences' (*Astronomie,* p. 7). This
view was echoed by the Comte de Fourcroy, who held the Chair
of Chemistry of the *Jardin du Roi,* and who was responsible for the
two volumes on chemistry in the *Bibliothèque.*

The scientists who follow this line are merely being logical and
consistent: if they have taken the trouble to prepare scientific
works for women readers, it can only be because they are convinced that women can understand and profit from such works.

These writers also state or imply that it is desirable for women to study such subjects simply out of interest, and not because they will derive any social or practical benefit from their study.

The *Bibliothèque Universelle des Dames* is a strange and incoherent phenomenon: ambitious in certain respects, but often treating its public with condescension; shaped to some extent by the hope of financial profit, yet pursuing an idealistic goal; furnishing a bread-and-butter job for a few second-rate *littérateurs* while also attracting contributions from distinguished scientists of the day. No single comment will suffice to sum it up, except perhaps the inconclusive observation that by its very contradictions and conflicting views, the *Bibliothèque* stands as valid testimony to the variety of ideas, in the late eighteenth century, on the proper education of 'la plus belle moitié de la société'.

II

WOMEN IN LITERATURE

Duclos's
Histoire de Madame de Luz:
Woman and History

P. M. HALL

Georges May, in *Le Dilemme du roman au XVIIIe siècle*, establishes with persuasive evidence the connexion that existed in the eighteenth century between attitudes towards women and towards the novel. Hostility towards the novel goes hand in hand with a misogynist attitude and, inversely, a more tolerant attitude towards the novel with greater sympathy for women and their social role.[1] If one compares the diametrically opposed views of two eighteenth-century critics on this connexion, one finds that, on the one hand, Lenglet-Dufresnoy—writing under the pseudonym of Gordon de Percel—could argue in one of the most important chapters of *De l'usage des romans* that the novel's superiority to history consisted in the greater prominence it gave to women,[2] whilst, on the other hand, a bitter opponent of the novel, l'Abbé Jaquin, could go so far as to argue that the novel, in its exaltation of women, was dangerously subversive: 'Les romans ne tendent pas seulement à troubler la paix des familles, ils renversent encore l'ordre le plus nécessaire pour conserver la société. La volonté du Tout-puissant, en formant la femme, étoit d'en faire la compagne de l'homme et l'ornement de l'univers. Les Romans au contraire en font, et les tyrans des hommes, et les idoles du monde.'[3] In the view of both Jaquin and Lenglet, the novel, by its very nature, is bound up with the position of women in society; both critics, for instance, attempt to relate this connexion to the development of civilizations in which the novel enjoys popularity and to the social status of women. Their contrasting views of women and the novel stem not from a different interpretation of the evidence but from the moral judgement they pass on contemporary social developments: the subversion of the traditional superiority of man over woman is for Jaquin an abomination, for Lenglet a desirable and just redressing of the balance.

If, for the hostile critics of the novel, the ascendancy of women in fiction was such a matter for concern, it was because, with a greater or lesser degree of explicitness, their view of women's position in society relegated the woman to an inferior position where, indeed, her very appearance in writing might be suspect. This suspicion about the appearance of women in writing has been discussed by René Démoris in his recent work on the first person narrative in the classical period.[4] Referring specifically to the first person narrative, Démoris argues that the female 'mémoires' differ radically from the male 'mémoires' by the fact that putting pen to paper, for a woman, constitutes a problem, if not a scandal. Discussing the *Mémoires* of Hortense Mancini, Démoris writes: 'Hortense n'ignore pas que le seul fait de rédiger ses souvenirs plaide contre elle, puisqu'une des preuves de la vertu féminine est justement de ne pas faire parler d'elle.'[5] The point though made in the context of the first person narrative can be generalized. Thus Rousseau, in the *Lettre à M. d'Alembert*, referring with approval to the maxim of antiquity that 'la femme la plus honnête était celle dont on parlait le moins',[6] gives an unambiguous statement of the proposition that the virtuous woman is the woman who has no 'history'. In effect, the 'history' of a virtuous woman is a nonsense and she is condemned to remain anonymous.

For the hostile critics of the novel, then, the 'genre' was doubly condemnable, committed as it was to the representation of women: immoral because it introduced women of, by definition, suspect virtue and compounding this by elevating them to a position of superiority. If, however, we return to Lenglet-Dufresnoy, the reasons for the hostile critic's odium are transformed into the greatest merits of the novel. The second chapter of Lenglet's *De l'usage des romans* has the following instructive title: 'L'Imperfection de l'histoire doit faire estimer les Romans. Les femmes, quoique mobile essentiel des Grandes affaires, paroissent à peine dans l'histoire.'[7] The argument which Lenglet advances in support of this proposition is in general outline that upon which the historical novel of the late seventeenth and early eighteenth century relies for its justification: history, the history of historians, that which tells of kings, reigns, treaties, wars and martial activity, is untrustworthy in the facts it presents and defective in its interpretation of those facts. These inadequacies are the result of an excessive disregard for the part played by women in history. Here, we enter the realm of the 'histoire secrète'. Briefly defined, the 'histoire secrète' can be described as an alternative history, a filling in of the blank spaces of history, as Démoris puts it.[8] What goes into these blank spaces is almost invariably an explanation of historical causality alternative to that of the historians, one based on the importance attached to the influence of various passions, but above all love, in the making of history. The novel—and for Lenglet, whose sights are turned to the seventeenth century, this means the historical novel—is superior to history because it substitutes for an essentially masculine interpretation of history and historical causality one which promotes the woman to a position of primary importance. Masculine activity, from being the only possible subject of history, becomes a symptom of female influence.

Lenglet's justification of the prominence given to women in the novel rests on the reference to contemporary social reality: 'On ne sauroit disconvenir que le sexe ne fasse plus de la moitié du monde raisonnable, et qu'il ne soit la portion la plus essentielle de toutes les Cours: Mais j'ose encore assurer qu'il a souvent dans les grandes affaires plus de part que les Ministres mêmes' (i, 83). This reality he finds reproduced in the novel: 'J'y vois briller les femmes . . . en tout ce qu'il y a d'essentiel en matière d'intérêt public, et dans les plus grands mistères des affaires' (i, 115). Significantly, Lenglet stresses the paramount role of mistresses in contemporary life as justification of the historical novel: 'Et puisque les femmes légitimes ont tant de crédit, quelle autorité n'a point une maitresse? ça été dans tous les gouvernemens le grand mobile des grandes affaires (i, 101). The mistress, the illegitimate object of affection, is given the greatest importance even though hierarchically inferior to the legitimate consort and the princess. In this reversal of the hierarchic positions rests the kernel of the second accusation of subversiveness that can be raised against the woman of the historical novel. Not only is male activity undermined by being projected as a symptom of feminine influence, but the nature of this dominance runs against accepted morality and, indeed, any social norm. Lenglet-Dufresnoy, this time writing under his own name in his own refutation of *De l'usage*, stresses this anti-social aspect of women's role in the novel: 'On ne les y voit [i.e. les femmes] . . . occupées que d'elles-mêmes, et jamais du bien general',[9] and contrasts this with the more public-spirited role they supposedly perform in history. For Lenglet-Dufresnoy then, in spite of all the caveats he enters about the need to distinguish between virtuous and wicked manifestations of passion, the woman's role in history carries subversive implications both in respect of the relative status of man and woman (Jaquin's accusation) and in respect of the nature of the influence women exert.

Before passing from these theoretical considerations to the *Histoire de Madame de Luz*, we may ask to what extent, in practice, the same picture emerges from the actual novels of the period and how, for instance, the novelists of the period treated the princess and the mistress. What emerges tends to point to the general timorousness of novelists in their approach to their subject. The royal mistress, as one might in fact expect, is by no means the glorious embodiment of female superiority Lenglet hints at. On the contrary, she is usually viewed with suspicion and hostility. Following the outline provided by Mme de Lafayette's portrait of Diane de Poitiers in *La Princesse de Clèves*, later novelists stress the power and influence the favourite exercises over the King. Mlle de La Roche-Guilhem in her *Histoire des favorites* of 1697 presents a gallery of famous mistresses most of whom are thoroughly unpleasant characters. The first tale, which deals with the reign of Pedro the Cruel, offers a sharp contrast between the King's mistress, Marie de Padille, 'la plus détestable femme qui eût jamais été', and the saintly, persecuted wife of Pedro, who, in spite of her secret love for her husband's half-brother, remains faithful to her wicked husband. The contrast could not be more striking: the mistress uses her sexual influence 'sans pudeur', resorts to poison, is completely selfish and ungrateful. The queen, unable to influence her husband, is chaste, suffers and is murdered. Sexual activity and evil confront virtuous passivity and the renunciation of sexual fulfilment.

In general, this contrast defines the respective roles of mistress and princess. In the *Anecdotes du seizième siècle*,[10] Mlle de La Force refers to the infidelities of Gabrielle d'Estrées, Henri IV's mistress, in a tale which centres on the theme of the sacrificed princess—Henri's sister, Catherine—who is forced to renounce a promised marriage to the man she loves for a political marriage. The same theme of the princess recurs in Mlle de Lussan's *Marie d'Angleterre, Reine-Duchesse* (1749) and Baudot de Juilly's *Germaine de Foix, Reine d'Espagne* (1701). In both cases the same defining features recur: a reciprocated love precedes and is thwarted by the project of a political marriage. After the heroine has sacrificed herself to her duty, widowhood soon afterwards offers a further chance of happiness. Marie, in Mlle de Lussan's work, defying her brother, Henry VIII, and English opinion, exclaims: 'je n'écoute plus les loix du devoir! . . . dans ce moment l'amour au désespoir en triomphe' (p. 252). A clear enough statement: Marie opts out of any historico-political role and becomes a private person. The significance of this revolt is that it makes explicit the demand for individual freedom which Jean Decottignies has claimed to detect in the ostensibly 'virtuous' submission of heroines in the novel of the early eighteenth century.[11] The princess of the historical novel is basically no different from the passive heroines of such authors as Catherine Bernard,[12] the apparatus of the 'raison d'état' which oppresses them being an extension of the domestic or private tyranny which weighs down on, for instance, the heroine of Mme de Tencin's *Comte de Comminge*. However, what the contrasted figures of mistress and princess in the novels mentioned above clearly indicate is the limits which are imposed on the representation of women as active participants in history. History remains above all the privilege of the male; female participation is passive, influencing the course of history only in so far as it provokes male activity. Where this catalytic function is translated into a more active response, it immediately becomes suspect and liable to censure.[13]

To discuss Duclos's *Histoire de Madame de Luz* in the context of the historical novel of the period 1670–1750 is to beg the question of whether it really belongs in the same category as the novels of authors like Mlle de Lussan, Mme de Gomez or Baudot de Juilly. Critics have argued that the historical background is more or less a matter of background 'atmosphere' or a distancing technique comparable to that of classical French tragedy.[14] Alternatively, the early seventeenth century, which Duclos is writing about, can be seen as a camouflage behind which Duclos, with deliberate anachronism, attacks contemporary *mores* and institutions.[15] Moreover, the historical setting is only apparent in the first part of the novel, effectively ending after the first of the three assaults which Mme de Luz's virtue suffers.

In justification of an approach which considers the *Histoire de Madame de Luz* in the context of the historical novel, two points can be made. First, the nature of the action—the sexual submission forced on Mme de Luz—is, with one exception which will be referred to later, unique in this type of novel yet in a sense highlights an important aspect of the whole genre. Second, the way in which Duclos introduces the historical dimension goes beyond any mere background or stage setting, since there is a well-defined connexion between the historical events mentioned and the 'histoire' of Mme de Luz herself.

The opening pages of Duclos's novel establish a familiar grouping of characters. The heroine, during her childhood and adolescence, has been brought up in close friendship with her cousin, Saint-Géran. Familiarity turns insensibly to love, but before the cousins have become aware of their true feelings for each other, the heroine, 'fort jeune', is married to the older and not very attractive Baron de Luz. The scene is thus set for the development of the 'mal-mariée' triangle. Saint-Géran, taking the opportunity of a private conversation declares that the marriage of Mme de Luz and her consequent inaccessibility have made him aware of his true feelings and of his loss. Mme de Luz, after an interval, responds by admitting a reciprocal intensity of feeling but resists Saint-Géran's advances. In doing so, she puts forward a view of woman's responsibility and duty which, with some justification, has been seen as deriving from the theme of 'repos' in *La Princesse de Clèves*. For Mme de Luz, the world of sexual relations is immediately dangerous. The woman must remain on her guard, constantly seeking not so much to overcome her feelings as to restrain them. Caution, restraint, withdrawal, the search for 'tranquillité' define Mme de Luz's attitude. Her behaviour towards Saint-Géran is marked by a defensiveness which is one of the themes underlined by Duclos at the beginning of the novel.[16] Her strategy consists in persuading Saint-Géran to accept the renunciation of any adulterous relationship in the higher name of 'amour-estime': 'Je veux que mon honneur vous soit aussi cher qu'à moi-même et j'ai plus de confiance dans la fidélite de votre amitié que de crainte de la vivacité de vos désirs' (p. 16). This recognition of her own frailty is characteristic of Mme de Luz and indicates her descent from the Princesse de Clèves. In similar fashion, she admits her inability to control the emergence of certain feelings, while accepting the social and ethical demand that she restrain them. This humility makes it difficult to accept Meister's interpretation of the novel in terms of the punishment of an 'héroisme bien cornélien', of a 'caractère inhumain' whose hubris is punished by subsequent events in the novel.[17]

Saint-Géran accepts Mme de Luz's plea that he respect her honour and the relationship between them moves towards a sort of equilibrium; some kind of resolution has been attained, a resolution that sacrifices the satisfaction of the senses to the seemingly tranquil pleasures of a clear conscience: 'Insensiblement, M. de Saint-Géran s'était fait aux idées et à la vertu de Mme de Luz. Il semblait que son amour ne fût plus qu'une amitié tendre, une jouissance de l'âme, qui renaît d'elle-même, toujours nouvelle' (p. 19).

It is at this point that Duclos introduces the historical element. What is apparent is the break in continuity: 'C'était ainsi qu'il vivait avec Mme de Luz, lorsque le maréchal de Biron arriva de Bourgogne' (p. 20). The historical dimension, 'la grande histoire', recorded and chronicled history, has so far played no part (except that the Baron de Luz's career had furnished convenient opportunities for the lovers' tête-à-tête). Mme de Luz's and Saint-Géran's affair has been shown against the sketchiest of court backgrounds with little of the back-drop which Mme de Lafayette uses. Moreover, Duclos chooses to make the starting point of the 'machine infernale' which overwhelms Mme de Luz as remote and complicated as possible. We begin with the struggles of Henri IV and Spain, pass on to the role of the Duke of Savoy, caught between the two great powers and seeking to seduce the French King's favourite, Biron, from his allegiance. Biron's plots

with Savoy against Henri IV involve his lieutenant in the government of Burgundy, the Baron de Luz. In the atmosphere of
suspicion, jealousy and double-cross which the plotting engenders, Lafin, one of Biron's subordinates, betrays the plot and
reveals to the King the Baron de Luz's collaboration in Biron's
activities. With the appointment of Thurin, a magistrate who has
been rebuffed in his advances to Mme de Luz, as the judge with
responsibility for investigating the case of the Baron, history and
Mme de Luz meet, the public and the private domain are brought
into contact. Thurin, with written evidence of Luz's treason,
blackmails Mme de Luz, threatening to reveal the guilt of her
husband unless she will submit to him. Mme de Luz, isolated and
unable to find help, at first refuses, but finally yields when faced
with the machiavellian arguments of Thurin, who undermines her
hope of obtaining redress by exposing him, and who advances
the argument that the king as a practical ruler would overlook the
private activities of a useful and flexible servant. In the flush of
success, Thurin then gallantly destroys the evidence against M.
de Luz, and presents earlier documents in which Biron had
emphasized the Baron's fidelity to the King. The upshot is not
merely the release of the Baron, but his public vindication, a
triumphal procession through Paris and his appointment as
lieutenant-governor of Burgundy. (The Baron, of course, knows
nothing of what has produced this reversal of fortune.)

A number of points may be made here. First, Duclos, far more
than the majority of his predecessors or contemporaries writing in
the tradition of the 'roman historique' would do, goes to considerable lengths to elaborate the details of the conspiracy of the
Maréchal de Biron. Secondly, until Mme de Luz's involvement,
he eschews any interpretation in the traditional novelistic mode,
that is by reference to secret passions. Indeed, he underlines this
by referring to Biron's purely formal 'galanteries' when presented
to Mme de Luz (p. 20). No woman is involved in the plot, the
motives of the protagonists are dictated by ambition or—in the
case of the Baron—misconceived loyalty. The world of 'la grande
histoire' is thus an exclusively masculine one, without significant
reference to women. It may be mentioned here that one of the
defining features of the *Histoire de Madam de Luz* is the virtual
absence of any other female character: the only other women are

a certain Mme de Noirmoutier mentioned by Saint-Géran and Mme de Luz's maid. There is no theme of feminine rivalry or jealousy, no intercalated stories such as one finds in *La Princesse de Clèves*. The second point to be made concerns the relationship of historical event to private life. We are taken down a narrowing chain of causality from European to French to private political disputes and intrigues. Duclos stresses the part played in this sequence by the motives and choices of the figures involved, Biron, his henchman and betrayer Lafin, the Baron de Luz. History is still conceived in terms of the classical model as the unravelling of the various secret strands of individual motivation, but the purpose of this elucidation of the secret reality of history is not to explain Mme de Luz's fate. What happens to Mme de Luz is not just the last link in a well-ordered and comprehensible historical sequence which explains the events of private life in terms of historical causes. On the contrary, in spite of the apparatus of historical concatenation, it is by a dreadful coincidence, the appointment of Thurin as examining magistrate in a case about which Mme de Luz, although an interested party, knows nothing at all, that her downfall comes about. The realms of the personal and the public, the feminine struggle of Mme de Luz in her relationship with Saint-Géran and the masculine struggles of Biron, Henri, Lafin do not possess any continuity except through coincidence.

Mme de Luz's relationship with Saint-Géran brings us to the feature of the work which most clearly links it to the 'nouvelle' of the late seventeenth century, the 'mal-mariée' triangle. In particular, the influence of *La Princesse de Clèves* seems to pervade Duclos's novel. The similarities are indicated by Brengues: 'Mlle de Chartres and Mlle de Saint-Géran ont en commun d'avoir été mariées jeunes et sans amour: toutes deux se refusent, par vertu et par éducation, à l'homme qu'elles aiment et dont elles sont aimées et si même la princesse de Clèves ne souffre pas tous les malheurs de Mme de Luz, elles se retrouvent être souvent dans des situations semblables' (p. xxxviii). However, the differences are, if anything, more striking. Quite apart from the fact that the *modus vivendi* which Mme de Luz achieves with Saint-Géran goes beyond anything that Mme de Clèves would consider ('toutes les fois que ces amants se trouvaient seuls, leur amour faisait la matière et le charme de leurs entretiens', p. 17), the experience of Mme de Luz at the hands of Thurin constitutes a break in the novel unmatched in *La Princesse de Clèves*. Mme de Clèves's relationship with Nemours, in all its vicissitudes, remains the central problem of the novel. In Duclos's novel, the violent irruption of quite unexpected factors brings about a radical change in the relationship with Saint-Géran. Indeed, for most of the rest of the novel he is absent, returning only at Mme de Luz's death. The significance of this discontinuity lies in the fact that in a sense it questions the fundamental assumptions of Mme de Luz's life. She has sought, above all, to live privately, conceiving the problems she faces in terms of a set of purely personal relationships. In this, finally, lies her miscalculation: when Thurin, scorning her threat to carry to the King the facts of his blackmail, asks her: 'pouvez-vous imaginer que la grâce d'un rebelle [i.e. her husband] soit le prix de votre vertu qui importe peu au salut de l'Etat?' (p. 33), he presents her with the brutal truth that in the context of the political realities of the time and the historical conjuncture a private life is not possible.

The role of M. de Thurin in Mme de Luz's life brings us to some of the more general implications of the novel as an historical novel and to its relation to the historical novels of the preceding decades. As mentioned earlier, when he has got what he wants from Mme de Luz, Thurin arranges matters so that the Baron de Luz is restored to favour. There is a certain irony to this turn of events, a parody even of the most basic convention of the 'histoire secrète'. For what defines the 'histoire secrète' is the idea that the facts of 'History' are in reality symptoms of a series of events which remain hidden from the record. The historical novel is written in the blank spaces of history and consists largely in subordinating historical incident to secret emotional factors. In a sense, this is what happens in the wake of Mme de Luz's surrender to Thurin. By way of compensation, Thurin 'rewrites history'. Mme de Luz becomes the 'cause' of the events which culminate in the Baron de Luz's promotion. In this, albeit in spite of herself, Mme de Luz influences the course of history, but this is not the triumph of the feminine principle in history such as Lenglet celebrates. On the contrary, the triumphal procession through the streets of Paris which testifies to Mme de Luz's 'influence' is the celebration of her downfall as chance victim of historical events over which she has no power.

Duclos's *Histoire de Madame de Luz* thus functions in a sense as a critical commentary on certain conventions underlying the historical novel of the classical and early eighteenth-century period. In concluding this discussion, it may be useful to compare this novel briefly with another very successful and similarly scandalous historical novel which appeared at almost the same time, Mme de Tencin's *Siège de Calais* (1739). The scandal of both works consisted in the same theme of a woman who unwillingly gives herself to a man other than her husband. In *Le Siège de Calais*, the virtuous heroine, married to a man she does not love and attracted to the handsome and 'aimable' M. de Canaple, is the victim of a case of mistaken bedrooms: Canaple, returning in the dark to the household of M. and Mme de Granson, strays into her room and she, half asleep, takes Canaple into her bed under the impression that she is—rather grudgingly—allowing conjugal rights to her returning husband. The misunderstanding is revealed and, like Mme de Luz, Mme de Granson is revolted by the man she feels has defiled her, a feeling made more complicated than Mme de Luz's by the fact that she continues to be attracted at the same time to this man who has taken advantage of her. The novel —leaving aside the numerous sub-plots—develops the relationship of Mme de Granson and Canaple who by his submissive and adoring behaviour wins some relaxation in her severity towards him. M. de Granson in the meantime dies, and the obstacle to any union between the otherwise well-assorted couple rests solely in Mme de Granson's attitude to Canaple. It is the events of the Hundred Years War that give the book its title and that form the background to the central relationship. Compared to Duclos, Mme de Tencin is very cavalier in her treatment of history, making little or no attempt to convey the medieval period—this, however, is in keeping with the practice of contemporaries such as Mme de Gomez or Mlle de Lussan, and unremarkable. What does give rise to comment is the basic function served by the historical setting in structural terms. The climax of the book takes place at the siege of Calais. When Edward III, accepting the French surrender, requires as hostages six burghers, Canaple substitutes himself for Eustache de Saint-Pierre's son. Mme de Granson, realizing that this sacrificial gesture is made as evidence of his repentance and love for her—the aggressive male of the first pages now the passive suffering figure—intercedes on behalf of him and his companions, secures the safety of all six and finally forgives and marries Canaple.

In the manner then of the 'histoire secrète', Mme de Tencin explains recorded history by reference to an unknown, hidden cause. As René Démoris has pointed out[18], *Le Siège de Calais* substitutes for a number of the bourgeois protagonists of the chronicle aristocrats who act, at least in part, for private motives. The epic and symbolic quality of the six burghers' action is subordinated to the working out of private affairs between aristocratic men and women. History, in exemplary fashion, becomes significant as a manifestation of female activity. As in Mme de Luz's case, Mme de Granson's experience is one of suffering at the hands of the active male (if not in the physical act, at least in the subsequent feeling of defilement). In contrast to the *Histoire de Madame de Luz*, however, the resolution of Mme de Tencin's novel in the historical events of the siege of Calais reverses the pattern of male aggression and female passivity. The male submits, renouncing any action in his penitential garb; the female then for the first time in the story takes independent action, on his behalf, and in so doing, acts upon history, transforming events rather than being their victim.

The two novels are thus, in a sense, mirror images of one another. The *Histoire de Madame de Luz* offers a narrowing perspective, taking us from the political struggles of late sixteenth-century Europe to the agony of one woman, on the receiving end, so to speak, of history, the 'fait du mâle'. At the same time, by a bitter twist, Mme de Luz's agony results in a significant revision of historical truth. Her passivity is transformed, in spite of herself, into activity, but activity which is a parody of true activity. In *Le Siège de Calais*, we have a perspective which widens out from the particular—the assault of the male on the female—to the general—the resolution of the siege, which is also the resolution of the problem posed by the initial act of male aggression. The work demonstrates in clear fashion the revenge of the female on male history.

Le Siège de Calais and the *Histoire de Madame de Luz* have been considered in their relation to some of the important themes of the historical novel of the period 1670–1750. Their appearance respectively in 1739 and 1740 indicates that they belong to the last generation of this kind of fiction. After the first half of the eighteenth century, whilst isolated examples of the third-person historical novel continue to appear, they enjoy little success in the face of competition from other forms of prose fiction, and when historical fiction reappears in the late eighteenth century as a popular option for novelists, the forms and themes it adopts make it very different from the earlier historical novel. Of the two novels discussed, *Le Siège de Calais* can be said to represent the culmination of a tradition. In spite of the innovation which made it notorious, it operates within the themes and conventions of the genre. In contrast, Duclos's *Histoire de Madam de Luz*, as well as anticipating in a number of ways future developments of the novel,[19] offers a critique of the historical novel of the preceding decades, whilst working within its terms. In its investigation of the relationship of personal experience to historical event, particularly feminine experience, the novel above all refuses the convention of the passive heroine elaborated by the successors of Mme de Lafayette. Mme de Luz, prepared at the beginning of the novel to accept a life based on renunciation of sexual fulfilment in the name of norms received passively and without question, is denied even this modest satisfaction by a sequence of events characterized by their irreducibility to any significant order.

12

The
Paradox of Sophie and Julie: Contemporary Response to Rousseau's Ideal Wife and Ideal Mother

P. D. JIMACK

Although Sophie in Book 5 of *Emile* was created specifically as the ideal mate for the ideal man—or perhaps precisely because she was so intended—the view of woman that emerges from Rousseau's educational treatise might appear to a twentieth-century feminist to represent little advance over that of Molière's Arnolphe. Rousseau began by a careful attempt to defend himself against any charge of asserting the inferiority of women, arguing that men and women were either equal, or, in so far as they were different, not comparable; but the quibble does not even begin to conceal the fact that, in this work at least, he clearly saw women as an inferior species. The brave independence of mind which he had so assiduously cultivated in Emile was quite inappropriate for a woman: Sophie must be submissive—to her parents, to her husband, even to public opinion. There was indeed one rule for men and another for women: men could and even should fly in the face of public opinion, whereas for women, 'il ne suffit pas qu'elles soient estimables, il faut qu'elles soient estimées' (*Emile*, Garnier-Flammarion, p. 475). And this was not just because of the different social consequences for women: their natural capacity itself was too limited for them to achieve independence of mind. After the powerfully argued affirmation of man's right to judge for himself in religion, and of the consequent need to delay

religious education till he is old enough to judge, Rousseau
claimed that the religious education of girls should begin at an
early age; for there was no point in waiting similarly in their case:
's'il fallait attendre qu'elles fussent en état de discuter méthodique-
ment ces questions profondes, on courrait risque de ne leur en
parler jamais' (pp. 491–2). Their religious 'opinions' will thus be
settled by the authority of mothers and husbands: 'Toute fille doit
avoir la religion de sa mère, et toute femme celle de son mari'
(p. 492).

But regardless of the question of the inferiority of women,
Rousseau's whole view of feminine education was based on the
subordination of women, on their more or less total dependence
on men. In the opening pages of 'Sophie ou la Femme', he had
immediately established—as a law of nature—that 'la femme est
faite pour plaire à l'homme' (p. 466), and the consciousness of this
relationship between the sexes seems to underlie virtually all that
follows. If Rousseau improves on Arnolphe by wanting to give
Sophie knowledge and skills beyond those necessary for mere
good housekeeping, it is not for *her* satisfaction, but so that she
can become a more charming companion for her future husband.
And if he does at least touch on the fact that the girl will one day
herself become a mother, it is only to use this, in an extraordinary
piece of logic, as a further proof that woman's whole existence
must be conceived in relation to men: 'De la bonne constitution
des mères dépend d'abord celle des enfants; du soin des femmes
dépend la première éducation des hommes; des femmes dépendent
encore leurs mœurs, leurs passions, leurs goûts, leurs plaisirs, leur
bonheur même. Ainsi toute l'éducation des femmes doit être
relative aux hommes. Leur plaire, leur être utiles, se faire aimer et
honorer d'eux, les élever jeunes, les soigner grands, les conseiller,
les consoler, leur rendre la vie agréable et douce: voilà les devoirs
des femmes dans tous les temps, et ce qu'on doit leur apprendre
dès leur enfance' (p. 475).

It might of course be argued that, given the social reality of
woman's existence in the eighteenth century, Rousseau's attitude
was the only conceivable one. But in the education of Emile, he
had emphatically refused to be limited by what was generally considered feasible, and it was the uninhibited originality of his ideas
which both brought forth so many contemporary accusations of

impracticability and made the work such an important landmark in the history of educational theory. In any case, even Fénelon's *De l'éducation des filles* (1687), with which Rousseau's 'Sophie' has much in common, placed far less emphasis on the subordination of women to men, and saw the girl more in her future social and family role as educator and head of a household. Besides, there were precedents, if Rousseau had wanted any, for seeing women as truly equal to men. Poulain de la Barre, in *De l'égalité des deux sexes* (Paris 1673), had deplored the usual masculine view of women, namely 'qu'elles ne sont faites que pour nous' (p. 7), and attacked the traditional limiting of women, as he had already done in his *Education des dames*, arguing that they could succeed in the professions and other careers traditionally closed to them if only they were given the chance. And much the same views were expressed in Rousseau's day by the abbé Dinouart, in a work entitled *Le Triomphe du sexe, ouvrage dans lequel on démontre que les femmes sont en tout égales aux hommes* (1749).

The cautious conservatism of Rousseau's views on feminine education is borne out by the response of his contemporaries. In addition to the numerous theological condemnations and refutations which greeted the publication of *Emile*, there appeared a number of criticisms of the work as a treatise on education, mostly attacking it as impracticable as well as morally and socially pernicious. But when it came to the education of Sophie, they tended either to ignore it, no doubt finding little to attack, or to give it grudging approval. Grimm devoted many pages of the *Correspondance littéraire* of 1762 and 1763 to a discussion of Rousseau's book, and, probably influenced by personal dislike, his comments were nearly all hostile; almost the only aspect of the pedagogical system of *Emile* that he found to praise was in fact the education of Sophie. D'Alembert, too, in his 'Jugement sur *Emile*', considered Rousseau's feminine education much more useful than the rest of the work: 'presque tout ce qu'il dit à ce sujet est vrai, bien pensé, et sur-tout praticable' (*Œuvres posthumes* (Paris 1799), i, pp. 135–6). Even Formey, whose *Anti-Emile* was the most detailed of the refutations, conceded that the portrait of Sophie was 'moins chimérique que celui d'Emile' (*Anti-Emile* (Berlin 1763), p. 190).

When contemporary critics did attack Rousseau's theories on

the education of women, it was not because they were too radical,
but because they were unacceptably repressive and illiberal.
Formey himself, whose conservatism may be judged by the fact
that he was almost alone in defending the practice of moulding
the heads of new-born babies and the use of the *maillot*, had just
such reservations: he deplored Rousseau's denial of a woman's
right to choose her own religion, and as for his insistence on
woman's subservience to man, this was 'dégrader et avilir le sexe'
(*Anti-Emile*, p. 191).

The years between the appearance of *Emile* in 1762 and the
outbreak of the Revolution saw the publication of a great number
of works on education. Although *Emile* was still banned, Rousseau quickly came to be regarded as an authority in education,
and many of his key ideas were soon widely accepted, at least by
theorists. But the progress in pedagogical thinking made his ideas
on feminine education seem increasingly reactionary, and there
were few writers who could accept without major reservations
the fundamental attitudes of 'Sophie ou la Femme'.

One who seemed to be able to was the anonymous author of
L'Elève de la Raison et de la Religion (Paris 1773), a curious com-
pendium of sometimes contradictory passages drawn from a
variety of sources. It is true that, at one point, the author complains that 'le préjugé nous crie qu'il n'est pas bon que la femme
soit l'égale de l'homme', with the result that 'les femmes languis-
sent dans une ignorance qui fait leur malheur et notre ennui' (iv,
p. 359). The 'notre ennui' is no doubt a revealing addition, but
in any case, the predominant attitude is one of endorsement of
the very prejudice here under attack. Whereas the borrowings
from the first four books of *Emile* were fairly sparse, and confined
to details, the section entitled 'l'Education des Filles' reproduced
page after page of Book 5—including the passage quoted above
concerning the duties of women—and the conception of feminine
education that emerges from the work is unmistakably Rousseau's.

The spectre of Molière's 'femmes savantes' seemed to haunt
eighteenth-century writers on education, but Joly de Saint-Vallier,
writing some ten years later, went further than most in severely
limiting the formal education to be allowed to girls. He argued
that it would be a waste of time for them to study seriously, since
women are incapable of succeeding in literature, science, etc.:

'Les femmes n'ont ni *le tems*, ni *la force*, ni *la réflexion* nécessaire pour soutenir de pareils travaux' (*Traité sur l'éducation des deux sexes* (London 1783), p. 90). They are intended by nature to be 'adorées' and to make men happy. And a similar view was expressed the following year in the Marquis de Lezay-Marnézia's *Plan de lecture pour une jeune dame* (Paris 1784). Instead of studying sciences which were not merely not useful to them but positively harmful, women should concern themselves with pleasing men: 'charmer est leur devoir, comme il est leur destin' (p. 3).

Like Rousseau, these authors were of course referring only to women at the upper end of the social scale. For those at the other end, however, an even more limited education was obviously called for. Philipon de la Madelaine, in his *Vues patriotiques sur l'éducation du peuple* (Lyon 1783), accepting that 'nos femmes', the 'femmes du monde', were 'plus faites pour plaire à leurs maris que pour les aider' (p. 310), saw that the graces and accomplishments which they properly cultivated were totally inappropriate for the 'femmes du peuple'. Of what use would such adornments be, he asked, to a husband whose 'vêtemens délabrés offrent mille issues à la rigueur des saisons' (p. 322)? Philipon's 'femme du peuple' should be trained to become a kind of housekeeper-cum-work-horse, who would be taught at school only to sew and spin.

The most consciously and emphatically anti-feminist writer of the period was probably the prolific Restif de la Bretonne, a great admirer of *Emile*. The function of women, said Restif, is simply to please man, on whom they are necessarily dependent, and their most effective way of earning respect, 'c'est de vénérer le premier sexe jusque dans le dernier de ses Individus' (*Les Gynographes* (La Haye 1777), p. 45). The consequence for education is obvious: 'Il faut de bonneheure inculquer aux Jeunes-filles qu'elles sont destinées pour l'Homme, qui est le Chèf et le Souverain de la société' (p. 63).

But these extreme views were principally a protest against the increasing feminism of contemporary society. Restif was all too conscious of the fact that his attitude was quite outmoded in a century whose 'grand axiome' was to consider the sexes as equal (p. 41), and he complained bitterly that woman had already usurped man's place in society.

In fact, most writers on feminine education made at least some concessions to the principle of the equality of the sexes, and some went virtually as far as Poulain and Dinouart. Riballier, for example, maintained that women were potentially capable of as much as men, arguing, like Dinouart, that they were made of similar matter and had a similar soul and similar powers of reason. If in practice they seemed physically and morally inferior, it was merely the result of their defective education, which almost everywhere reduced them to being a 'seconde classe', unjustly subordinated to men ... though Riballier perhaps spoiled his case by what he claimed to be the extreme consequences of this injustice: 'De l'absurde système de notre supériorité exclusive, sont nés tous les maux qui désolent la surface du globe que nous habitons' (*De l'éducation physique et morale des femmes* (Paris 1779), p. 5). Not surprisingly, he rejected completely Rousseau's attitude to feminine education: although in other respects he admired *Emile* greatly, he complained sadly that the picture of woman in the fifth book was both 'humiliant' and 'avilissant' (p. 23).

Leaving aside the debatable question of woman's potential, there was of course no evading the reality of her subordination to man, at least in the married state. But it was certainly possible, while still recognizing this subordination, to see the relationship between the sexes very differently from Rousseau and Restif. If, for instance, the Comte de Caraman's view of woman in his *Projet d'instruction pour assurer la paix parmi les hommes* (1786) was more realistic than Riballier's, he none the less avoided the opposite extreme. Far from emphasizing her dependence on man, Caraman described a dignified partner, 'une compagne destinée à partager nos peines et nos plaisirs' (p. 68). He did not deny the husband's authority over the wife, but he saw the relationship in practice as a meeting of equals: 'la raison exposée sans humeur ni émotion, doit être le point de réunion de tous les différends' (p. 69).

Besides, it was perfectly possible to devise a programme of feminine education which did not have as its sole or even main objective the formation of the ideal wife. The abbé Fromageot's *Cours d'études des jeunes demoiselles* (1772–5) was unimaginative and conventional enough, no doubt, yet at least he thought it worthwhile teaching girls matters which were not directly related to their future role as wives. A few years later, the Comte de Golowkin began the outline of the plan of education he proposed for his daughter by affirming that the education of women should be based on their dependence on men; yet he was clearly considering his daughter as far more than a trainee wife when he prescribed a programme of study considerably more ambitious than Fromageot's, including foreign languages, natural history, physics, mathematics, anatomy, etc.—though, like Fromageot, he was careful to deny any intention of forming a 'femme savante'. Indeed, instead of wanting to train her to please a husband, he explicitly aimed at teaching her self-esteem, and even self-sufficiency: 'notre jeune personne [doit] toujours se suffire à elle-même, et trouver dans son cœur son premier bonheur' (*Mes idées sur l'éducation du sexe* (London 1778), p. 72).

Understandably, however, it was the women writers of the period who were the most conscious of the need to reconcile the unavoidably dependent situation of woman with the self-respect and dignity of an independent human being. Mlle d'Espinassy, who had been prompted by reading *Emile* to write her *Essai sur l'éducation des demoiselles* in 1764, approved of much that Rousseau had written on the subject, but disagreed strongly with the limitations he imposed on the education a girl should receive (she herself proposed a comprehensive list of studies), and with his view of the destiny of woman as one of continual submission to a husband. And some fifteen years later, Mme de Miremont, while trying to reconcile woman to her lot by arguing that in society everyone is inevitably dependent, nevertheless sought a compromise between the two extreme positions: 'Les Femmes ne sont pas nées pour commander. Les préjugés voudroient les assujettir à obéir. Entre ces deux extrêmes, il y a un milieu, il dépend de leur dextérité de le saisir' (*Traité de l'éducation des femmes* (Paris 1779–89), i, p. 289). She wanted thus to see women better equipped to deal with the problem of social living, and proposed extensive studies for girls, justifying the inclusion of sciences such as physiology on the grounds that they would help to counteract the traditional faults of women, their timidity, their hypochondria, and the host of petty prejudices so many of them are dominated by.

But it was Mme de Genlis, in her *Adèle et Théodore* (Paris 1782), who provides us with what was certainly one of the most interesting and adventurous discussions of feminine education to be written in the eighteenth century, though her attitude was basic-

ally the same as Mme de Miremont's. She recognized all too well
the limitations imposed on women by society and the consequences they had for their education. If they were to be happy,
they must be trained to accept their lot in life, avoiding anything
which might lead to frustration and discontent: 'on doit éviter
avec soin d'enflammer l'imagination des femmes et d'exalter leurs
têtes, elles sont nées pour une vie monotone et dépendante. Il leur
faut . . . des goûts modérés et point de passions. Le génie est pour
elles un don inutile et dangereux; il les sort de leur état, ou ne
peut servir qu'à leur en faire connoître les désagrémens. . . . Le
goût des sciences les singularise, les arrache à la simplicité de leurs
devoirs domestiques, et à la société dont elles sont l'ornement'
(Vol. i, Letter 9).

Yet the ideal is less restricted than one might suppose. To cope
with her various duties, a woman needs far more than 'des goûts
modérés': 'Faites pour conduire une maison, pour élever des
enfans, pour dépendre d'un maître qui demandera tour-à-tour
des conseils et de l'obéissance, il faut donc qu'elles ayent de l'ordre,
de la patience, de la prudence, un esprit juste et sain, qu'elles ne
soient étrangères à aucun genre de connoissances, . . . qu'elles
possèdent tous les talens agréables, qu'elles ayent du goût pour
la lecture . . .' etc. (ibid.). The education she proposes for Adèle
is therefore an ambitious one. If at the age of twelve she will seem
to know far less than many children of her age, the restriction is
not because she is a girl, but simply because she is a child, and
because her mother shared the views Rousseau had expressed in
Books 2 and 3 of *Emile* about the dangers of premature instruction. Like Emile, Adèle 'aura peu d'idées, mais n'en aura pas une
fausse' (i, Letter 11), and indeed, her education is in many
respects based on Rousseau—though Rousseau writing about
Emile rather than Sophie. But Mme de Genlis did not carry
Rousseau's ideas too far, and Adèle in fact was to learn a remarkable amount from an early age: she would speak several languages,
being taught English while still a baby, read the Bible by seven,
and learn at least a smattering of the sciences; at the same time,
she would acquire all the usual adornments such as drawing, as
well as the knowledge and skills needed for running a household.

Mme de Genlis recognized herself how ambitious her educational programme was; for when, near the beginning of the book,

the Baronne d'Almane, Adèle's mother, described to her friend
the ideal woman she intended to make of Adèle, the friend found
the ideal too lofty to be attainable, and feared that she might well
be asking too much of her daughter: 'J'ai quelques doutes à vous
proposer sur l'article de votre Lettre qui concerne les femmes: il
me semble que vous les jugez trop d'après vous, et que vous en
exigez une réunion de qualités, d'agrémens et de talens, qui ne peut
jamais être le partage que d'un très-petit nombre' (i, Letter 10).

And the friend is of course right: the Baronne's ideal is mod-
elled on herself; it is she herself who illustrates to the reader what
Adèle is to become, and so validates, as it were, her own pedagogical system. For in a sense, the book is far more about the
parents than the children, and it is the character and personality
of the Baronne, and through her of the author, which act as the
focal point of the whole work, the mother figure in her dual
function of educator and educational objective. No doubt the
picture of Adèle's mother goes beyond the purely realistic, but it
does represent a dignified ideal which was in no way incompatible
with the subordinate social situation of woman. Intelligent
motherhood was perhaps the only really constructive and reward-
ing career normally open to eighteenth-century women . . . and
it is significant that the Baronne d'Almane had deliberately
renounced Parisian society to devote herself to bringing up her
children.

Now although Mme de Genlis dealt more extensively than
others with the role of the mother, she was of course by no
means the first or only writer of this period to stress the positive
pedagogical aspect of motherhood. In fact, many authors emphasized the importance of the noble duties of the mother, sometimes
showing a rather different view of woman in her exalted role as
educator than appeared from the details of the restricted education
they thought appropriate for girls. The *Elève de la Raison et de la
Religion*, for example, underlined the contribution that could be
made to a happy family life by a mother who was at once virtuous
and educated. And while Bernardin de Saint-Pierre, writing in
1778, shared Rousseau's view of the difference between the sexes,
stressed the weakness and timidity of women, and thought they
should be kept firmly in their place, he had an elevated enough
view of the social responsibilities of the wife and mother, 'chargée

de faire régner autour d'elle l'ordre, l'abondance, d'assurer pendant toute sa vie la félicité de ses amis, de ses domestiques, de ses enfants et de son époux' (*Comment l'éducation des femmes pourrait contribuer à rendre les hommes meilleurs*, in *Œuvres complètes* (Paris 1818), xii, p. 166). Mlle d'Espinassy had gone further, seeing the ideally educated woman as the instrument of social regeneration: she would earn the love and respect of her husband and would bring up her children to resemble her, so that 'après quelques générations, nous verrons la vertu prendre la place du vice, et les femmes généralement respectées et aimées' (*Essai*, pp. 83–4).

Most of all, however, it was Rousseau himself who was the great proponent of the overwhelming importance of the mother, whatever his views in Book 5 of *Emile* on the subordinate status of women, and there is little doubt that his influence was a major contributing factor in creating what was almost a cult of the mother figure in the years that followed. The most obvious aspect of this influence was no doubt his persuasion of mothers to breast-feed their babies. In *L'Enfant dans la société du 18e siècle avant l'Emile* (Paris 1961), R. Mercier has shown that long before the publication of *Emile*, the advocacy of maternal breast-feeding as a law of nature had become a commonplace; and in the face of the widespread belief that the fashion of breast-feeding was due to Rousseau's influence, several contemporary writers, among them Diderot in the *Essai sur les règnes de Claude et de Néron*, protested that well before Rousseau, the majority of moralists and doctors had urged mothers to feed their children themselves. But as Mercier pointed out, whatever the views of the theoreticians before Rousseau, the vast majority of mothers among the wealthy urban classes had recourse to wet-nurses; whereas there is ample evidence, including the protests just referred to, to show that maternal breast-feeding did subsequently become fashionable, and that this was popularly attributed to the influence of Rousseau's impassioned pleas in Book 1 of *Emile*. In the words of Mme de Staël, 'C'est l'éloquence de Rousseau qui ranima le sentiment maternel, dans une certaine classe de la société' (*Lettres sur Rousseau* (No place, 1788), p. 39). When Buffon was reminded that he had demonstrated before Rousseau that mothers should breast-feed their babies themselves, he is reported to have replied: 'Oui, nous l'avons tous dit, . . . mais M. Rousseau seul le commande et se fait obéir' (Corancez, *Journal de Paris*, 30 October 1778).

Indeed, the fashion was such that there were numerous protests that it had gone too far. Mme de Genlis, for instance, thought that the practice was scarcely compatible with the usual social round of balls and receptions, and in any case objected to breast-feeding in public on the grounds of decency (*Adèle et Théodore*, i, Letter 21). And a number of doctors complained that in following the fashion many women were endangering their health, as well as that of their babies. Tissot, for example, the eminent author of the *Avis au peuple sur sa santé*, significantly devoted the entire article 'Du nourrissage' in his *Traité des nerfs* (Paris 1778–80) to the dangers of breast-feeding: while he accepted that healthy mothers should of course feed their babies, he asserted that there were many exceptions, and that in misguided response to the dangerous declamations of certain (unnamed) idealistic moralists, many women were making themselves ill and starving their babies.

But such warnings were the exception rather than the rule, and far more common was praise for Rousseau for having effected a reform which had far-reaching moral and social consequences. In Book 1 of *Emile*, Rousseau had stressed not only the advantages to the health and happiness of mothers and babies, but also the morally regenerating effect on family life, and consequently on the whole of society, and this view was echoed by many subsequent writers, often with due acknowledgement to Rousseau. Carpentier, for example, in his *Plan d'éducation* (1775), and Landais, in a *Dissertation sur les avantages de l'allaitement des enfans par leurs mères* (1779) which was awarded a prize by the Paris Faculty of Medicine, both quoted and paraphrased *Emile* extensively on the advantages to family life of mothers feeding their children themselves; and Mme Panckoucke, in her *Sentiments de reconnoissance d'une mère*, expressed what seemed to be the general opinion: 'si les Familles deviennent plus unies; si les Enfans aiment davantage ceux à qui ils doivent plus que le jour; si les unions deviennent plus douces par le spectacle d'une Mère entourée de ses Enfans, c'est à toi, Rousseau, que l'humanité doit tous ces bienfaits' (in Rousseau, *Œuvres* (Neuchâtel 1779), x, 280).

But it was not only in the field of baby-care that Rousseau contributed to the ideal of the mother. Emile's mother, it is true, has vanished from the scene, and little attention is given to Sophie's, although she appears to have been largely responsible for bringing up her daughter; as for Sophie herself, it is doubtful whether the woman Rousseau seems to be trying to create in her would ever serve as an effective educator of her own children. Yet a perfect example of the double function embodied in Mme de Genlis's Baronne d'Almane is to be found in Julie de Wolmar, the ideal mother-educator who represents at the same time the ideal human being education seeks to realize. When Saint-Preux returns from his travels, he finds Julie, as wife and mother, more beautiful than ever. Almost her first action on meeting him again is to present to him her two little boys, for whom Saint-Preux's wish is that they should grow up to resemble their parents. More specifically still, Claire not only designates Julie as the model for her daughter's education, but actually asks her to bring her up in her stead. Just as Jean-Jacques acquired all the rights of Emile's parents, so Claire announced to Julie, 'je résigne en tes mains le pouvoir maternel', adding: 'et pour me la rendre plus chere encore, fais en s'il se peut une autre Julie' (Rousseau, Œuvres complètes (Pléiade), ii, 439).

There is indeed a remarkable contrast between the ideal of woman in Book 5 of *Emile* and that in *La Nouvelle Héloïse*, as Riballier pointed out in his *Education des femmes*: 'O vous, . . . dont les savantes leçons avoient enrichi de tant de vertus, de tant de connoissances, l'heureux naturel de la fille du Baron d'Etanges! quel a donc été votre but quand, sous le spécieux prétexte de donner à votre Emile une compagne digne de lui, vous nous avez fait un portrait si humiliant, si avilissant, du plus beau, du plus ravissant des ouvrages du créateur? (p. 23). The difference between the two is nowhere better illustrated than on the question of religion. Whereas Sophie must meekly embrace the opinions first of her mother and then of her husband, the dignified and independent Julie has an intensely personal religion which is in fact intended by Rousseau to serve as a contrast, and even corrective, to Wolmar's atheism.

The explanation of the striking difference between Sophie and Julie de Wolmar is not hard to find. In the second half of *La Nouvelle Héloïse*, Rousseau was consciously trying to counterbalance the erotic extravagances of the first half by the evocation of the ideal family. The creation of Julie thus precedes that of her husband, and far from her being 'faite pour plaire à l'homme', it is Wolmar who is made for her, to provide her with the circumstances she needs to find fulfilment in her role as mother and spiritual head of a family. *Emile*, in contrast, is a totally male-oriented work. Riballier answered his own question when he referred to Rousseau's 'spécieux prétexte': Sophie was designed to be a companion for Emile, no more than that. By this point in the work, with Emile approaching maturity, Rousseau was beginning to identify with him in much the same way as he had with Julie and Saint-Preux, and in Book 5 he embarked on the quest for the ideal mate rather than the ideal woman, still less the potential ideal mother. The picture of woman at the end of *Emile* is thus a kind of erotic fantasy—in contrast, ironically, to the sober, domestic ideal portrayed in the latter half of *La Nouvelle Héloïse*. It is for this reason, surely, that Emile becomes himself Sophie's academic tutor, emulating Saint-Preux at the beginning of *La Nouvelle Héloïse*.

The extent to which the conception of Sophie was subordinated to Emile and her education far from ideal is perhaps borne out by the events of the continuation of *Emile, Les Solitaires*, in which we learn of Sophie's 'faute'. For her infidelity was not even used as a comment on the frailty of woman; it served in fact as a therapy for Emile, who was thereby painfully taught the full meaning of the 'sagesse' his tutor had once tried to inculcate in him. As Mme de Staël observed in discussing Rousseau's attitude to Sophie, 'Il a condamné lui-même son éducation; il l'a sacrifiée au désir de faire valoir celle d'Emile' (*Lettres sur Rousseau*, p. 45).

But it was Julie and not Sophie who captured the attention of the public: whereas, in complete contrast to *Emile* as a whole, the feminine education of Book 5 came to be increasingly ignored, the immense success and sustained popularity of *La Nouvelle Héloïse* is well-attested and well-known. When the author of some *Considérations générales sur l'éducation* (Bouillon 1782) wrote that it was Rousseau 'qui a donné aux femmes leur juste place dans la société, en faisant sortir, d'une manière ravissante, leur bonheur, leur empire même, de la pratique de leurs devoirs' (p. 21), he was most probably thinking of the care of young babies, and breast-feeding in particular. But if the first book of *Emile* had done much to emphasize and dignify the essential role of the mother, the idyllic picture of the Wolmar household, dominated by the noble figure of Julie, had surely contributed at least as much. Whereas the portrait of 'Sophie ou la Femme' had contributed practically nothing at all.

13

D'Antraigues's Feminism: Where Fact and Fantasy Meet

COLIN DUCKWORTH

The comte d'Antraigues, the revolutionary aristocrat who is either vilified as a royalist turncoat or praised for his disengagement from the parliamentary machine when the Revolution took too repressive a turn for his liking, was obsessed with a particular social injustice which, for a George Sand, would have placed him firmly on the side of the angels: the victimization of woman in a male-dominated society.

It is not in his political tracts that this strand of his thought reveals itself, but in his unpublished memoirs and novels. How can we account for this preoccupation? How did he treat the problem? Whence did he draw his material? What is the connection between his relationships with certain women—English and Polish—and the imaginative structures he created in the form of novels and of memoirs (in which the line between fact and fiction, confession and fantasy, is very difficult to define)?[1]

In an earlier study[2] the *Soliloques* and *Henri et Cécile* were examined as records of d'Antraigues's inner life, and as means of understanding his extraordinary compulsion to pour out romanticized autobiography and semi-autobiographical fiction. Several aspects lay outside the scope of that study, and further documents and information have since come to light, with which the present study will deal.

If d'Antraigues's dating of his manuscripts is to be believed, the earliest extant attempt at fiction was *Talmi et Eliza*, which bears upon the title page: 'par J. J. Rousseau/le 7 janvier 1772 et 11 avril 1773/ardet que in virgine virgo/pub. ovid. meta. Li ix ver 724'.

The attribution to Rousseau must be treated with the scepticism due to all such claims written on d'Antraigues's manuscripts.[3] The handwriting is undoubtedly that of the writer of the *Soliloques*. In this exchange of imaginary letters between Talmi and Eliza we find ourselves immediately plunged into what appears to be a commonplace story of unrequited love and rejection, but the sapphic overtones, for which the quotation from Ovid prepares us, are established from the first line, in which Talmi's sex is revealed: 'Vous m'avez cruellement trompée Madame . . .' The extent of Eliza's passion for her, and the outraged shock sustained by Talmi, leave no doubt that this is an overt physical lesbian attraction. Talmi continues: 'On ne peut être plus aimable et plus perfide que vous et la fraieur que vous m'avez inspirée est telle qu'elle me force à renoncer à ce charme de votre amitié. Eh, quels sont vos principes si le langage de l'amitié n'est chez vous que le voile d'une passion effrénée dont vous ne manifestez les excès que lorsque vos séductions de tout genre vous ont attiré une confiance entière et une amitié sans défiance?' Her horror for 'ce penchant dépravé' and Eliza's threat to do away with herself lead Talmi to recount to Eliza her own life story, in the hope that she can replace passion with friendship in Eliza's heart. Her autobiography constitutes, in fact, the body of the novel. Although now a widowed duchess, she was brought up in relatively mediocre circumstances by her father, whom she adored. They lived in the Vivarais (in a château at first called Baladesti and later La Bastide). Her father never recovered from his wife's death (when Talmi was one year old), and made his daughter, from the age of six, wear his wife's clothes and sleep in her room. He gave her a sound education ('comme il eût élevé son fils'), and 'il développa en moi une sensibilité qui me cause bien des tourments'. Her reason was affected 'par la lecture d'une foule de romans qui exaltèrent mon imagination et me jettèrent dans un monde idéal dont je ne suis jamais revenue'.

She married a man of her own choice, enjoyed a satisfying relationship with him, but was dealt a double blow with the deaths of her father and husband within two years. On her return from Paris to La Bastide she meets her *frère de lait*, a young man of angelic beauty, and falls in love with him. Going through her father's papers together they find a paper revealing that he had

always hoped they would marry. After a night's anxious ponder-
ing, she comes to an irrevocable decision.[4] She takes Lilier up a
snow-covered mountain, where they swear their mutual love in
terms prefiguring the tenets of female emancipation: 'Jure-moi',
she commands, 'une constance que je sens qui m'est due et une
obéissance sans réserve. Je te jure un amour éternel et de n'em-
ploier qu'à nostre bonheur l'empire que j'accepte et la toute
puissance que je reçois'.

Talmi then prepares her father's old bedroom as a nuptial
chamber. The ambivalent tones of incest and filial devotion are
strong in the precise description of the sensations experienced by
Talmi as she prepares the bed: 'Ce choix du premier rendez-vous
de l'amour dans la chambre où vécut mon père le plus tendrement
aimé, où il passa sa vie à former toutes mes opinions, à me créer
telle que je suis. Ce lit où en des jours plus heureux je devins le
gage du plus tendre amour et où je vis ses derniers regards se
fixer sur Lilier et sur moi, ne devait-il pas devenir le lit nuptial
des enfants qu'il voulait unir . . . ? Enflamée de ces idées j'allai
seule dans cette chambre y préparer cet autel . . . Quelle volup-
tuese occupation!' She ceremonially adorns and perfumes herself
as 'la victime sur l'autel' ready for the sacrifice. Follows a night
of passionate and mutually satisfying activity, described with
considerable emotional fervour but little physical detail.[5] The
terminology used to describe their changed relationship is
exclusively one of domination and defeat or submission: 'Le règne
de la fuite allait finir, j'élevais moi-même les trophées du vainqueur
et je préparais ses triomphes . . . là finissait mon empire et com-
mençait celui du maître que j'allais me donner . . . Ce Lilier si
soumis, si timide, si bien façonné à la servitude était devenu tout
à coup un maître hardi, impèrieux . . . Jamais sultan ne trouva
d'esclave plus soumise . . . Au milieu des ténèbres je trouvai un
moment de calme où l'esclave prête à redevenir un maître sévère
put expliquer à celui qui allait reprendre sa chaîne ce qu'elle aviat
décidé pour leur mutuel bonheur . . . Alors l'esclave de la nuit
confia à l'esclave des jours la volonté du maître.'

Talmi outlines her philosophy of love at some length, in order
to explain her determination to retain her social and psychological
superiority over Lilier uncompromisingly during the day: by
remaining an untouchable goddess by light of day, to be adored

and respected, her lover will never take the willing slave of the night for granted: 'C'est ainsi que ramenant les plaisirs des sens à tous ceux de l'imagination j'ai mis sous la protection du sentiment la perpétuité et l'existence de mon bonheur comme l'on couvre d'un cristal ces objets délicats dont on veut conserver les formes fragiles et les éclatantes couleurs.'

Thus she becomes two distinct persons: master by day, mistress by night. A hint of sexual ambiguity in Talmi shows itself again in her choice of two pretty girls as her companions. Under her aegis they have soon 'maîtrisé leurs amants'. They become one 'voluptueuse famille', and Talmi likes to be 'vêtue touchée par ces mains toutes tremblantes de plaisir'.

But with a perverse subtlety redolent of Genet, d'Antraigues accompanies Talmi's insistence that her maids should share her delights with a determination that they remain conscious of their inferiority: 'Pas une délicatesse qu'elles ne partagent, pas un raffinement qu'elles n'éprouvent; seulement j'ai réservé pour montrer à leurs yeux ma supériorité le luxe dans tout ce qui m'a fort réussi . . . ce plaisir des yeux n'en est pas un pour moi, c'est seulement une prééminence qu'il me donne sur elles.'

Talmi now returns to Paris ('cette ville où règne l'opinion et la vanité') for six months in the year in order to appreciate all the more the pleasures of life and love amid luxury and Nature at La Bastide for the other six. Through her eyes d'Antraigues comments (as he does in *Mes Soliloques* and *Henri et Cécile*) on the intellectual and social life of Paris: 'La littéreature est séparée en deux classes, car la nature aime les hiérarchies. Elle est ennemie de l'égalité. La classe suprême, composée de quelques individus très distingués, offre de grands génies réunis à de grands moyens en tous genres pour le développer. Mais les J.-J. Rousseau et les Buffon sont des phénomènes et les d'Alembert, les Diderot sont communs.' The latter are destructive, poisonous vipers, 'le dépôt mortuaire de l'esprit humain'. She avoids them, and 'tous les autres avec ces manières polies et froides qui satisfont la vanité sans altérer le sentiment', and 'les femmes auteurs', and all the men of Paris, who 'ne m'inspirent que de la froideur et du mépris'. Her contempt for this 'essaim de frelons bruiants et dorés', and her revelling in their hatred for her, enable her to sympathize with Eliza's rejection of men: 'Je ne doute pas que le dégoût qu'ils inspirent . . . ne soient une des principales causes de l'erreur de tes gouts . . . Tu cherches un cœur dans ton propre sexe comme on devait chercher un objet dans un autre univers'.

But Talmi is beyond temptation. She no longer frequents the Court because the King 's'était laissé persuader qu'il fallait me remarier'. Rather death! 'Quel homme me paraîtrait digne d'être mon maître'. Even if the man had all Eliza's qualities of heart and mind, she would reject him: 'dans ce cœur il n'y a qu'une place, elle est occupée'.

Her advice to Eliza is given as from one who finds the Parisian high society male as despicable as Eliza does: 'Jeune, belle, charmante, adorée, si le ciel t'accorde une âme tendre, des sens impérieux, daigne rendre un mortel heureux et l'élever jusques à toi sans avilir ton amie par tes vœux . . .'

The rest of the story is missing: we do not know why Eliza's revolt has taken the form of lesbianism, but we have only to imagine Talmi without the solace of her rural lover to understand the temptation. D'Antraigues makes it quite feasible that Eliza should be attracted by the imperious, contemptuous man-hater, Talmi, in whom the masculine, dominating qualities arouse Eliza's homosexual instincts. The sexual ambivalence of Talmi, although more covert and subconscious than that of Eliza, derives from her genesis: she is d'Antraigues himself, the owner of La Bastide,[6] a bitter critic of Parisian society, constantly fleeing to the rugged seclusion of La Bastide, always contemptuous of men,[7] but capable of great passion for women. In fact, the origins of this story, with its theme of lesbianism *versus* disciplined and respectful heterosexual love, as ways to female emancipation, are to be found in *Mes Soliloques*, where d'Antraigues recounts at length his amorous dalliance with a close relative of his, la comtesse de Barral. A great beauty, openly bisexual, 'sans vertu, sans honnêteté, sans aucune décence', she led the willing d'Antraigues into a turmoil of total debauchery together with the Opéra dancer Cécile Dumesnil. His comments about the society Mme de Barral encouraged round her closely resemble those of Eliza with regard to Talmi's: 'Sa société, composée de tous les gens dont les goûts étaient les plus opposés au mien, devait me déplaire. Une foule de jeunes étourdis, de beaux esprits de province, des fammes sans mœurs et sans agrément . . . Je prostituais ignominieusement le peu de talents que dieu m'a donné aux plaisirs de cette canaille' (*Mes Soliloques*, ff. 193-4). Talmi's contempt for the society kept by the lesbian Eliza is, then, an expression of d'Antraigues's contempt for that kept by the lesbian Mme de Barral. Talmi's rejection of Eliza's *mœurs spéciales* is the realization in fantasy-form of his own ultimate horror at the depraved conduct which, encouraged by the licentious Mme de Barral, had almost led him to an early death. The feature that should retain our attention, however, is the desire for individual liberty and the violent dislike of authority, for it is this that will prove the link with the other heroines of d'Antraigues's real and imaginary worlds.

The obstacle to love in *Talmi et Eliza* is sex. At this stage, d'Antraigues does not complicate human relationships with social pressures. In every other case, however, true love is thwarted by despotic authority—and in each case it is the woman who suffers. Who, or what was it that triggered off these female-emancipatory salvoes—each destined to remain unpublished until a century and a half after his death? To reach a partial answer we must look as far afield as Cumberland and Warsaw.

I have already written in some detail about the relationships between d'Antraigues and Anne Howard of Corby Castle in Cumberland.[8] What was once mere speculation has now been established by coincidences which would otherwise be inexplicable. However, a common feature of d'Antraigues's imagination is that his women acquaintances inspire stories of victimization and humiliation by fathers, and of passionate love-affairs with d'Antraigues. This is true of 'milady Howard', and of Princess Potocki. Princess Poninski is spared the latter attentions only by her spirited appeal to his better self as he invades her bed: 'Ah, Dantraigues, est-ce ainsi que vous me protégez?'[9]

Having been able to corroborate and extend the opinion of Cobban and Elmes (art. cit.) that Mrs Philip Howard was the original 'Cécile' of 'Corbi'—together with her daughter, Catherina, possibly leading d'Antraigues to the creation of a composite character—one was puzzled by the lack of any similarity between the Howards' happy, stable marriage, and the vicissitudes of the love-affair between Henri and Cécile, kept apart by his snobbish father's objecting to the girl's lower social status. The connexion became clear on reading the thirty-eight letters, now kept at Corby

Castle, written by Charles Howard of Greystoke and Mary Anne Coppinger of Cork, between 1766 and 1768. Charles's father objected to the match from the start, and when in 1763 he unexpectedly came into direct (lateral) line to be tenth Duke of Norfolk (which he became in 1777), the objections were reinforced by Edward, ninth Duke of Norfolk, who interviewed Miss Coppinger on 29 March 1767. The two young people refused to give way, however, and the Duke finally withdrew his opposition. They were married on 7 July 1767, but the marriage was sadly brief: Mary Anne died in childbirth on 28 May 1768.

This was only two years before d'Antraigues (he claims in *Mes Soliloques*) first met Philip and Anne Howard, in Montpellier. It may safely be assumed that the unhappy affair would have been a point of conversation among the English visitors there (including, according to d'Antraigues, Georgiana, Duchess of Devonshire, and Lady Spencer). How did these letters find their way to Corby? Because the Howards were a close-knit family, and the antiquary Henry Howard (1757–1842)—eldest son of the Philip and Anne Howard whom d'Antraigues knew—became a close friend of Charles and admired him greatly.[10] He ran the Corby estate from about 1785.

The relevance of the letters (which in any case have an intrinsic value for eighteenth-century social history) lies not only in the resemblance of the circumstances with those of *Henri et Cécile* (in which the young lovers are separated by the English Channel, as Charles and Mary Anne were by the Irish Sea) but also in the fortitude and strength of mind of the two young women, and in the determination of both couples to resist authority. We find the same fears by the young ladies that they are demanding too great a sacrifice of fortune and social reputation from their lovers, the same expressions of doubts, of suffering and of detestation of the father's prejudices, the alternate periods of depression, exaltation, and mutual moral support through love (marked by the repeated refrain in the Corby letters, *'but the time will come'*). Let us recall that Cécile lives at 'Corbi', and that Henri, a young English nobleman, has been told to forget her and sent to France where (like Henry, the son of Philip and Anne Howard) he was educated.

One major difference is that the Howards devote great attention to seeking practical (financial) ways of escaping from the power of

Charles's father, whereas their French counterparts are apparently powerless to avoid the risk of Henri's being sent out to Jamaica if he disobeys.

A few samples must suffice (see *Appendix*) in order to give some taste of these testimonies to the resistance of love when confronted by the despotism of social prejudice.

Two other cases of female persecution and victimization to which d'Antraigues devotes much of his attention have been touched on in my previous paper (pp. 632–3). The same concern and pattern are to be observed in his unfolding of the story of Princess Sophie Alexandrie Potocki (Potocka).[11] Here again the line between fact and fantasy is very hard to define. Here is his summary of the circumstances which led her to be staying in Lausanne in 1776, whence (claims d'Antraigues) they both visited Voltaire at Ferney, and played *Tancrède* and *Adelaïde Du Guesclin* with Lekain: 'Mde Potoska, fille unique d'un des plus grands seigneurs de Pologne, réunit sur sa tête des biens immenses et plusieurs principautés souveraines sous la protection de la Pologne. Unie malgré elle au plus vil des hommes elle ne vit son époux présenté par son père que comme un tiran. Il l'était en effet. Ce barbare instruit par elle de son goût pour un jeune seigneur de sa famille n'en persista pas moins à l'épouser et le père de la princesse fit célébrer ce mariage sous ses yeux. Ce père dénaturé mourut un an après. Alors sa fille, âgée de 18 ans, dégagée de ses chaines, maitresse d'une fortune prodigieuse à laquelle son mari n'avait nul droit suivant les usages et les loix de leur contract, aulieu de punir son époux de ses violences lui confia son autorité. Il en abusa et bientôt elle fut forcée de l'en priver. Alors ce lâche courut servir la Russie qui dévastait la Pologne. Son épouse, aigrie par ce forfait, s'en vengea avec cette magnanimité qui n'existe que dans un pais libre. Elle adopta les deux neveux[12] de ce même homme qu'elle avait tant aimé, qu'on lui avait refusé pour époux et qui mort depuis avait laissé 2 neveux porteurs de son nom et de ses vertus. Depuis cette époque elle n'a pu souffrir que son mari s'approche des lieux qu'elle habitait. On verra bientôt quel était son projet pour s'en débarrasser. Jeune, aimable, fêtée, aiant beaucopu d'esprit et un cœur tendre elle devait des sacrifices à l'amour et bientôt elle lui en offrit. Elle eut plusieurs amants. Sa tournure romanesque la rendit infortunée, elle ne trouva nulle part l'homme sélon son cœur' (*Soliloques*, ff. 211–12).

D'Antraigues's relationships with Mme Potocka quickly developed on both the amorous and the political planes. 'En me parlant des intérêts de la Pologne et de la haine pour le tiran qui en est le roi elle m'instruisit de la forme de ce gouvernement singulier que j'ignorais, de ses lois et de son institution.' She inspired him with hatred for Catherine ('la femme criminelle qui y tient un sceptre'); very soon he had become 'polonais à ses pieds et dans ses bras', for she was imbued with the strengths and qualities of the ideal liberated woman: not only uninhibited and generous, but 'Roman': 'Le cœur d'un romain semblait animer cette figure charmante et ce mélange étonnant de vigueur dans les discours et de grâces dans la personne composaient l'être le plus intéressant qui peut-être ait existé'.

If one hesitates to believe in the reality of this relationship, one's credence is driven to an extreme when he claims that she invited him to write speeches for her and her 'enfants' to deliver before 'diettes et diétines'; but 'le seul que je lui offris fut celui qu'elle eût dû prononcer le jour de son adoption' (*Soliloques*, f. 219).

As so often with d'Antraigues, it is when one thinks his fantastic *folie de grandeur* has gone too far that some detail corroborates his claims. In this case, one is surprised to find among his papers still kept in private hands the following document: 'Manifeste de [sic] très Excellente et très haute princesse Sophie Alexandrie Comtesse de Potoski princesse de Wilna grande maréchale de la Couronne née Potoski'. It is not in d'Antraigues's writing, but it is corrected and signed by him, and dated 1778. Over four thousand words long, it is an account of her enforced marriage to Adolphe Potoski by her father (Alexis Potoski) despite her attachment to another relative, Commene Potoski. The story is much as summarized by d'Antraigues above, with the added detail that Commene died in France eight months after her marriage. One is surprised to see her husband aided and abetted in her attempted assassination by 'les princes Sulkuski'—presumably Auguste and François Sulkowski, who were certainly rather unsavoury conspirators.[13] Having thrown her husband into prison for this attempted murder, she is now pleading her case for doing this. It is written with the same rhetorical indignation as parts of *Henri et Cécile*, and it follows d'Antraigues's usual procedure (e.g. Mr and Mrs Howard become 'milord' and 'miladi') of raising her rank to 'souveraine', ruling a 'patrie'. Wilno could have been suggested to him by Wilanow. Magnates the Potockis were, but not sovereigns! With splendid majesty she addresses her husband, pictured as standing in the dock: 'Avant de prouver que j'ay pû vous juger, Comte Potoski, répondez à ces trois questions: qu'êtes-vous? qui suis-je? Et en quel pays vivez-vous? Chaque réponse établit mon droit; et en effet je suis votre souveraine, vous n'êtes que mon premier sujet et vous habitez ma principauté . . . Je suis la fille de votre maître . . . La loi fondamentale accorde l'empire à tous les descendants des comtes Potoski mâles ou filles . . . Vous êtes l'époux de la princesse mais non pas le prince.'

Her indignation is occasioned, it must be said, as much by his violation of the citizens' rights as by his infamous conduct towards her. Her final plea is for mercy: 'Mon malheur fut assez cruel de vous avoir pour époux. Ils n'y mettront pas le comble en versant votre sang par la main d'un bourreau.'

This impassioned tirade contains no precise facts regarding her husband's crimes, but as a final speech for the prosecution it could be admissible. There is little point in pressing its veracity, however. Once again, d'Antraigues used real people and places as *points de départ*, and elaborated a story which in this case involved the betrayal of a woman's confidence and generosity. Like Cécile she has been made to suffer by a despotic male—but whereas Cécile was reduced to passivity and resignation, Sophie represents the triumph of the female through the natural superiority of high birth—which, to the feudal revolutionary d'Antraigues, would incorporate the noble qualities of mercy and gentleness.[14]

The necessity to adopt a descriptive approach at this stage, when dealing with generally inaccessible unpublished material, leaves little space for assessment. The time will come, no doubt, when these writings are in print, to decide whether or not d'Antraigues deserves a larger place in the history of the epistolary novel[15] and of feminism. Although he was far more enlightened on this matter than his avowed master, the author of *Emile*, and although he viewed female subjection on a different plane from the hackneyed seduction-betrayal level popularized by Richardson, he succeeded only momentarily, in Mme Potocki's *Manifeste*,

in systematizing in political terms his horror of prejudice and
tyranny by fathers and husbands, and of enforced female dependence. But then, even the *philosophes* (whom he detested, but with
whom he is at one regarding female servitude) also failed to reach
the clarity of view of a Condorcet and an Olympe de Gouges
regarding the political rights of women.[16]

Appendix

I. Extracts from three of the Howard-Coppinger letters

II. Extracts from three letters of *Henri et Cécile*

(Orthographical eccentricities have been retained)

1. Charles Howard to Miss Copinger [*sic*], 19 May 1766

[. . .] Can you forget how, during my father's being at Dublin, you encouraged me and bid me not despair; the many convincing proofs you then gave me of the sincerity of your regard for me encouraged me to proceed in a plan which tho' attended with difficulties I trust in god will yet succeed, at least I see nothing on this side of the water at present likely to prevent it, if we lose courage at every trifling obstacle, we cannot hope for happiness either in this life or the next; providence has order'd man to earn his Bread by the sweat of his Brow were that only to be understood in a literal sense, it coud not affect those whose Birth has placed them in a state of affluence, which would not seem consistent with the just dispensations of the allwise being, who directs every thing for the Best, and while we do not act contrary to what he commands, we may always hope for a Blessing on our endeavours, and any loss we might sustain, woud be a perpetual monitor to remind us of our duty to God and to love and be faithful to each other, and might perhaps be the cause of more happiness, than all the riches in the world, en tout cas nous ne serions, selon ce monde, que des infortunés, non pas des malheureux ni coupables.

You mention having wrote a letter to me at Greystock which I have not yet received, do not direct to me any more there as my father is going there; if you choose you may direct under cover to me at Mr Ryder's No. 1 Lincolns inn, which will be better than that direction I mention'd before. I am going to night to see Tancred and Sigismunda I think there are a great many refind sentiments and striking images which cannot but move, tho at the same time one cannot help being vexed at her despondency on account of that unfortunate Letter he read in council, if you have not the play by you I reccomend it to your perusal; I need not tell you who I shall be thinking off while I see it how pleasing woud every place appear in your company, and how insipid is every thing without it, this disagreeable business I have here to go through, wou'd become delightfull if after the plague of the day I coud have one hour to sit and converse with *ou* to tell *ou* how much I loved the pleasure I coud take in gazing and hearing *ou* talk, the very thinking of it affords me a delight I cannot express believe me the time will come when we shall be entirely free to cherish and cultivate an affection that I hope is mutual nay had I ten times more to suffer, it wou'd be more than repaid, in obtaining your heart, but without that I shoud be miserable, but I am not so, my love will not desert me; her assurances last year in the time of my distress convince me of the contrary; I cannot say more at present being sent for by my father believe me I love you and you will always find it C.H.

2. Miss Coppinger to Charles Howard, 26 May

You have by this time rec'd my letter, and was no doubt Struck, at my having Seen the play of Tancred almost at the Same time you did, and I am Convinced our thoughts were much the Same, I have this instant read it over, and I will not tell you how much I wish'd to point out to you, every Sentiment that pleased me to make every reflection, the Conformity of her Situation and mine in Some particulars occasioned; but by letter 'tis impossible; I Coud not explain my Self without entering upon Circumstances that it woud be imprudent to mention, but I never was So much affected with a play, I joyn with you in Condemning her for believing Tancred Cabable of being So Cruelly false, for I think no proof whatever Shou'd affect a person that really loves, and I think the greatest test of regard, is to have Such an opinion of the person as to disbelieve every Seeming evidence to the Contrary, from a firm dependance on his truth—his honour,—you imagine I easily dispair—you mistake me, I wish I Cou'd Clear up Some parts, I am Sure you do not understand, or do not See in the light I did but once more all explanations must be differed till we meet, tho this delay distress's me; there is a thousand things I want to talk to you, to ask your opinion upon, and even in my own

thoughts many Contradictions, I want you to Clear up, I am not
Satisfied with my Self, it is So hard to distinguish between what
may be the effects of pride, or realy proceed from delicacy, that I
own my self at a loss but you are too much used to reflection to be
puzzeld about it, besides there is not as many little niceties to be
Considered in your Situation as in mine, but a thousand triffles
hurt me Now, which I Shou'd not think of, were we on the Same
equallity as when our acquaintance first begun, but the difference
of your Situation gives me a Constraint, the idea of the world will
in Spite of me occur, and that a thousand things might be mis-
construed into Selfish, interested motives, yet I look on it as
meaness, to be affected with Such low Considerations, wish—but
Cannot reason my Self above it, the last part of your letter gave
me real Satisfaction, your Seeming So Convinced of my regard, it
frightened me when you Seem'd even to hesitate about it, and I
feelt my Self almost grow angry; had you not concluded as you
did I Shou'd Certainly have Scolded, but now Howard will you
not in reality Scold me, if I own to you this misterious Sort of
Correspondence vexes me if it is justifiable, why conceal it, if not,
nothing Shou'd tempt me to go on with it [. . .].

3. Miss Coppinger to Charles Howard, 16 April [1767?]

en verité mon cher ami, votre nom et l'idée du plus aimable, du
plus Sincere de touts les hommes Sont pour moi inséparable[s],
Mais comment vous exprimer ma reconnoissance, ma façon de
penser à votre égard, Selon moi c'est impossible, car quand l'on
Sent vivement, les Sentimens perdroi[en]t trop, à vouloir les
définir, c'est au cœur Seul à le pouvoir faire, je me recommande
donc au vôtre, et comme je lui donne Carte blanche je le prie
d'être discret, car je ne voudrois point qu'il vous en dise trop.
[. . .] Believe me, nothing but your letter, and Such a one as the
last cou'd have given me Spirits, you will Scold me but I Cannot
help it, I CAnnot have a Doubt of you, but think how many Causes
I have for uneasiness, or rather think how many I have made for
my Self, and an impression once made is hard to be removed, for
the Mind much taken up with one object, tho painful it dwells on
it, with a malincholy Sort of pleasure, and every triffle is magnified
by fear, but do not mind me 'tis only phantoms of my own

creating and the produce of an imagination busy in tormenting itself I am alarmed I Cannot tell you why, but I have thought of ten thousand things that may happen and fancy you have concealed many from me, least being acquainted with each Circomstance might hurt me, but remember I will not allow you Such tenderness, I entreat you tell me all, and believe me I have resolution enough to hear every thing that can happen, except the loss of your affections, this I know will never happen, it is not vanity, it is my attachement to you that persuades me of it. but one of the things I have pictured to my Self is your fathers having forbid you to think of me you do not mention him what does he Say how will he act, then Howard every thing you may lose the Disobliging all your friends, I know you have too much real greatness not to be above every Consideration of interest, but Shall I not feel every Sacrifice you make me, this you know we have already talked over, but I am not Satisfied every different reflection occasions an inquietude I Cannot conquer.

je borne mon ambition à celle de Clarice dans l'ambitieux, un Séjour sans éclat, une vie innocente avec un tendre époux, qui content de mon cœur, en me donnant le Sien put faire Son bonheur. that my beloved friend is *ou*, does not *ou* remind you of a thousand delightful days, tho I do not think we have had many realy So, *but the time will come* and *ou* will *to me*. it wou'd be rediculous to tell you in how much better Spirits *ou* has put me, I realy was monstrously oppressed when I began to write but I have not been very well, and had in Settling my drawer, met with all your letters when we first parted, I cou'd not help reading them over, nor being affected tho tis now past but what a painful recollection all you have Suffered, what tenderness do I not owe you, with what Sensibility do I not reflect on every proof of your attachement, nay Howard I envy you the giving me Such Glaring marks of it, but do not think I am of So passive a disposition as tamely to allow *ou* the Superiority, as to affect[ion] believe me you are not entitled to it, nor will I ever give up this one point, does not this Stubborn disposition frighten you, at least 'tis Candeur to acquaint you with my faults, but the Candeur that reigns thro this whole letter almost frightens me, but who cou'd listen to prudence and resist the pleasure of assuring one So deserving of tenderness, of the most Sincere the most unalterable affection—Cop.

1er cahier

Henri à Cécile, 20 juillet 1766 à Douvres

Quel fut cet homme de fer qui put sans pitié séparer l'amant de son amie, qui vit répandre les pleurs de l'amour malheureux sans en être ému? Quel fut ce barbare qui remit entre les mains d'un père inflexible, la despotique autorité des plus cruels tirans? Oh douleur sans cesse renaissante. J'aime et je te fuis. J'étais aimé, je voyais mes jours s'écouler à tes pieds dans le délire du bonheur et de l'innocence. Je ne demandais au ciel que la renaissance des mêmes jours ou la mort. Un père, mon bourreau, vient m'arracher la vie. Oh que dis-je, ce n'est pas ma mort qu'il veut, c'est mon suplice puisqu'il me laisse exister en m'éloignant de toi. Quelle horrible distance trois jours ont mis entre nous et ils ne sont pas contents. La mer doit nous servir de bourreau heureux. Si elle pouvait me servir de tombeau pendant ces trois jours. Ah que ton ami a souffert. Ses tourments ne peuvent se décrire. Ils ne peuvent s'imaginer. Il faut avoir son cœur pour aprétier ses maux. Famme adorée c'est toi qui me conserve la vie, c'est ton image chérie qui vivifie ce cœur qu'on réduit au désespoir. Dans les transports de ma colère quand je songe aux violences dont je suis l'objet, tout mon cœur se soulève et s'irrite en un moment de rage. Il n'est aucune sorte de vengeance en dessus de mon courage et qui ne soit au dessous des maux que l'on m'a fait. Alors je sais mon impuissance. L'enfer est dans mon cœur avide de liberté et impatient du joug et de la servitude. [. . .] Il faut s'habituer au malheur de l'absence pour sentir le bonheur d'écrire à ce qu'on aime. Dans les premiers moments je l'éprouve. L'aspect de ce papier fortuné où je trace mes douleurs les ranime, les aigrit, je songe que cette feuille que je touche, que je baigne de pleurs, sera touchée par celle que j'aime [. . .]

Londres   [Cécile à Henri]

Ta lettre m'est parvenue cher Henri. Mes regrets moins expansifs que les tiens n'en sont pas moins douloureux. Le présent m'est horrible, l'avenir m'effraie. J'ai vu notre bonheur se dissoudre. Qu'on me ravisse le souvenir du passé et je cesserai de vivre. Mon respectable père pleure avec moi. Notre espoir mutuel est en tes vertus. Pour nous rendre les plus infortunés des mortels il faut que tu cesses d'être le plus honnête des hommes. Oh que dis-je? Tel est le langage d'un père. Oserais-tu te méprendre? Non, ce n'est pas ainsi que parle une amante. Ce n'est pas ta probité qui peut me rendre heureuse, c'est ton amour [. . .] Qu'ils sont insensés, ces hommes barbares qui crurent en te séparant de moi briser les nœuds qui enlacent nos cœurs. Ils ont pour me nuire les préjugés, l'opinion, les richesses, ce ton de mépris prodigué par l'opulence à l'honorable médiocrité. Moi je n'ai pour me défendre que mon amour, que la connaissance de ton cœur, et je leur résisterai. [. . .] Lis souvent cette lettre, elle te ramènera à des moments que tu ne dois jamais oublier. [. . .] Je pars demain pour Corbi [. . .].

2ème cahier

Paris   [Henri à Cécile]

Depuis trois jours je mourais de langueur et d'impatience. Ta lettre m'a ranimé, j'y ai retrouvé avec les témoignages de ton amour les précieux souvenirs qui me rendent encore la vie désirable. [. . .] En lisant celle que tu m'as écrite puis-je te dépeindre quels sentimens se partageaient mon cœur? Je sentais toute ta supériorité sur moi. J'étais ébloui de l'éclat de tes vertus, ton éloquence m'entraînait. [. . .] Eh bien tant de gloire, tant d'avantages ne m'humiliaient pas. Etonné de la distance où tu es placée, je sentais que mon amour me raprochait de toi. [. . .]

3ème cahier

(*Henri's father proposes a brilliant match for him*)
Versailles   Henri à Cécile

[. . .] Que de pleurs, j'ai répandu en lui répondant [. . .] que je dédaignais la fortune qu'il m'offrait et l'alliance qui devait m'y conduire, que jamais miladi ne serait mon épouse et que je mourrais libre ou ne porterais d'autre chaîne que celle de Cécile.

Je m'attends à ses fureurs et je les brave. Le respect pour les pères ne s'étend pas au dévouement absolu, à leurs volontés. Ce n'est pas pour notre suplice qu'ils nous donnent la vie, il ne leur appartient pas d'avilir leur ouvrage. [. . .]

14

Cleopatra's Nose and Enlightenment Historiography

J. H. BRUMFITT

Enlightenment historiography has often had a bad press and in particular its theories of causation have been criticized by writers as different as the Marxist G. V. Plekhanov[1] and the Crocean idealist R. G. Collingwood. Of eighteenth-century historians in general, the latter has this to say: 'It was these historians, for example, who invented the grotesque idea that the Renaissance in Europe was due to the fall of Constantinople and the consequent expulsion of scholars in search of new homes; and a typical expression of this attitude is the remark of Pascal that if Cleopatra's nose had been longer the whole history of the world would have been different—typical, that is, of a bankruptcy of historical method which in despair of genuine explanation acquiesces in the most trivial causes for the vastest events.'[2] It is not my intention to defend Collingwood's view. On the contrary, I would suggest that the overall development of Enlightenment historiography is characterized by an increasing concern to discover, within the complex pattern of human events, a theory of causality which is both 'rational' and 'social'. Yet the Cleopatra's nose philosophy of history (if one may dignify it by such a title) exercised its seductions on many Enlightenment historians. It is the manifestations of this seduction (particularly in a French context) that I wish to explore. Moreover, since this volume is devoted more particularly to the role of women in eighteenth-century French society, I wish to suggest that it was not accidental that Cleopatra should have given her name to this particular theory of history and that there is a statistical (and perhaps causal) link between the theory itself and contemporary views on the role of woman.

Pascal, of course, did not invent the idea that minute causes could lead to great events. One can find it, for example, as Pascal himself may well have done, in Montaigne. In the *Essai* 'De Mesnager sa volonté' (iii, 10) the latter writes: 'Nos plus grandes agitations ont des ressorts et causes ridicules. Combien encourut de ruyne nostre dernier Duc de Bourgongne pour la querelle d'une charretée de peaux de mouton? Et l'engraveure d'un cachet, fut-ce pas la première et maistresse cause du plus horrible crollement que cette machine aye onques souffert? Car Pompeius et Caesar, ce ne sont que les rejettons et la suitte des deux autres. Et j'ai veu de mon temps les plus sages testes de ce Royaume assemblées, avec grande ceremonie et publique despence, pour des traitez et accords, desquels la vraye decision despendoit ce pendant en toute souveraineté des devis du cabinet des dames et inclination de quelque fammelette.' It is interesting to observe that Montaigne ends up on a 'feminine' note. So too, of course, does Pascal. Number 162 of the Brunschvicg edition of the *Pensées* reads as follows: 'Qui voudra connaitre à plein la vanité de l'homme n'a qu'à considérer les causes et les effets de l'amour. La cause en est *un je ne sais quoi* (Corneille), et les effets en sont effroyables. Ce *je ne sais quoi*, si peu de chose qu'on ne peut le reconnaître, remue toute la terre, les princes, les armées, le monde entier. Le nez de Cléopâtre: s'il eût été plus court, toute la face de la terre aurait changé.' Repressing a desire to speculate why Pascal's 'plus court' has become 'longer' in Collingwood's memory, let us rather emphasize that both Montaigne and Pascal are writing as *moralistes* and not as philosophers of history. This may be one reason why their views evoked little echo in seventeenth-century historians. Other reasons, however, were perhaps more important.

If there was an 'orthodox' view of historical causation in the late seventeenth and early eighteenth centuries, it was the one which found its fullest expression in Bossuet's *Discours sur l'histoire universelle* (1681), but which was still being accepted by men like Rollin or Dom Calmet over half a century later:[3] the course of history was controlled by divine Providence and 'le doigt de Dieu' was everywhere manifest. It is true that if one did not read Bossuet's text with what Pascal would have called 'les yeux de la charité', one might feel a little uneasy when, for example, one found the fall of the Roman Empire being explained by the fact that 'Dieu enfin se ressouvint de tant de sanglants decrets du sénat contre les fidèles'.[4] God, certainly, was no 'petite cause', but what about whatever it was that had jogged his memory? And when Boulainvilliers, in the generally sympathetic account he gave of the rise of Islam in his *Vie de Mahomed* asserted that the Prophet had been sent by 'God' to punish the misdeeds of bad Christians etc., it seems possible, given Boulainvillier's heterodoxy, that his tongue was in his cheek.[5] Yet if such reflections occurred to any-one at the time, it must have been to a tiny minority who took good care not to publish their views.

The antiquarians—those *érudits* from Mabillon and Montfaucon onwards who did so much to perfect scientific methods of his-torical enquiry—would probably, since they were in large part devout churchmen, have subscribed to Bossuet's views. But their eyes were mostly glued to their texts and speculation about causation was not their *forte*. In a very different category were the popular historians of the day—men like Varillas, Vertot, or Saint-Réal. They were not unduly concerned with accuracy (cf. Vertot's proverbial 'J'en suis fâché, mais mon siège est fait'), but aimed, like many another writer of the age, to *plaire et instruire*.[6] Instruction, however, they conceived of primarily in moral terms. History should teach the reader, and more particularly the 'Princes' into whose hands they were always hoping their books would fall, to follow the precepts of virtue and prudence. If history was to teach a moral lesson it must, by and large, exemplify a moral order in which virtue was rewarded and crime punished. Any systematic acceptance of a world in which minute causes led to disproportionate effects would obviously have run counter to their aims. Yet their desire to please led them, not surprisingly, to a wish to tell exciting stories in which the element of the unexpec-ted played no small part. As a result, though they did not accept, or at any rate propound, a 'Cleopatra's nose' view of history, they moved somewhat nearer to it in practice. This tendency is observ-able, for example in the histories of 'revolutions'—those of Sweden, Portugal, or the Roman Republic—by which Vertot made his name. Here, in a *coup d'état* situation, a brilliant decision or a slight mistake on the part of an individual could make or mar a whole enterprise. Yet perhaps the best example of this type of

historical writing was Saint-Réal's *Conjuration des Espagnols contre
la République de Venise* of 1674. In this taut and indeed exciting
narrative there is no place for theories of causation, but the way
in which the elaborately-contrived plans of the Spanish Ambassador are brought to naught by a series of mischances and finally
revealed by a character who only appears in the concluding stages
of the story serves to emphasize the unpredictability of events.
And although this is a predominantly 'male' narrative, it is
interesting to observe that one of the figures in the plot is a
courtesan with a grudge against Venice and that her role is high-
lighted, to the exclusion of those more important figures, in
Saint-Réal's concluding remarks.[7]

With the advent of historical Pyrrhonism, epitomized in the
figure of Pierre Bayle, we are, of course, in a different world.
Bayle's opposition to theories of historical causality is at times so
radical (see, for example, the opening of his *Critique générale de
l'histoire du Calvinisme*[8]) that a 'Cleopatra's nose' view of history
seems to be swept away with all the rest. And in the *Pensées diverses
sur la comète* he is on the whole more concerned with refuting
theories of causation than with propounding one of his own. Yet
this work contains a chapter (ccxxxvi) entitled 'Combien sont
quelquesfois petites les causes des plus grands événemens'. Here,
in order to refute the predictions of astrology, Bayle asserts that
'il est certain que la cause des grands armemens, et des guerres les
plus importantes n'est quelquefois qu'un caprice, qu'un dépit,
qu'une Amourette, qu'un rien' and illustrates this theme with
about half-a-dozen examples.[9] Surprisingly, perhaps, Cleopatra
herself does not figure among these, but Helen of Troy does, and
all the others, with one exception, illustrate the importance Bayle
gives to the female role in these cases of incalculable causality.

The *Dictionnaire historique* is somewhat less explicit on the dis-
parity between minute causes and great events—at any rate in
those places where one might expect to find the theme mentioned.
There is no article on Cleopatra, and though that on 'Fulvie'
remarks that 'Les passions de femme avoient eu part à la guerre
qu'elle excita contre Octave', Bayle is content to leave his readers
to draw their own general conclusions, as he is, too, in the case
of 'Hélène'. But if Cleopatra's nose does not dominate Bayle's
historical thinking, its role is sufficiently important to ensure the

transmission of the theory to those of the *philosophes* who read his work so avidly.

Yet if Bayle remained influential, his deeply sceptical attitude to historical truth went further than most contemporaries, and still more the later *philosophes*, were prepared to follow. If we are looking for the sources of Enlightenment historiography in the more positive sense of the term, we are more likely to turn to Fontenelle, to Fénelon, to those who sought to explain 'l'histoire de l'esprit humain' and the nature and development of society—and ultimately, of course, to Montesquieu.

None of these writers are devotees of the 'Cleopatra's nose' theory; yet it continues to cast its shadow over all of them. That this is true of Fontenelle would probably not be apparent to the reader of the *Histoire des oracles*, for that work is a model of what one is tempted to call positive Cartesian historiography. Fontenelle demolishes the evidence in favour of the miraculous origin of the oracles and then proceeds to offer a convincing rational explanation in its place. The famous parable of the golden tooth, with its conclusion 'assurons-nous bien du fait avant de nous inquiéter de la cause'[10] could well be interpreted as a rejection of some of the more extravagant examples of the 'small causes—great events' theory. And was not Fontenelle, in the *Digression sur les anciens et les modernes*, one of the progenitors of the theory of progress? Yet while this is true, it is also true that the author of *De l'Origine des fables*, or the fragment *Sur l'histoire* was less interested in explaining societies or events than in understanding what was basic and unchanging in human nature. 'Ce n'est point l'histoire des révolutions, des états, des guerres . . . qu'il faut étudier, mais sous cette histoire, il faut développer celle des erreurs et des passions humaines.'[11] Fontenelle, too, is a seventeenth-century *moraliste* as much as an eighteenth-century *philosophe*. It therefore becomes less surprising to find that he can, especially in the *Nouveaux Dialogues des morts*, find himself in agreement with Pascal. In the dialogue between Charles V and Erasmus, for example, the latter can answer the former's proud assertions by insisting that 'Toute cette grandeur n'estoit, pour ainsi dire, qu'un composé de plusieurs hazards' and proceed to demonstrate the role which chance played in the Emperor's rise to power.[12] And the dialogue between Hélène and Fulvie (and here again we return to *das ewig Weibliche*) ends with Fulvie saying: 'Ainsi vont les choses parmy les Hommes. On y voit de grands mouvemens, mais les ressorts en sont d'ordinaire assez ridicules. Il est important, pour l'honneur des évenemens les plus considérables, que les causes en soient cachées.'[13]

In many ways, Fénelon is more of a traditionalist than Fontenelle. An *ancien* rather than a *moderne* (even though he tries to keep an open mind), his historical precepts often re-echo Cicero and his concern for form and style and the avoidance of any unnecessary display of erudition exemplify the extent to which he is rooted in the humanist classical tradition. At the same time, however, the emphasis he places, in the *Projet d'un traité sur l'histoire* of the *Lettre à l'Académie,* on the importance of the exact study of social and constitutional history (particularly French) plays a significant part in the development of interest in the origins and nature of institutions which characterizes men like Boulainvilliers, Dubos, Montesquieu and Mably, and plays an important part in the development of French historical and political thought. These different themes are developed in the argument of the *Lettre à l'Académie* and it comes as something of a surprise that, after having expounded them, Fénelon should, as it were, call them in question. Yet he almost seems to do so at the very end of the letter in his criticism of Tacitus who, he says, 'raffine trop; il attribue aux plus subtils ressorts de la politique ce qui ne vient souvent que d'un mécompte, que d'une humeur bizarre, que d'un caprice.' And he adds the general reflection that 'Les plus grands événements sont souvent causés par les causes les plus méprisables.'[14] In contrast to the majority of the cases we have so far considered, there is no 'feminine' principle discernible in Fénelon's observations: though when one reflects on the role played in his own career by Mme Guyon, it is difficult not to perceive a certain irony in the contrast.

It would be perverse to suggest that Montesquieu really merits a seat in Cleopatra's galley. One of the most famous quotations from the *Considérations sur les Romains* begins: 'Ce n'est pas la fortune qui domine le monde: on peut le demander aux Romains', and the whole book is devoted to showing the relationship between the maxims and constitution of the State on the one hand and its growth and subsequent decline on the other. *De l'Esprit*

des lois is in large measure concerned with explaining the determining factors which go to make up the *esprit général* of a nation
and the way in which this in its turn determines that nation's laws
and history. At the same time, one should not forget that it was
Montesquieu who created the sparkling antitheses of Rica and the
tragic irony of Usbek. One should therefore not be too surprised
to read in the *Pensées*: 'On verra dans *l'Histoire de la Jalousie* que ce
n'est pas toujours la Nature et la Raison qui gouvernent les
hommes, mais le pur hasard, et que certaines circonstances qui ne
paroissent pas d'abord considérables, influent tellement sur eux et
agissent avec tant de force et d'assiduité, qu'elles peuvent donner
un tour d'esprit à toute la nature humaine.'[15] Montesquieu's
Histoire de la Jalousie was probably written in 1732 or earlier,[16]
but the text has not come down to us and the short references in
the *Pensées* do not provide enough information for us to form a
clear idea of its content. That a serious historical and sociological
purpose was not absent from Montesquieu's mind is suggested by
the few examples of jealousy and its impact on society given in the
Pensées. But that it may not have been uppermost is suggested not
only by the quotation I have already given, but also by the introductory remarks: 'Je lis quelquefois toute une histoire sans faire
la moindre attention aux coups donnés dans les batailles et à
l'épaisseur des murs des villes prises; uniquement attentif à
regarder les hommes, mon plaisir est de voir cette longue suite de
passions et de fantaisies.'[17] Montesquieu, too, then, is not totally
blind to the seductions of Cleopatra's nose.

However, the greatest and most prolific of French Enlightenment historians fell more deeply under her spell. 'Simbolo
pur esso della concezione storica di Voltaire', remarks
Giarrizzo, discussing the 'Cleopatra's nose' theory in relation to
Gibbon.[18] La Beaumelle, the first critic of *Le Siècle de Louis XIV*,
took Voltaire to task over his predilection for 'petites causes'[19]
and a much later and generally more sympathetic editor of the
same work, Emile Bourgeois, could be led, after a consideration
of other examples, to characterize Voltaire's mature theory of
history as 'infiniment mesquine'.[20] It was no doubt Voltaire whom
Collingwood had principally in mind when he wrote the paragraph
with which this paper opens.

I shall not even begin to catalogue the many cases in which

Voltaire makes use of the principle of minute causes leading to great events, for this has already been done, adequately if not exhaustively, by many writers on Voltaire's historical works[21] and some examples, like the 'jatte d'eau' which the Duchess of Marlborough splashed on Mrs Masham's dress, thus causing the downfall of the Whig administration and saving France from invasion, are too widely known to need comment.[22] It is more important to try to situate the precise place of the theory in Voltaire's historical thinking and the precise form it takes. In the first place it does not constitute the essence of Voltaire's view of history, but is only one element among many. It is hardly to be found in the *Histoire de Charles XII* (except, perhaps, in muted form when Charles' sudden death is described), for in this work Voltaire is concerned with pointing out the folly of aggressive war, with a certain amount of social investigation, and above all with telling a good story. It plays no part in the original conception of *Le Siècle de Louis XIV*, when Voltaire's eyes are firmly set on the cultural achievements of the age, and very little in those chapters (last to be written) on the arts, sciences and principal religious disputes. One does not find it in those important chapters of the *Essai sur les mœurs* which deal with the customs, inventions, etc. of past ages. It is absent from all Voltaire's serious writings about the theory of history. To accept Giarrizzo's view would be to obtain a totally false impression of Voltaire historian as a whole.

Yet it does form an important part of Voltaire's view of history. Many of those whose preoccupation with Cleopatra's nose we have examined are (like Pascal himself) primarily concerned not with history, but with 'les effets effroyables' of human passion. This is not the case with Voltaire. His theory of 'petites causes' may be a muddled one—chance, destiny, caprice and the determinism of the inexplicable and unforeseeable can all be adduced to back up the 'explanation'—but it can be said to constitute a historical theory, for though at times it appears purely gratuitous, it rests on two firm foundations. The first of these is negative: though Voltaire never directly attacked Bossuet's theory of 'le doigt de Dieu', the absence of Providence from the historical writings of one who could call himself a deist shows how completely he rejected it.[23] Every example of the illogicality and unpredictability of history was a further nail in Bossuet's coffin. On the positive side however, Voltaire was, at any rate in his later years, a convinced determinist who felt that causal explanation must always theoretically be possible. If no such explanation could be provided in demonstrable terms, recourse to the affirmation of 'un enchaînement fatal des causes' was better than nothing. Even more than in the historical works themselves, this view is exemplified in the *Dialogue entre un Brachmane et un Jésuite*.[24]

But let us end consideration of Voltaire by taking one particular example which has a certain general interest as well as raising a number of problems. In the first chapter of the *Précis du siècle de Louis XV* (a work in which *fatalité aveugle* and *petites causes* abound) Voltaire describes the Cellamare conspiracy in which the Spanish ambassador was engaged, principally with the Duchesse du Maine, in a plot to overthrow the Regent, Philippe d'Orléans. In its main outlines, the plot had been described in the first edition of the *Précis* in 1768, and indeed, as part of a chapter outlining events from the Peace of Utrecht to 1750, it even found a place in *Le Siècle de Louis XIV* of 1751. Between 1768 and the second edition of the *Précis* in 1769, however, Voltaire added a new dimension to his story:[25] 'La fortune fit évanouir tous ces vastes projets; une simple courtisane découvrit à Paris la conspiration, qui devint inutile dès qu'elle fut connue. Cette affaire mérite un détail qui fera voir comment les plus faibles ressorts font souvent les grandes destinées.' The details which follow tell the story of the abbé de Porto-Carrero who was entrusted by Cellamare with despatches for Spain, but who, before setting off on his journey, had occasion to make use of the services of 'Une femme publique, nommée Fillon, auparavant fille de joie du plus bas étage, devenue entremetteuse distinguée'. Fillon combined her lucrative profession with that of the possibly even better-paid job of agent of the Foreign Minister, Dubois. Whilst Porto-Carrero was more pleasurably engaged, she succeeded in having some of his papers removed and they were sent to the Duc d'Orléans. Porto-Carrero was later arrested on his way to Spain and full details of the plot were discovered.

This story provokes a number of interesting questions: is it true? Did Voltaire know of it before the 1769 edition of the *Précis* and if so, why did he not mention it earlier? Did this *petite cause* really bring to naught a conspiracy which might have over-thrown the Regency? To none of these questions can I give a completely satisfactory answer, but it is at least possible to throw some light on them all.

The relationship of Dubois to Fillon is vouched for, though hardly in the most flattering terms, by Barbier. Mentioning Dubois's death in his *Journal* he remarks: 'On dit que c'est la Fillon, fameuse maq . . ., qui doit faire son oraison funèbre, comme ayant été dans son temps fameux maq . . .'.[26] However, the earliest version of Voltaire's story to find its way into print, a letter from Caumartin de Boissy dated December 1718, leaves Dubois out of the picture, speaks of a direct relationship between Fillon and the Regent himself and states that it was the Spanish Ambassador, not his envoy, who was assiduous at Fillon's establishment and whose overheard conversations led to the dis-covery of the plot.[27] Duclos's *Mémoires secrets* offer yet another version of the incident.[28] Saint-Simon, writing in 1718, thinks that Porto-Carrero was arrested *en route* for Spain because he was unwise enough to travel with a bankrupt Englishman[29] and La Mothe La Hode speaks of an accident to Porto-Carrero's coach after which the latter was so concerned for the safety of his trunk that suspicions were aroused.[30] According to Piossens and Bacallar y Sanna, on the other hand, the plot was revealed to Dubois by a certain Buvat whom the Spanish Ambassador had employed for the transcription of documents.[31]

The incident then, if not perhaps the perfect example of the *petite cause*, could certainly, if Voltaire had investigated it further, have afforded him rich material for a disquisition on 'le pyrrhon-isme de l'histoire'. But was there a *petite cause* at all? More recent historians such as Baudrillart and Leclerq have shown that Dubois knew at least the essence of what was going on from information received from Stanhope who in turn got it from the Spanish Ambassador in London. But whereas Baudrillart[32] is prepared to hedge his bets and concede that the final revelation might have come from Fillon or Buvat, Leclerq[33] thinks that once Dubois was in the know, he controlled the situation for his own ends and that the ending of the plot was rather 'la conspiration de Dubois'.

But what of Voltaire? He did not have access to all this information, but what did he know and when? It seems unlikely that he discovered the Fillon story between 1768 and 1769. Though there is nothing to link him directly with the Cellamare conspiracy, he was in close contact with the Duchesse du Maine and her entourage and probably heard at the time most of the rumours that were circulating. Did he, in 1769, remember them and decide to give Cleopatra's nose an extra pull? One suspects he did.

Though this story concerns a woman of ill repute, the links between *petites causes* and femininity are, on the whole, far more tenuous in Voltaire than in most of the writers we have been discussing. They come back into their own, however, in the last work we shall consider. The name of Adam Richer hardly merits a place beside those of Montesquieu or Voltaire, yet his book entitled *Les Grands Evénemens par les petites causes*, published in Geneva in 1758 constitutes not the final word on the subject (there is no final word), but at least a general view in which this central theme is abstracted from its many different contexts. Richer, moreover, shows a becoming modesty which is by no means always present in Voltaire. 'Mon but est d'amuser, non d'apprendre l'histoire', he tells us in his *Avertissement*, and this confession dissipates any impression we may get from the somewhat more dogmatic tone of: 'Les plus légers motifs les [les hommes] excitent aux entreprises hardies et leur font faire les plus grands efforts. Les moindres circonstances renversent des Trônes, détruisent des Empires et en élevent de nouveaux. Enfin les plus grands Evénemens sont souvent produits par les plus petites causes.'[34] Richer illustrates his case with fifty examples. They range from ancient history to the eighteenth century and include some we have already met with elsewhere—those of Helen of Troy, of Fulvia and of Buckingham (cited by Bayle) are among the most obvious. Curiously, perhaps, Richer omits Cleopatra, and it is also interesting to observe that his most modern incident: 'Un coup de canne donné par un Allemand à un Génois qui regarde l'affut d'un mortier qui s'est rompu dans une rue de Gènes, est cause que les Autrichiens sont chassés de cette ville, et que la République de Gènes recouvre sa liberté...'[35] deals with an event described by Voltaire in the *Précis du siècle de Louis XV*, but which the latter had been at pains to present as the occasion rather than the cause of the Genovese revolt.[36]

Richer's stories are naively, if pleasantly told and he has nothing new to offer the philosopher of history. Yet it is interesting to find, at this relatively late date, a whole collection of *petites causes* stories being gathered together and published. It is also interesting to observe that the *petites causes* principle, which with Voltaire had tended to become 'unisex', is now once again exemplified principally by stories in which 'quelque fammelette', or some deeper sexual passion, plays the central role (well over half, certainly, and with a little good will one could include many more). No doubt this is in large measure explained by the fact that Richer's avowed aim is primarily to amuse. Yet this is probably not the whole explanation of the general correlation we have observed between the *petites causes* principle and the role of women. History, surely (though Collingwood would not agree here),[37] is essentially concerned with military, political, constitutional and governmental affairs and throughout its course, the role of women in these matters has tended to be a secondary one. Mme du Châtelet observed with some regret that women were 'exclues par leur état de toute espèce de gloire', from government, diplomacy and 'l'art de la guerre'.[38] If 'normal', 'predictable' history has been very much a masculine concern, it is hardly surprising that the unusual and the unpredictable should be more particularly associated with the feminine. It was with the normal and the predictable that Enlightenment historians were primarily concerned, but they were never so rigid as to close their minds to the opposite principle. So Cleopatra's nose continued to exercise its fascination.

III
FIVE WOMEN

15

Voltaire and Ninon de Lenclos[1]

MARK WADDICOR

Voltaire's interest in Ninon de Lenclos, 'cette fille si singulière', as he called her (M i, 71),[2] whose long life spanned the greater part of the seventeenth century and the early years of the eighteenth, is well known; it is also fairly common knowledge that he was taken to see her shortly before her death, and that she left him a sum of money in her will (Best. *V*, 28 and 42, Desnoiresterres, i, 34). Less well known are the precise facts concerning the meeting or meetings of Voltaire and Ninon, the extent to which truth and falsehood are mingled in the many pages he wrote about her, and the causes and nature of what amounts to his fascination with this celebrated exemplar of feminine emancipation. It is our purpose, in the following pages, to throw some light on these questions.[3]

In *La Défense de mon oncle* (1767), Voltaire claimed that 'Personne n'est plus en état que moi de rendre compte des dernières années de Mlle de L'Enclos' (M xxvi, 384). However, when we are confronted with the often conflicting and sometimes vague pieces of information which he gives about her, we have the impression that what he says is not altogether reliable.

In April 1751, Voltaire wrote to Samuel Formey on the subject of Ninon de Lenclos. (This letter was published in 1765 in the *Nouveaux mélanges* and appears in the Moland edition under the title *Sur Mlle de Lenclos, à M. + + +*). In the letter, he describes his first meeting with 'Mlle de Lenclos'; he does not give a date, but refers to the respective ages of Ninon and himself. As regards his own age, he states: 'L'abbé de Châteauneuf me mena chez elle dans ma plus tendre jeunesse. J'étais âgé d'environ treize ans' (*N*, 512); after telling a little anecdote about Châteauneuf, who, he claims, became Ninon's lover on her seventieth birthday, he continues: 'Pour moi, je lui fus présenté un peu plus tard; elle avait quatre-vingt-cinq ans. . . . Sa mort suivit de près ma visite . . .'

(*N*, 512). Already, we are aware of a certain *flottement* in Voltaire's memory, for how can an interval of fifteen years be described as 'un peu plus tard'? The confusion becomes even greater if we look at other works where Voltaire refers to his visit or visits to Ninon. In a note (which first appeared in 1751) to the *Dialogue entre Mme de Maintenon et Mlle de Lenclos*, of 1750, he said that she was eighty-eight when she died (M xxiii, 497), which is in contradiction with what he said in the letter to Formey. In *La Défense de mon oncle* he stated that he saw Ninon when she was in 'les dernières années de sa vie' (M xxvi, 384), which is not in accordance with the earlier statement: 'Sa mort suivit de près ma visite', since it implies a number of visits over several years. In an article of the *Questions sur l'Encyclopédie* (1771), he says: 'J'ai beaucoup vu dans mon enfance . . . Mlle Lenclos [*sic*]', and implies that this was when she was about eighty (M xviii, 354): 'mon enfance' certainly does not tally with the statement, in the letter to Formey, that he was thirteen, and the two texts are at variance over Ninon's age at the time. Finally, in the *Commentaire historique* (1776), the visit is said to have taken place when Voltaire was about twelve (M i, 71).

Commentators have drawn attention to some of these contradictions, and tried to unravel them. Louis Moland does not get very far (M xxiii, 497, n. 2, and 512, n. 2). G. Desnoiresterres concludes that Voltaire may have been eleven at the time of the meeting (i, 34). Theodore Besterman, in his biography of Voltaire, has come closest to the truth about young Arouet's age, but is quite wrong about his hostess's: 'He was ten and she ninety' (Best. *V*, 42).[4] Let us now look at the facts, as far as they can be ascertained.

The *acte de baptême* of Anne de Lanclos, whom we call Ninon de Lenclos,[5] was not discovered till the nineteenth century; it shows that she was baptized on 10 November 1620 (Magne, 17-18, n. 2); her death is certified by Voltaire's father as having taken place on 17 October 1705 (Desnoirresterres, i, 34, and Magne, 256). Thus, provided that the date given by the *acte de baptême* is correct (this is not absolutely certain[6]), and assuming that Ninon was born, say, one day before the *acte* was drawn up, she was, on the day of her death, aged 84 years, 11 months and 8 days. On the same day, Voltaire, who was born on 21 November 1694 (M i,

294, and Best. *V*, 24–6), was aged 10 years, 10 months and 26 days. Voltaire says that Châteauneuf took him to see Ninon because the abbé was impressed by some verses the boy had written at school (M i, 71); it is fairly certain that Voltaire entered the Collège Louis-le-Grand in 1704 (Best. *V*, 31), perhaps at about the time of his tenth birthday, in November of that year.[7] So it seems probable that he went to see Ninon between late 1704 and October 1705, at which time she was eighty-four, and he was ten.

It was not simply bad memory which caused Voltaire to give contradictory and inaccurate chronological information regarding what was for him a memorable encounter; other factors were at work, among them his habit of making fanciful statements about his date of birth and his age (Best. *V*, 24–5), and perhaps also a desire to make the image of the precocious poet admired by the ageing Ninon more plausible, by advancing his own age by a couple of years; as regards Ninon's age, it is not surprising that he should be uncertain about that, since the true facts were not known in the eighteenth century.[8]

In our eyes, Voltaire's real age at the time of the meeting serves to underline his precociousness: the verses (M i, 72) give evidence of considerable skill in versification, and of wit. It is not at all improbable that Châteauneuf, on the strength of these lines, took the boy to Ninon's house in the rue des Tournelles. Her salon, in the late seventeenth and early eighteenth century, was a gathering-place for the lettered aristocracy, for men of letters, for philosophers with a disposition towards *libertinage*, and for young men wishing to acquire the social graces.[9] But besides the literary and social reasons which may have prompted the visit, there were personal ones too. As Voltaire says: 'Mlle de Lenclos avait autrefois connu ma mère, qui était fort amie de l'abbé de Châteauneuf. . . . L'abbé était le maître de la maison [de Ninon]' (*N*, 512). Madame Arouet died in July 1701; however, Voltaire's father continued to visit Ninon till the latter's death. His visits may have had a cultural motive, for he was interested in literature (Desnoiresterres, i, 12), but the principal reason was that he acted for Mlle de Lenclos in a legal capacity: he helped her to draw up her will, in December 1704, and was appointed as her executor, as can be seen from this extract: 'Je supplie très humblement

M. Aroüet de vouloir bien, par la bonté qu'il a pour moi, de ce [*sic*]
charger d'exécuter mon testament, et de me permettre de laisser
à son fils, qui est aux Jésuites, mille francs pour luy avoir des
livres; c'est une grâce dont je luy seray fort obligée'.[10] When
Voltaire said, in the letter to Formey, that Ninon bequeathed him
'deux mille francs pour acheter des livres' (*N*, 512), he was wrong
about the amount of the bequest, but right about its motive,
though it seems likely that the gift was at least partly intended as a
'thank you' to the executor,[11] (and indeed, young Arouet's visit
may not have been unrelated to the fact that his father was helping
Ninon with her will). In a letter written by Voltaire to Formey
shortly after the letter *Sur Mlle de Lenclos*, the truth about the
motive of the bequest becomes distorted: 'elle m'a mis sur son
testament pour m'engager à faire des vers: je n'ai que trop
exécuté sa dernière volonté' (Best. D 4802); and in a further letter
to the same correspondent, he implies much the same: 'elle me
laissa deux mille francs; j'étais enfant, j'avais fait quelques mauvais
vers qu'on disait bons pour mon âge' (Best. D 4867).[12] These
statements, which are at variance with what he said in the letter
Sur Mlle de Lenclos (and with the truth), can perhaps be attributed
to false modesty on the part of Voltaire, concerning his poetic
talent.

Another confused aspect of Voltaire's meeting with Ninon is
the question of who took him. In the letter *Sur Mlle de Lenclos*
(*N*, 512), and in the *Commentaire historique* (M i, 71), he said it was
Châteauneuf, but in *La Défense de mon oncle* (M xxvi, 384), he said
it was the abbé Gédoyn, who himself had only recently started to
frequent her salon. Both men were well aware of Voltaire's talent,
both were well acquainted with his family as well as with Ninon,[13]
so it is equally possible that either or both accompanied him on
visits to the rue des Tournelles.

There is yet another uncertainty in connection with what
Voltaire says about the ageing Ninon, though, in this case, we
have no hope of arriving at the truth. The anecdote, in the letter
Sur Mlle de Lenclos, about Châteauneuf becoming her lover on her
seventieth birthday, is directly contradicted in the second of the
two further letters he sent to Formey on the same subject, less
than a year later: 'C'est ce même abbé de Châteauneuf qui avait
été son dernier amant, mais à qui cette célèbre vieille ne donna

point ses tristes faveurs à l'âge de soixante et dix ans comme on l'a dit' (Best. D 4867). This contradiction was itself contradicted by Voltaire some years later, when, in 1765, he came to revise both the letter *Sur Mlle de Lenclos* and what is now Best. D 4867, for publication in the *Nouveaux mélanges*, for he altered the text of the letter to read: 'C'est ce même abbé de Châteauneuf qui avait fini son histoire amoureuse, c'est lui à qui cette célèbre vieille fit la plaisanterie de donner ses tristes faveurs, à l'âge de soixante et dix ans.'[14] Two years later, in *La Défense de mon oncle*, he is much more sceptical about these autumnal amours, and tries to arrive at a more balanced assessment of the truth. He attacks the assertion, made by P. H. Larcher in his *Supplément à la Philosophie de l'histoire*, that Gédoyn became Ninon's lover in her old age: first, in her 'dernières années' she was 'sèche comme une momie', so Gédoyn 'était fort éloigné de sentir des désirs pour une décrépite ridée'; second, 'Ce n'était point l'abbé Gédoyn à qui on imputait cette folie: c'était à l'abbé de Châteauneuf', but the event would have taken place when Ninon was but sixty and 'encore assez belle'. Voltaire adds: 'Voilà la vérité de cette historiette, qui a tant couru, et que l'abbé de Châteauneuf, mon bon parrain, . . . m'a racontée souvent dans mon enfance, *pour me former l'esprit et le cœur*' (M xxvi, 384-5). By using the word 'historiette', and by alluding ironically to Châteauneuf's motives, Voltaire is in effect inviting us to see the whole story as a piece of self-indulgent imagination on the abbé's part.

The reasons for Voltaire's changes of mind regarding Châteauneuf and Ninon are perhaps not hard to find. The original letter *Sur Mlle de Lenclos* was a reply to Formey's request for information about the lady.[15] At first sight, it seems a little strange that such a man should make such an enquiry: Formey, a Protestant pastor, and permanent secretary of the Berlin Academy[16] was conventional, not to say narrow-minded in his moral and religious outlook.[17] However, besides his official functions, he had a passionate interest in French life and culture, which found an outlet in his journalistic activities. Between 1750 and 1758, he edited a review entitled *Bibliothèque impartiale*. In the September–October 1750 issue he had reviewed the spurious *Lettres de Ninon de Lenclos au marquis de Sévigné*. His review shows that he was shrewd enough to realize that the work was not authentic, but that he had con-

siderable admiration for Ninon herself.[18] His subsequent inquiry
to Voltaire was perhaps prompted by the appearance, in March
1751, of two *Mémoires* (that is, biographies) of Ninon, one by the
playwright A. Bret, the other by a certain Douxménil:[19] Voltaire,
recently arrived in Prussia, and a known authority on French
history, was the obvious person to go to for information.

The two men had met, and they had not yet quarrelled, as they
were to do later.[20] Voltaire must have sensed, in the Academician,
an apparent contradiction between his moral and religious ideas,
and his interest in the unreligious, and, by conventional standards,
immoral, Ninon de Lenclos. We can tell this from a letter he wrote
to D'Argental: 'Il y a ici un ministre du saint évangile qui m'a
demandé des anecdotes sur cette célèbre fille: je lui en ai envoyé
d'un peu ordurières, pour apprivoiser les huguenots' (Best. D
4480); and from the first paragraph of the letter *Sur Mlle de
Lenclos*: 'Je suis bien aise, monsieur, qu'un ministre du saint
Evangile veuille savoir des nouvelles d'une prêtresse de Vénus.
Je n'ai pas l'honneur d'être de votre religion, et je ne suis plus de
l'autre; mais j'ai voulu laisser passer le saint temps de Pâques
avant de répondre à vos questions, jugeant bien que vous n'auriez
pas voulu lire ma lettre pendant la semaine sainte' (*N*, 507). It is
obvious from this that Voltaire wished to tease his correspondent.
The anecdote, at the end of the same letter, about Châteauneuf
becoming Ninon's lover on her seventieth birthday can be seen as
further evidence of such teasing: as a minister of the church,
Formey ought to have been shocked by the story. The reason
why Voltaire subsequently denied, in Best. D 4867, that the event
had taken place when Ninon was seventy, was probably that he
was there intent on pouring scorn on the *Mémoires* of Bret and
Douxménil, which tell a similar, though not identical story, about
Ninon and Gédoyn.[21] The reason for the revision of Best D 4867
in the *Nouveaux mélanges* was to avoid a flagrant contradiction, as
Voltaire admitted in his instructions to Cramer, who was printing
the edition (Best. D 13040). The *Défense de mon oncle*, although a
polemic work, shows Voltaire's critical opinion of the alleged
event.

Obviously, then, all is not true in the letter *Sur Mlle de Lenclos*;
but this does not mean that everything is false.

Among what is substantially true (leaving aside discrepancies of age, date and so on) is the information which is first-hand, such as young François-Marie's visit to Ninon and her subsequent bequest, the latter being in addition verifiable by a document which is very probably authentic. Secondly, there is information which, although it is not first-hand, finds confirmation in fairly reliable sources, and may therefore have a factual basis (in spite of inaccuracies of detail): in this category are the statements that Ninon was friendly with Saint-Evremond (N, 508),[22] that she was visited by the Queen of Sweden (N, 509),[23] that she had a son called La Boissière (N, 509),[24] and that she had been acquainted with Mme Scarron in the 1650s (N, 509).[25]

In a different category, mid-way between fact and fiction, must go a story which is alleged only by not altogether reliable sources, namely, the Queen Mother's threat to have Ninon sent to a convent for misconduct, and her witty retort (N, 508).[26]

In the category of the purely *romanesque* must surely go the alleged offer by Mme de Maintenon to Ninon, to share her boring life at Versailles (N, 510-11): apart from the fact that it seems highly improbable, it is not attested by any seventeenth-century written source, and probably emanated, as the note added to the *Dialogue entre Mme de Maintenon et Mlle de Lenclos* states, from Châteauneuf. (It is possible, however, that the two women occasionally had contact after Mme Scarron had been widowed).[27] In the same category we must also place the allegations about Châteauneuf's successful courtship of the elderly Ninon, about Richelieu having been her first lover (N, 507), about the suicide of her son (N, 509),[28] about her act of fidelity towards Gourville (N, 510),[29] and about the visit of Huygens (N, 508).[30] Some of these allegations are to be found in the *Mémoires* of Bret and of Douxménil, as well as in the (authentic) *Mémoires* of the Duc de Luynes, who attributes them ultimately to Gédoyn, but to whom they were recounted by an un-named intermediary at Versailles in 1745—Voltaire himself perhaps?[31] By the 1740s, there seems to have been a highly-developed Ninon myth, to which Voltaire may well have contributed, by his retelling of the words of Châteauneuf and Gédoyn.

All in all, Voltaire has invented very little, if anything, about Ninon de Lenclos, but would probably have vouched for very little if he had been seriously challenged. An indication of this is the fact that he did not see fit to include any mention of her in *Le Siècle de Louis XIV*, although we know from Mme de Graffigny that he had originally intended to refer to certain aspects of Ninon's life (Best. D 1681). The reason for the suppression of any allusion to Ninon can perhaps be inferred from a passage in the *Supplément au Siècle de Louis XIV* (1753), where, talking of Mme de Maintenon, he says: 'Je pouvais parler des hommages que sa beauté et son esprit lui attirèrent dans sa jeunesse, en ayant été très informé par l'abbé de Châteauneuf, le dernier amant de la célèbre Ninon ma bienfaitrice,[32] laquelle avait vécu, comme on sait, avec Mme Scarron plusieurs années dans la familiarité la plus intime; mais un tableau du siècle de Louis XIV ne doit pas, à mon avis, être déshonoré par de pareils traits. J'ai voulu dire des vérités utiles, non des vérités propres aux historiettes' (M xv, 135). By using the word 'déshonoré', Voltaire shows that the exclusion of Ninon was partly based on a concept of *bienséance*, but the phrase 'des vérités propres aux historiettes' would seem to indicate, at the same time, that he was not certain enough, in his critical mind, of the facts of Ninon's life, to wish to refer to them in his 'tableau'.

Voltaire's refusal to include, in a historical work, stories about Ninon of dubious authenticity, contrasted with his readiness to retell them in the letter *Sur Mlle de Lenclos* and elsewhere, probably shows that he distinguished between historical facts, guaranteed by reliable documents and by the criterion of *vraisemblance*,[33] and unverifiable or incorrect facts which may nevertheless be instructive as well as amusing. The letter *Sur Mlle de Lenclos* may not contain many 'vérités utiles', but it might be fair to describe it as a *fiction utile*, in that Voltaire uses it to express various aspects of his own outlook on life. This use of fictional material reminds us of the *contes*, except, of course, that there is no narrative thread in the letter, merely a series of anecdotes arranged according to a loose sort of analytic order.

What are the 'truths' which emerge from the letter, and why was Voltaire interested in Ninon de Lenclos?

A preliminary answer to this question can be given by eliminating those aspects of her life which did not particularly interest him: these aspects emerge clearly when the letter is compared with the *Mémoires* of Bret and of Douxménil, the aim of which was undoubtedly to appeal to the general reading public, and not to emphasize any attitude to life.

Unlike Bret (1–6, 29–31) and Douxménil (7–13), Voltaire spends no time at all on Ninon's mother, or her childhood, or even her loss of religious belief. He makes only a passing reference to her beauty (N, 508), of which Bret (4), though not Douxménil, had given a detailed if fanciful description. His account of her son's suicide (N, 509), is brief and witty, in contrast with the dramatic approach adopted for this episode (as well as for many others) by Bret (89–98) and Douxménil (64–9).

Like Tallemant[34] and Saint-Simon,[35] Bret and Douxménil (*passim*) place great emphasis on Ninon's reputed sexual freedom, giving detailed accounts of many of her relationships. This is an aspect which Voltaire treats comparatively little,[36] though he does briefly mention her liaisons with Richelieu (N, 507), Saint-Evremond (N, 508), Villarceaux (N, 509), Sévigné (N, 510), and, of course, Châteauneuf. There is some common ground in this field, however, for, like Bret (10–12) and Douxménil (107–13), Voltaire is interested in her attitude towards sexual relations, which seems to have been that love is a mere pleasure, of little consequence compared with the all-important relationship of friendship. Voltaire sums up this outlook in a few phrases: 'On la quittait rarement; mais elle quittait fort vite, et restait toujours l'amie de ses anciens amants' (N, 508).

It is Ninon's attitude to the art of living which above all attracts Voltaire. He admires her aim of living a life of moderate luxury, without ambition, and surrounded by a circle of polite, intelligent, and cultured friends:

> Les plus beaux esprits du royaume et la meilleure compagnie se rendaient chez elle (N, 508).

> Elle resta chez elle, paisible avec ses amis, jouissant de sept à huit mille livres de rente, . . . et n'aurait pas voulu de la place de Mme de Maintenon . . .; elle ne se plaignit jamais de son état (N, 510–11).

> Sa maison était sur la fin une espèce de petit hôtel de Rambouillet, où l'on parlait plus naturellement, et où il y avait un peu plus de philosophie que dans l'autre (N, 511).

This existence, Voltaire implies through the Gourville incident, led not to selfishness but to honesty and generosity. At the same time, Ninon's 'philosophie' led her to view with equanimity the possibility of death, and to avoid superstition: 'Sa philosophie était véritable, ferme, invariable, au-dessus des préjugés et des vaines recherches. Elle eut, à l'âge de vingt-deux ans, une maladie qui la mit au bord du tombeau. Ses amis déploraient sa destinée . . . "Ah, dit-elle, je ne laisse au monde que des mourants." Il me semble que ce mot est bien philosophique' (*N*, 508). Her aim, Voltaire is suggesting with approval, was to live the good life on earth, a life where physical and intellectual enjoyment go hand in hand with a strong sense of secular morality.

It is not unreasonable to suppose that Voltaire admired, in this graceful, cultured, intelligent and emancipated woman some of the characteristics for which he had loved Mme du Châtelet, like Ninon a 'philosophe' and an 'honnête homme'.[37]

16

Madame de Tencin: an Eighteenth-Century Woman Novelist

SHIRLEY JONES

'Je n'ai d'autre dessein en écrivant les Mémoires de ma vie, que de rappeller les plus petites circonstances de mes malheurs, et de les graver encore, s'il est possible, plus profondément dans mon souvenir.'[1] It is with these arresting words that Mme de Tencin made her début as a novelist in 1735 with the *Mémoires du Comte de Comminge*. The story is simply told: the hero, while travelling incognito to collect some papers proving the validity of his father's claim to an inheritance against that of a hated kinsman, meets and falls in love with the beautiful Adélaïde, whom he then discovers to be the daughter of his father's rival claimant. Inspired by his passion, Comminge destroys the documents he had been sent to recover and, on his return to his father's house, is punished by being locked up. After a while, a letter is smuggled to him from Adélaïde, telling him that she must marry another man as the price of his freedom. When he has recovered from his initial shock and despair, Comminge decides that he must see Adélaïde again and contrives to gain access to her husband's house, disguised as a workman. It is thus that he is discovered by Benavides, the jealous husband, at Adélaïde's feet as he is bidding her an eternal farewell. Having wounded Benavides in the ensuing *mêlée*, he has to go into hiding and is sheltered by a kindly monk. Comminge eventually joins the Trappist Order, where he can nurse his grief in suitably sombre surroundings,[2] until one day the bell tolls for the impending death of a fellow monk, who turns out to be none other than Adélaïde, whom Comminge believed to be already dead, and who dies confessing her undying love for Comminge.

The theme of the *Mémoires du Comte de Comminge* is one which has been treated by some of the greatest novelists of the eighteenth century, from Prévost to Rousseau, that of family and conjugal relationships, representing the demands of society upon the individual in conflict with private passion. However, Mme de Tencin's story, dwelling as it does on violent emotions played out against the gloomy backdrop of prisons and monasteries, indicates that her aim was to conjure up a series of situations calculated to play on the readers' sensibilities and to cause them to shed delicious tears rather than to reflect that such misfortunes must have their counterparts in real life. In other words, Mme de Tencin, in this her first excursion into prose fiction, treads closely in the footsteps of Prévost, not only in the form in which she casts her tale—the highly emotive first-person narrative, reminiscent of the *Mémoires d'un homme de qualité*—but also in casting her hero in the same mould as Prévost's most famous 'jeune aveugle', the Chevalier des Grieux.

This is not, however, to suggest that Mme de Tencin's novel is merely a pale imitation of Prévost. A feature of the *Mémoires du Comte de Comminge* which constitutes its originality in 1735 and which is one of its chief artistic merits is the delicate balance achieved in the presentation of the two views of suffering: on the one hand that of the rash and thoughtless hero who, acting totally on impulse, brings about his own and others' unhappiness; and on the other, that of the virtuous heroine, who, while prepared to sacrifice her own happiness and even her life, will make no compromise with her conscience, which dictates that she, as a woman, must blindly obey the rigorous code of behaviour laid down for her as a daughter and as a wife. The particular blend of sensibility which was thus created, which was perhaps all the more effective in that it was expressed in perfect classical prose, doubtless helped to ensure the success of the *Mémoires*. The eclipse which Mme de Tencin's fame has subsequently suffered has to some extent been atoned for by recent scholarly opinion, which has tended to find resoundingly in her favour.[3]

The broader issues relating to Mme de Tencin's place in the history of the eighteenth-century novel clearly cannot be tackled here, thus this paesent discussion will attempt to isolate those features of her work which have bearing on the fact that she was a woman novelist, working within the social and literary conventions of her time.

Looking for a moment at the question of Mme de Tencin's indebtedness to her predecessors and contemporaries in the novel, one is immediately struck by the fact that her debt to the latter is negligible. The 1730s witnessed, with the emergence of brilliant exponents like Duclos and Crébillon, the evolution of the novel of manners which, while using the techniques of classicism, portrayed the world of the aristocracy, and particularly its female members, in an overall unflattering light. The brilliantly witty and elegantly brutal world which we glimpse in the pages of Duclos and Crébillon, giving as they do a new meaning to the term realism, are light-years away from the love-lorn fantasy of the Comte de Comminge.

Expectations of finding similarities between the art of Marivaux and that of Mme de Tencin are, in the last resort, bound to be disappointed, notwithstanding their shared taste for moral exclusiveness and *précieux* psychological analysis. Marivaux's main characters differ radically from those of Mme de Tencin in their rationality (in spite of Marianne's much vaunted sensibility) and in their—essentially bourgeois—preoccupation with social acceptance. In some important respects, Marivaux's novels have more in common with those of Duclos and Crébillon than with those of Mme de Tencin in that they deal with one of the great themes of the eighteenth-century novel (and one which one could qualify as realist), that of socio-sexual initiation. Whilst Crébillon doubtless provided the masterpiece in that subject with his *Egarements du cœur et de l'esprit*,[4] the underlying theme of both *La Vie de Marianne*[5] and *Le Paysan parvenu*[6] is basically *le moyen d'arriver*, which constitutes a fundamentally bourgeois variant.

Having acknowledged Mme de Tencin's debt to Prévost, one is inevitably led to the question of Prévost's literary ancestry, or rather their common literary ancestry, since both have their roots in the novel of sensibility, which flourished at the end of the seventeenth century and which ultimately derived its inspiration from *La Princesse de Clèves*.[7] That is to say, Mme de Lafayette's masterpiece as viewed through the prism of moral and literary conventions of the period—and all literary conventions must of necessity be the faithful reflection of prevailing moral conventions.

Thus *La Princesse de Clèves*—or rather, the uncomprehending prestige which it enjoyed—encouraged the development of a type of novel dedicated to the depiction of an unswerving virtue which served as the cornerstone to tales of unhappy, oppressed innocence (a fundamental misunderstanding of Mme de Lafayette's text which was to prove fruitful in its literary consequences). From this cult of virtue—and since the moral intransigence which was the hall-mark of these novels precluded much psychological development—there arose the cult of suffering, which in this context is synonymous with that of sensibility. The heroines of these novels are invariably virtuous and are equally invariably pursued by a hostile Fate or a hostile family (or both together).

The second feature of this type of novel which grew up in the shade of *La Princesse de Clèves* is the historical *décor* which is adopted, and which scores primarily as a distancing device.[8] The stage on which the rather cardboard characters of a Mlle de La Force,[9] a Mme Durand,[10] or even at times Mme d'Aulnoy,[11] play out their diminutive dramas, is nominally that of a remote, often medieval and invariably *postiche* Past. Much has already been written about Mme de Lafayette's use of historical background. In one respect only does she follow established literary tradition in *La Princesse de Clèves*, and that is in her inclusion of the story of the unhappy loves and life of Anne Boleyn. The intercalation of this episode in the main plot, which can only with difficulty be justified on artistic grounds, may well have been prompted by the apparent interest which the novel-reading public took in English history, particularly that of the Tudor period. Stories dealing with the darker side of English history and the English character continued to appear and the genre—if that is not too grandiose a term—was clearly given a fillip by the treatment it received at the hands of its most gifted exponent, Mme d'Aulnoy, in two of her best novels, the *Histoire d'Hypolite, comte de Duglas,* published in 1695, and *Le Comte de Warwick,* which first appeared in 1703. Thus, long before Voltaire appeared as the apostle of English thought and longer still before Richardson's novels made their mark on French sensibilities, English themes were a commonplace in the novel.

One of the most significant features of this branch of the novel is that its chief exponents were women, from talented novelists like Mlle Bernard[12] and Mme d'Aulnoy, to the less gifted Mlle de La Force and Mme Durand. Naturally, given the favour which their works apparently found with the novel-reading public, they attracted men writers to their ranks. Irrespective, however, of the relative merits of a novel by Préchac as compared with one by Mlle de La Force, for example, the category as a whole remains inalienably feminine in its moral inspiration. It is this factor which informs the particular view of history to be found in these novels.

Before we discuss Mme de Tencin's second novel, *Le Siège de Calais,*[13] a further general question remains to be posed: why did women novelists, including Mme de Tencin, writing in the 1730s, choose to cling to a musty historical *décor* when the novel was beginning to emancipate itself from the shackles of classical æsthetics and move towards a more immediate view of reality? The answer, it might be suggested, is twofold: in the first place the woman novelist's predilection for 'history' was due to the fact that it was the literary terrain *par excellence* which she was deemed eligible to exploit, since she would appear to have been effectively barred, for moral and literary reasons, from exploring the newly-opened up avenues of realism. And if this claim appears to be extravagant, one only has to consider that such novels as are known to have been written by women during the eighteenth century are all, without exception, characterized by rigorous moral conservatism. It is really rather ironical to reflect that women writers, much more than their male counterparts, remained faithful to the classical concept of *bienséance* in the novel. Indeed, the importance of literary convention can scarcely be over-emphasized when discussing the role of women writers in the eighteenth-century novel. That the reality of their own lives had no bearing on what they wrote is amply demonstrated by the highly adventurous careers of Mlle de La Force or Mme d'Aulnoy, for instance.[14] Whatever the nature of the private reality, women writers showed themselves as submissive in their acceptance of literary conventions as their heroines did of those imposed on them by society.

A second cogent reason for women's choice of 'history' is surely that it could also be made to serve as an instrument of revenge for the circumscribed role assigned to them in life. It is stating the

obvious to point out that the role allocated to women in eighteenth-century society was essentially a passive one and that women
like Mme de Tencin, who tried to circumvent this convention
by exercising influence through becoming the mistresses of such
powerful men as Dubois, were seen as a threat to the social
order.[15] What more natural than that women should proceed to
rewrite history in their novels so that it became in their hands a
chronicle of female domination? Hence what was seen by outraged critics, from the reactionary misogynist Boileau to the
democrat sceptic Bayle, as the trivialization of history, viewed
from another angle may be seen to represent the glorification of
Woman, for whose good graces—but not for whose favours—
wars were fought and won and kingdoms lost. Finally, the frequent choice of a nebulous medieval background for these sentimental novels is eminently understandable when one considers
that the Middle Ages were associated, in the minds of late-
seventeenth-century audiences, with the concept of chivalrous
love which women writers sought to extol. When one adds to
this the belief, current at the time, that the Middle Ages were also
a period of gloom and violence, one readily understands its appeal
for exponents of the sentimental novel.

The continuing popularity of what can, then, be termed the
feminine historical novel—not entirely surprising when one considers the frequent assertions that the majority of the reading
public were women—is attested by the acclaim which Mme de
Tencin's major historical novel,[16] *Le Siège de Calais*, received.
From the artistic point of view, the work is inferior to the *Mémoires
du Comte de Comminge*, where, as we have seen, the *précieux* element
of unswerving virtue on the part of the heroine was counterbalanced by the blind, passionate response of the hero. The
précieux psychology which sets the moral tone of *Le Siège de Calais*
is surely responsible for one of the key episodes, the involuntary
rape of the heroine, Mme de Granson by the hero, M. de Canaple.
This rather extraordinary event, which much displeased the
ineffably smug Mme de Genlis,[17] can only be seen as a kind of a
challenge, a counterblast to the view of women promulgated by
writers of the Duclos/Crébillon school. It also serves to eke out
the rather feeble psychological interest of the plot, since Mme de
Tencin, like her predecessors in the sentimental novel, obviously

had to grapple with the problem that absolute virtue is a total non-starter as far as keeping the story going from the psychological point of view is concerned.

As the title suggests, Mme de Tencin has chosen to present this very conventional (fortuitous nocturnal encounter apart) love story against an historical backdrop, that of the famous siege of Calais during the Hundred Years' War. However, as any reader of this kind of novel has come to expect, (for example, Mme Durand's *Mémoires de la cour de Charles VII*, which describes the love-idylls, in a suitably bucolic setting, of the Maid of Orleans and Dunois)[18] Mme de Tencin's treatment of history is cavalier, to say the least. All the protagonists are manifestly *habitués* of an elegant eighteenth-century salon rather than the participants in the events of the Hundred Years' War. Such local colour as is present only serves to render the anachronisms more farcical, as when Mme de Granson's 'chariot' conveniently overturns so that she can be rescued by the valorous Canaple. The authoress shows a total disinclination to weave historical event into the plot until the *dénouement*, when historical fact is wrenched around in grotesque fashion to transform Canaple, disguised as one of the burghers whose life was to be forfeit, into one of the heroes of the hour. At this juncture, the desire to take on a disguise reaches epidemic proportions among Mme de Tencin's aristocratic protagonists, causing Mme de Granson to disguise herself as a man and successfully to sue for her lover's life at the feet of the bloodthirsty English King.

René Démoris has already pointed out that Mme de Tencin's abuse of history here is deeply revelatory of her aristocratic inspiration.[19] If she seems to have re-written history in order to rob the bourgeois of his claim to heroism—an attribute to which the aristocrat laid sole claim—the underlying motive for this heroism is equally important since, in making the chivalrous love of the hero the basis of an important historical event, Mme de Tencin thus demonstrates her allegiance to the moral tradition of the feminine historical novel.

However, the very term 'feminine historical novel' serves as a reminder that an essential issue remains to be examined, in view of the particular focus which has been suggested for this discussion: that of Mme de Tencin's feminism. This is, moreover, an issue which has already attracted critical attention.[20] Jean Sgard, for instance, in discussing the general question of feminism in the 1730s attributes its resurgence during this period in part to the influence of Mme de Lambert. If, however, one consults Mme de Lambert's specific writing on the subject, her *Réflexions nouvelles sur les femmes*, which were published for the first time in 1730, one is immediately impressed by the conservatism of her attitudes on the subject, although in an initial statement on the condition of women she does touch on the vital question of education when she writes: 'nous gâtons toutes ces dispositions que la nature a donné aux femmes. Nous commençons par négliger leur éducation; nous n'occupons leur esprit à rien de solide, et le cœur en profite: nous les destinons à plaire et elles ne nous plaisent que par leurs grâces ou par leurs vices.'[21]

However, while condemning the injustice of male domination (unjust because it has been achieved by force rather than by moral superiority), she bewails the moral emancipation, or rather what she sees as the licence, which reigns amongst the female members of eighteenth-century society and advocates absolute chastity on the part of women as the only means of counterbalancing the prevailing inequality between the sexes.[22] It is this same conservatism which sets the tone in Mme de Tencin's novels.

In his analysis of what he sees as Mme de Tencin's feminism in the *Mémoires du Comte de Comminge*, which he regards as 'littérature insurrectionnelle', Jean Decottignies takes as evidence for his interpretation the psychology of the hero as opposed to that of the heroine.[23] Comminge is weak, whereas Adélaïde is throughout characterized by unswerving moral courage; he causes (involuntarily, it must be agreed) her sufferings, which she not only unflinchingly bears, but actually adds to. It is, however, rather debatable as to how far one is justified in taking at its face value this view of masculine humanity, unflattering though it may be from the moral point of view, when one is examining a work of literature. The primary weakness of such a critical method is that it fails adequately to take into account the literary traditions in which Mme de Tencin was working. Thanks to Prévost in particular, these traditions permitted the portrayal of a hero who was morally weak but apparently decreed that inviolate virtue was the *sine qua non* of the heroine.[24]

For its part, *Le Siège de Calais* expresses, even more acutely, the dilemma in which Mme de Tencin's position as a woman novelist placed her. In addition to the gynæcocratic orientation of the story, which has already been touched on, there remains the episode of the hero's inadvertently becoming Mme de Granson's lover. Extraordinary the episode undoubtedly is, but what, if any, moral message does it convey? A near-contemporaneous novel, Duclos's *Histoire de Madame de Luz*,[25] treating a similar theme, gives a radically different account of the realities of men's attitude to women; and the cynicism which is a key element in Duclos's work throws into relief the high idealism of Mme de Tencin's account of M. de Canaple's relationship with Mme de Granson. But when, on the other hand, one looks at the masterpiece of feminist literature, written fifty years after *Le Siège de Calais*, Laclos's *Les Liaisons dangereuses*,[26] one readily appreciates the gulf, not only in time, but in psychological impact, which lies between them. Laclos uses the theme of sexual violation—in this case the cold-blooded corruption of Cécile by Valmont—to illustrate his thesis that women are stultified and corrupted by society. The choice of Laclos as a term of comparison here is not a random one, since *Les Liaisons dangereuses* serves to illustrate the point that the effectiveness of the author's moral argument is directly related to the æsthetic form in which he or she chooses to express it. As Mme de Tencin's novels show, it was precisely this choice of 'history', drawing as it did a veil between the reader and the subject, which precluded any examination of moral issues which might have bearing on the real-life situation of women in eighteenth-century society.

It is surely significant that no woman novelist in the eighteenth century took up the gauntlet in such a daring manner as Laclos. Mme de Tencin epitomizes the attitude of women novelists who were content to shine in those realms of fiction where reality was rejected in favour of what could only ironically be termed history, since it represents a flight from reality, an illusion which is cosy and yet cruel. Thus the moral paradox expressed in *Le Siège de Calais* must surely constitute one of its cardinal points of interest for the student of the eighteenth-century novel since it illustrates how the choice of thematic material, motivated by the desire to present an idealized view of women, was precisely the factor which inhibited any discussion of the position of women in reality—the reality of eighteenth-century society. This, in a word, is what can be seen as the dilemma, not only of Mme de Tencin in *Le Siège de Calais*, but of all women novelists during the eighteenth century (and with certain notable exceptions, beyond). Georges May has brilliantly analysed what he has called the dilemma of the novel during the Ancien Régime;[27] and that women responded more acutely to the moral and æsthetic pressures which society brought to bear on the novel may clearly be inferred from their choice and treatment of material in their writings.

What, then, is Mme de Tencin's significance as a novelist, that is to say, as a woman novelist? In the first place she stands, from the point of view of her art, as well as that of chronology, between the historical novels of Mme d'Aulnoy and the *genre sombre* of Baculard d'Arnaud, who, incidentally, re-vamped her *Mémoires du Comte de Comminge*.[28] Furthermore, she exemplifies the force of literary conventions as they operated on women writers. Meekly, like her sister-novelists before her, she trod the well-worn paths; and it would be difficult to identify the author of those tear-stained tales, told in limpid prose, with Claudine-Alexandrine de Guérin, known to the world as Mme de Tencin; and one of the few women in that, or indeed in any other age, who could be said in her private life to have played both the role of Suzanne Simonin and that of Madame de Merteuil.

As for that protean phenomenon, feminism, particularly in relation to women's contribution to literature, clearly much territory still remains to be explored in this sphere, although Pierre Fauchery's work on the subject serves as a brilliant initial survey.[29] Indeed, the ramifications of feminism are endless. Would for instance, patient research lead one beyond the realm of flimsy hypothesis in understanding the tepidity of the *philosophes'* interest in the question of women in society? Is it significant that Marivaux, whom they regarded with hostility and contempt, was the ardent champion of feminism? And is there any significance to be attached to the fact that Diderot entrusted the article on women (from the moral point of view) to the frivolous Desmahis in the *Encyclopédie*?

A final word, then, on the importance of what I have called the feminine historical novel. Georges May, in an article on the relationship between the novel and history during this period, has declared that the novel became an instrument of revolution.[30] If one confines the definition of revolution to that which took place in the political sphere, then clearly the conservatism and escapism of these women novelists precluded them from playing a role of any importance in forging the novel into a weapon of revolt. But, on the other hand, the compensations from the literary point of view were great. The will-o'-the-wisp flame of aristocratic idealism and the particular view of history which they helped to keep alive were to be of seminal importance in the revolution of Romanticism. More immediately, during the eighteenth-century itself, those limitations which were imposed, or self-imposed, on women writers had positive consequences in that they kept before the public eye an alternative view of history to that promulgated by the *coterie philosophique* (and here one is tempted to wonder whether Voltaire's dislike of the romantic, idealistic novel was not at least in part attributable to that view of history which it presented). This aristocratic idealism, which was, then, one of the distinguishing features of the feminine historical novel, was of course yet another factor which would have rendered it inimical to the *philosophes*. That it is this idealism which sets these novels apart is demonstrated by the briefest comparison. What a gulf, for instance, lies between Mme de Tencin's heroes and titled louts like Crébillon's Versac (who, it must be stressed, however, are interesting precisely because of their loutishness).

Although she was not a writer of the first rank, Mme de Tencin's novels merit our attention not only because of the role they played in the subsequent development of the novel, but also because they serve to illustrate one of the most challenging aspects of the eighteenth-century novel, its infinite diversity. The co-existence and popularity of novels such as those of Mme de Tencin and Crébillon render it impossible to speak of 'the novel' in the eighteenth century and do moreover make it difficult to see the novel as solely the organ of the aspiring bourgeoisie, whose ascendancy in the 1760s coincided with its triumph as a *genre*, since, as Georges May has so aptly put it, in this particular house there are many mansions.

17

Marie Huber and the Campaign against Eternal Hell Torments

E. R. BRIGGS

Marie Huber first offered her views to the public in an anonymous work printed at Amsterdam (according to the imprint) in 1731, under the title *Le Monde Fou préféré au Monde Sage, en 24 Promenades de Trois Amis* (2 vols, 12°). This was put into English by an anonymous translator in 1736 as *The World Unmasked; or the Philosopher the Greatest Cheat; in 24 Dialogues* (London, 8°), a version republished in 1743 and 1786, which indicates a degree of success here. The essence of her next work, also published in the 1731 volume, reappeared in 1733 at Amsterdam and in 1739 at 'London'(?) with important modifications and additions, as *Le Sistème des Théologiens anciens et modernes, concilié par l'exposition des différens sentimens sur l'Etat des Ames Séparées des Corps, en quatorze lettres*. (No printer is quoted, the octavo has three different texts and paginations but with no indication of this being a *recueil factice* or made-up tome.)

As the long English sub-sub-title shows, the three friends mentioned in the French title of the first work are Crito a philosopher, Philo a lawyer and Erastus a merchant, their aim being to distinguish true virtue from its current counterfeits, to rectify many prejudices and errors concerning conscience and religion, and to prove the value of truth against all efforts to obscure it. It will not be possible in this short paper to follow the author in such a wide project, but its crux becomes clear in the 'epistolary treatise' which she added in all editions of these texts from 1733 onwards under the title *The State of Souls separated from their Bodies . . . and all objections against it solved*, and in her *Large Introduction evincing the same truth from the principles of Natural Religion*. Some preliminary remarks upon these titles taken generally will assist a scrutiny of the controversy about disembodied souls: firstly, the 'philosopher as the worst cheat' reflects the growing revulsion in the early eighteenth century against the prevailing abstractions of deductive Cartesianism, often expressed in quasi-mathematical terms in the manner of Spinoza, which were hindering both scientific advance (the introduction of Newtonianism into France) and efforts to remedy the defects of older orthodoxies by more adequate views of the human and divine natures; secondly, the appeal to the 'principles of natural religion' is equally characteristic of the period; and thirdly, the syncretic approach towards the reconciliation of older doctrines about human survival after death was more ahead of the time, but a tendency that was to flourish in succeeding generations.

A minor problem arises from the indication that the 'epistolary treatise' was an answer to an anonymous attack entitled *Examen de l'Origénisme, ou réponse à un livre nouveau intitulé Sentimens différens de quelques Théologiens sur l'état des âmes*. This duodecimo volume appeared at Lausanne in 1733, coming from Abraham Ruchat, a professor at the noted academy there. He thought he was refuting Béat de Muralt, a rationalistic mystic (an unusual but not unprecedented combination) whose thought resembles Marie's in some respects. Members of her family in Switzerland doubtless sent her this attack immediately after its publication, for she penned her reply quickly enough for its publication the same year in the second edition of the *Sistème*, though she was living in Lyon, where the French third edition marked 'London' may well have been printed secretly. However that may be, this little controversy was summed up by Pastor Vuilleumier as inconclusive, since Ruchat threw against her own biblical quotations other holy texts of apparently opposite meanings without attempting to weaken her more philosophical fundamental reasonings about the divine attributes and the destiny of human souls. After her rejoinder, Ruchat let the dispute end, apparently feeling unable to match her loftier flights, where she had argued that eternal hell torments are incompatible with perfect goodness but that justice flowing from goodness supports expiatory sufferings of varying length and intensity for varying transgressions, so that all humans may be brought to eventual redemption. Vuilleumier says that Marie, who had been a Pietist and even an inspired mouthpiece in her own view, was slipping through Socinianism into deism, but this calls for further consideration of her background and attitudes.[1]

The family of Marie Huber was important in more than one respect, and our present subject requires some knowledge of it for a balanced judgment of her role. For this purpose it is necessary to put together a number of details culled from various works of reference, since none has adequately perceived its significance in the philosophico-religious field. Her father was Jean-Jacques I (1661–1740), a rich banker who became a member of Geneva's *Conseil des Deux-Cents*, the ruling oligarchy, but he had spent part of his career in Lyon before returning to Geneva. He had relatives in Lyon, probably a brother, for his father Jacob I had been a resident there before returning to Geneva, where he also became a *Bourgeois* (1654) and member of its Council in 1661 and professor of theology, before dying there in February 1693. He had originally come from Schaffhausen near the Rhine Falls, and from there in the sixteenth century a branch of the same family had also come to Berne, in the person of Peter Huber, a schoolmaster who favoured the pro-Lutheran party. Peter's very able son Samuel (c. 1547–1624) had several children and could have been the uncle of Jacob I; he was first a Bernese pastor and then a Lutheran professor in Germany after a resounding controversy against Swiss disciples of Calvin and Theodore de Bèze, mainly about predestination and the cognate doctrines which were to preoccupy Marie.[2] She may therefore have been his great-great-niece.[3] She had two brothers, Jacob II (1693–1753), a banker like his father and member of the Geneva Council, and Jean-Jacques II (1699–1759), born in Lyon and the black sheep of the family, who was imprisoned for fourteen months by his father and later fled to Savoy, where he was converted in the same Turin hospice as J. J. Rousseau afterwards, then went to Paris and became a minor diplomat for France. Marie's nephew Jean (1721–86), son of Jacob II, served as an officer in Hesse-Cassel and Piedmont (1738–46) before becoming an influential member of the Geneva Council in 1752 and a member of Voltaire's circle, where he indulged his taste for painting by depicting many scenes of the life in that circle. But Marie resembled none of these, her only marked resemblance being to her mother.

This lady was born Catherine Calandrini into a notable Italo-

Swiss family of Geneva (which was also represented in London during the Civil War by a Calvinist pastor of that name). She was an ardent Pietist, the nearest approach on the Continent to our Quakers, and a correspondent of her uncle Fatio de Duillier, known in his country as *l'inspiré* and *le prophète* for his similar leanings. Her residence in Lyon had brought her into contact with French Protestant *illuminés* from the nearby Cévennes, whom she greatly helped by shelter and finance when they fled from fierce persecutions, as also later in Geneva when many settled there. Under great trials some Huguenots had become a classic example of mystical outpourings or 'prophecy' by the laity when deprived of their pastors, and such 'prophets' spread even to London in the early eighteenth century to influence some seers like Mrs Jane Leade and her 'Philadelphians'. Ruchat in fact more or less accused Marie of taking her ideas from Mrs Leade and from some of her German pietist followers like Dr Petersen, but this is doubtful. By direct experience in her family circle, and possibly by reading the works of her distant relative Samuel (although I have found so far no documentary proof of this), Marie had more than enough incitement to follow the path she chose. Her nature was clearly exceptional, her strength of mind quite remarkable. Precisely because she was rich and beautiful, she decided against marriage for life-long celibacy in virtual seclusion. The most sympathetic account of her character is found in the work of the Catholic Abbé Jacques Pernetti, who puts to shame the hostile or perfunctory mentions of her by most orthodox Swiss Protestants, and I cannot forbear from quoting him, since he wrote very soon after her death, with many eye-witnesses available to him even if he does not claim personal acquaintance:

'Morte le 13 juin 1753 âgée d'environ 59 ans, cette fille protestante . . . malgré sa modestie et le soin qu'elle prenoit de se cacher, a fait trop de bruit dans cette ville pour n'avoir pas place dans ces *Mémoires* . . . Sa beauté lui fit craindre dès l'âge de 17 ans les dangers dont elle est si souvent la source, elle se livra alors à une retraite austère et à la pratique des bonnes œuvres qu'elle n'a jamais interrompue . . . La seule liberté qu'elle se donnoit étoit d'écrire, n'ayant jamais eu de maître que son génie, ni point lu d'autre livre que la Bible. L'accord de ses œuvres et de sa croyance sur l'autre vie est un phénomène de morale. [Implication—one which shames most orthodox believers by her far greater consistency!] La crainte n'avoit nulle part à sa conduite, l'amour de l'ordre et de ce qu'elle croyoit bien paroit avoir été son seul principe. Voici sa façon de penser, telle qu'on l'a trouvée dans ses papiers: "Toute spéculation, toute discussion d'opinion à part, je me contente d'acquiescer de bonne foi et pratiquement à tout ce qui peut m'être connu pour vrai, bon et juste, réglant mes jugements et ma conduite sur cela quant au jour présent, prête à croire et à fair mieux dès demain et de jour à autre, sitôt que le mieux me sera connu. Voilà ma bonne grosse philosophie, ou si vous voulez, ma Religion. Si vous trouvez, Monsieur, qu'il manque quelque article à ce formulaire, vous me ferez plaisir de me l'envoyer" (1739). [To this she added in 1749:] "Vous vous figurez peut-être que rien n'est si facile que d'apprendre un formulaire aussi abrégé; mais vous vous trompez, du moins s'il faut parler de l'espérience que j'en fais depuis de longues années que je l'étudie, je ne saurois me vanter de n'y pas faire bien des fautes. Cela soit dit pour ne donner le change à personne." '4

These sentences express the very essence of her Cartesian suspension of judgment and of that open mind for the consideration of new evidence, even if it requires revision of earlier judgments, which is the most rational and scientific attitude of all, but also the most difficult to maintain consistently. Its dose of scepticism explains the coolness of all the orthodox towards her, and it illustrates her refusal to follow some contemporary Cartesians into a crude materialism, or the most orthodox into a blind traditionalism. Tabaraud though hostile in his *Biographie universelle* admits that 'on découvre à travers le désordre apparent des idées [de M. Huber], un système lié dans toutes ses parties et une dialectique très-subtile.' While it cannot be denied that her composition and style leave much to be desired, this is hardly surprising in one who appears almost an auto-didact, but cannot disguise her native intellectual power. At the same time, one can hardly take literally Pernetti's claim that the Bible was her only reading, for she refers to certain 'docteurs anglais' who had handled her subjects, and shows sufficient knowledge to refute the error that Thomas Burnet, Master of the Charterhouse, was a son of Gilbert Burnet, bishop of Salisbury. It is however quite credible that in her later years she confined her interest to the Bible.

Before looking more closely into her *Sistème des Ames Séparées*, it is worth notice that Jean-Jacques Rousseau possessed a signed copy of the 1739 London edition which is still in the Geneva library. Théophile Dufour concluded that he bought it during his visit there in 1754, and Eugène Ritter devoted some pages to the possible influence upon him of her ideas.[5] It is also quite possible that he had met her brother, his homonym 'l'abbé Huber', in Paris, since their experiences were so similar. The editions printed or translated in Holland, England, Germany and (probably) France are sufficient testimony to the interest of the reading public in Europe, and Ruchat's attack doubtless won it more readers, so when she published in 1738 and 1739 even more important works, alert young intellectuals like Rousseau could hardly remain ignorant of what had become *une cause célèbre* in the 1740s.

Like earlier critics of universal salvation after appropriate purgation, Ruchat alleged that it destroyed morality by favouring licence, but that argument had already been disposed of by Aubert de Versé, among others, and Marie did not need to give much space to this attempt to prejudice readers against her book before its arguments were seriously considered.[6] Similarly, she remarks that his use of 'Origenism' and 'Pietism' as condemnatory terms resembles the abuse of the term heretic among Catholics, as calculated to befog all issues, pointing out also that he argues from the authority of ancient judgments by theologians and popes, which is an unwise concession by a Protestant to the Catholic claim of infallibility. Their clash of contradictory biblical texts on salvation and punishment clearly showed the dangers of a biblicist reliance upon obscure wordings, often of doubtful authenticity, as the progress of biblical exegesis since the seventeenth century had already demonstrated, but Marie does not dwell upon this beyond remarking that English authorities have asserted the Hebrew and Greek terms for 'eternal, eternity, everlasting, never' are ambiguous and limited, meaning only 'of long or unknown duration', not 'without end'.[7] She notes also that while such defenders of orthodoxy insist upon the fullest meaning given to such terms in post-biblical times, they wilfully refuse the clear, natural meaning of phrases such as 'Christ came to save *all* men', and that the orthodox are divided between several interpretations of the texts concerning salvation and damnation. As a rationalist she seeks stronger foundations of a different kind, to raise the discussion to a higher plane than quibbling about the sense of single words and phrases probably destined to remain obscure, as the very ancient polemics on this subject prove. She makes the point that just as the Jews felt injured when ranked with the Gentiles, just so do Christians resent the availability of salvation to non-Christians, but quotes Thomas Burnet against Ruchat to the effect that the dogma of eternal torments will become no less odious to Protestants than that of Transubstantiation. She then goes on to explain in two letters about a *Conversation with a Deist* that many honest thinkers, discouraged by the uncertainties in Holy Writ and revolted by the intolerant claims of all churches and sects concerning their interpretation of these, are driven, not to the systematic doubts of the Pyrrhonists but to an honest deism which admits ignorance of the basis of such claims while retaining certain other fundamental beliefs. She makes telling distinctions between the forms of Christianity, the actual religious practice of most Christians' superficial view of self-interest, and the more sincere efforts of deists to separate the chaff of man-made theology from the good grain of natural religion.[8] For her, wilful incredulity based on the weaknesses of individuals or organizations (which she is emphasizing) is only a lazy or even criminal refusal to weigh the evidence for a small nucleus of fundamental beliefs, which are discussed in later works.

She sees the greatest stumbling-block for the honest enquirer after truth as the dogma of eternal torments for the great majority of human beings who ever lived, including those innocent infants who died without baptism, so she adopts a psycho-philosophical method to show the illogicality of traditional theories of such divine 'justice'. Her introduction to the *Sistème* is a dissertation upon God's goodness and justice considered in their origin, which argues that as all beings aspire to happiness, God could have created them only for that end. The dogma of original sin is a shadowy, if not quite unreal, idea for her and she tends to reduce the problems of evil and justice or penalties to simple human experience. For Adam and Eve before their fall, which she doubtless envisages as symbolical rather than historical, only the idea of equity or fairness could have existed as compatible with that of divine perfection; the ideas of justice, rigour and penalty could have arisen only after an offence, but even then should be regarded as instruments of divine mercy to bring offenders back into line with the fundamental laws of creation for their long-term happiness.[9] Goodness, mercy and perfection are the very stuff of the concept of the divine qualities to which none can refuse their assent, whereas justice is a means to maintain these, and secondary to them, not contradictory. Predestination to evil is a gross error upon both logical and psychological grounds: 'Avouons-le, naître malheureux nécessairement, et risquer de l'être à jamais, c'est à quoi nul homme ne peut acquiescer; toutes les idées d'équité qu'il trouve gravées chez lui se révoltent à cet aspect.' Once eternal torments are rejected, major difficulties disappear and the serious thinker can recognize deism or natural religion as inevitable; perfect goodness in accord with justice cannot change the course of free beings, for that would be a reversal of natural order, but such goodness strives within the limits of freewill to repair the damage man does to himself and others. It is free human choice of action which determines our suffering and punishment, calculated by the degree of our egoistic disregard of 'Do as you would be done by'. Evil is the result of human aberrance, not of a divine decree for individuals nor of a general providence.

From this reasoning it will be apparent why Marie did not accompany her parents when they returned to Geneva, the high temple of predestination, although she had never before left the bosom of her family. Other reasons also probably helped her decision to remain with relatives in Lyon for the rest of her life, one being that commercial links with Italy had long helped to maintain there neo-platonic tendencies similar to her own, another being the presence of Cévenol 'prophets' and unorthodox mystical currents beneath the surface of local Catholicism. It may also be added that Lyon as a publishing and bookselling centre may have seemed more promising to her as a vehicle for the dissemination of writings which she knew to be highly unorthodox. Little seems to be known of the relatives with whom she lived, but they were probably sympathetic to the Pietism which was persecuted in Geneva, notably in the case of her great-uncle Nicolas Fatio who in 1707 was driven to London and died a member of the Royal Society in 1753.[10] With the high degree of immunity conferred by her Genevan birth and nationality, she was actually freer to propagate her ideas in Catholic Lyon than she would have been in Switzerland, just as was the case for Rousseau in Paris a little later.

The explicit ordering of her ideas in the first edition of the *Sistème* situates her as an early leader of the Enlightenment, both in its Anglo-Dutch aspect of Arminianism and in its Leibnizian-Wolffian aspect of the *Aufklärung*. As early as 1731 she declares she will first treat of the rational grounds for her *Sistème*, then show the conformities of Holy Writ with these, plus such contrary biblical texts as would seem to render the Bible inconclusive; thirdly, some external truths will be used as independent support for her view of Bible teaching; fourthly, the nature and validity of those truths will be further discussed; and the last section will show that the *Sistème* is less conducive to sin and despair than the dogma of hell. This is an unmistakable expression of that 'naturalist' approach giving precedence to reason over the older christocentric or biblicist tendencies of Protestantism, a little before its appearance in the Swiss churches and academies, a little after the Berne government's crusade against Pietism as socially and politically subversive. When therefore Ruchat accused Marie of Pietism, he was invoking against her work the arm of government, but the latter could touch neither her nor her books published in other countries. His other accusation of Origenism was more theological but no more decisive; indeed, had Marie possessed more historical and patristic knowledge, she could have thrown it back in a crushing retort justifying her search for primitive and 'basic' Christianity, for here again Ruchat was unwittingly following the intolerance of Rome. Origen (A.D. 185–263) and his master Clement of Alexandria (c. 160–c. 220) had shown conclusively in the third century of the church that it had then no settled teaching concerning retribution after death; on the contrary, Origen suggested that the perfection of God and his creation required the eventual salvation of all creatures, even of Satan himself, after appropriate purgation, because without total triumph divine perfection could not exist and any total damnation would represent a triumph for evil over divinity, therefore a virtual denial of the latter. Since Origen's immense piety and knowledge of the Holy Land (where he resided for years) gave him prestige second only to that of Paul and the Apostles in his

lifetime, and since his condemnation after death by a jealous cabal
in some obscure regional synod could not be proved authoritative,
he could have been made her strongest ally against those later
'Fathers' called orthodox, who in fact knew far less than he of
the early Christian languages, usages, writings and beliefs; but the
revival of patristic studies had then not proceeded far enough for
an autodidact like Marie to be able to enlist such potent support
for her cause. What she did competently was to marshal in this
book most of the arguments already used against the dogma,
especially in England, and to give them a wider audience in her
homely French prose.

Limitations on space oblige us to pass quickly to Marie's last
and best-known work, although her *Sistème* had much else
deserving of notice. She prepared the transition to the longer
work by adding to the earlier text two letters which argue that
her reasons in favour of limited and graduated retribution also
support a purificatory process after death, and that these together
cohere with the concept of equity in both God and man which
will eventually convince all of the due proportionality of their own
lot, whereas the gulf between immediate paradise or torment in
orthodox Protestantism offends all sense of justice and proportion,
like doctrines of predestination. A few sentences from this second
letter will illustrate her mode of suddenly giving a limited topic
a much wider perspective: 'Qui ne voit que l'opinion de la
damnation éternelle sert de *pivot* aux disputes les plus opiniâtres,
aux controverses les plus épineuses? Sans [elle], l'infaillibilité de
l'Eglise se réduiroit à rien ... La prédestination et la réprobation
n'auroient plus de lieu, [il n'y auroit] plus de distinction entre les
Particularistes et les *Universalistes*; tous seroient *Universalistes* dans
le sens le plus accompli ...'

Her *Lettres sur la Religion Essentielle à l'Homme, distinguée de ce
qui n'en est que l'accessoire* (Amsterdam 1738, in two parts of 20
letters each) were quickly followed in 1739 by a *Suite de la Troisième
Partie sur la Religion Essentielle ... en douze lettres* ('Londres', with
no printer's name, and very likely printed in Lyon). It is preceded
by a few *Observations Générales* which indicate her three essential
articles of belief as God, Providence, another life in another
sphere, and which follow the Lockian line of argument in the
Reasonableness of Christianity (1695, translated by Pierre Coste

1696) that the Gospel is fundamentally simple, or as Marie phrases it, 'accessible to idiots and children'. All Christians agree on these three articles, but all others have given rise to endless disputes and to progressive obfuscation of religious realities because so contrary to logic and experience. Such a radical simplification of religion could not fail to evoke angry retorts, only one of which can be cited here. David Renaud Boullier, a young Swiss pastor, published anonymously, also at Amsterdam, two small volumes in 1741 entitled: *Lettres sur les vrais Principes de la Religion, où l'on examine* . . . *'La Religion Essentielle à l'Homme'*. Since he coupled this with a defence of Pascal against Voltaire and an analysis of the latter's philosophy, he was putting Marie in very lofty company and greatly assisting the publicity for her book. Voltaire himself assisted it as late as 1768 after earlier praise, in his famous *Lettre à S.A. Mgr. le Prince de* . . . *sur Rabelais et d'autres auteurs accusés d'avoir mal parlé de la religion chrétienne*, though with reserves about her abstract style and semi-geometrical mode of reasoning. Her last work is certainly more difficult to read and ranges more widely than her *Sistème*, albeit in developing the same ideas. It was in fact more radical in some respects than the ideas of Locke and Voltaire, whom she resembles in many respects;[11] for example, whereas they both retain the notion of a Redemption, she gently but firmly eliminates it, together with many other dogmas, as based on false analogies which are incompatible with, and injurious to, any sound notion of the divine nature. (See Letter XIX in Part I, and also the *Question* after Letter III, where she takes up one of the leading arguments of Archbishop Tillotson's famous thirty-fifth sermon of 1690.) One is astonished at the boldness of the thought of this modest, retiring lady of the deepest piety, in combating both the theologians and freethinkers for the establishment of what could be called 'basic religion', and of what closely resembles the belief of vast numbers outside the churches today. Few have attained such a balance of the rational and transcendental faculties in humanity, and it is difficult to justify the neglect which she has suffered since her death.[12] This short paper can seek only to 'situate' her in relation to her family, her city, her period and her main originalities in the 'History of ideas' which I believe she was the first to name.[13] One can only hope she will receive a full-length study.

18

Madame de Montesquieu with some considerations on Thérèse de Secondat

ROBERT SHACKLETON

Montesquieu's wife, Jeanne de Lartigue, is a largely unknown person. Only one letter attributed to her survives. It was kept at the Château de La Brède until the sale of the family's manuscripts in 1939 when, with many other letters, it was acquired by the municipal library of Bordeaux, where it has the shelfmark MS 1868 no 202. It consists of a single sheet of paper 22.7 cm long and 16.5 cm high, which was folded in two to create four pages, and folded again for despatch. It has been mutilated. Two holes exist in the fold, which do not interfere with the text in any serious way, but a corner has been torn off so that some words on p. 3 and part of the address have been lost. The text is as follows:

Je veux croire contre les aparences, mon cher ami, que mes letres te font plaisir. C'est pour cela que je ne veux point lesser partir Vigneau sens t'assurer que je t'aime comme ma vie. Tu m'as fait des impressions inefaçables et je sens bien que je ne saurois jamais changer. Que je serois heureuse si je pouvois me flater que tu es le meme a mon egard. /p. 2/ Mais enfin quant bien meme cela ne seroit pas, tu me fais un plaisir infini de me le dire. Je suis ravie lors que je reçois de tes letres et sens examiner si ce que tu me dis d'obligent est bien sincere je m'abandonne a des transpors de joye que je ne saurois t'exprimer. Tu auras esté surpris apparament de la commission que je te donné a la postille de ma derniere letre. C'est pour faire plaisir a une de mes amies qui m'assura t'avoir /p. 3/ entendu dire que l'intendent étoit de tes amis. Ce n'étoit aussi qu'a cette condition que je to priés de luy parler. Apres cela tu en seras le maitre et ta volonté sera toujours la mienne. Adieu mon cher ami, je t'aime cent fois plus que tu ne m'aimes. Tu verras a ce conte que je suis bien prodigue. Je ne le serois pas autant si tu le meritois moins. Au reste Mselle de Guionnet auroit-elle le sort de la comtesse? Je n'entens plus parler d'elle. Dis m'en (*torn*) premie (*torn*) |p. 4| Adieu je suis a toy plus qu'a moy meme.

Montesquieu

Ma tante te saluent et mes amies particulierement. Mes amitiés a la belle Denise, suposé qu'elle ait toujours autant de part dans tes bonnes grasses que par le passé. Je t'embrasse de tout mon coeur. Je ne t'ecrirai pas d'un an si tu ne m'ecris pas.

A Mon(*torn*)
Monsieur de M(*torn*)
President à M(*torn*)
A Paris

At the head of p. 1 is written '1726' in an old handwriting. The first line of the postscript shows a correction. The original reading was 'mes amies te saluent'. The words 'mes amies' were then changed to 'ma tante' but the plural verb 'saluent' was unchanged. The words 'et mes amies particulierement' were added. In the transcription punctuation, almost wholly absent, has been added, capitalization has been regularized, and the modern distinction between 'i' and 'j' and between 'u' and 'v' has been introduced. The original spelling has been maintained.

The letter was published in the first edition of Montesquieu's correspondence, in which it is no 299.[1] It was reprinted in 1955 in the Nagel edition[2] where it bears the number 309 (iii, 1032–3). The editor of the correspondence in the Nagel edition was again François Gebelin. In each case the letter was attributed to Madame de Montesquieu and the date 1742–3 was editorially supplied. The 1914 edition printed the text with modernised orthography and punctuation; the Nagel edition retained some features of the eighteenth-century spelling.

The letter is deeply moving, particularly if addressed by a wife to her husband, and it has frequently been quoted by those who have written on Montesquieu. In the valuable article by Emile de Perceval, which gives more information about Madame de

Montesquieu than any preceding writing, it is reproduced *in extenso* and the writer comments: 'D'après cette belle et émouvante lettre, Jeanne de Lartigue s'est peinte à nous en son intimité—et nous pourrions d'ores et déjà clore ce récit'.[3] It is quoted again by Pierre Barrière, who goes on to avow: 'Cette mélancolie discrète, cette indulgence pour un homme honnête mais faible en face des tentations du monde, nous font aimer Mme de Montesquieu.[4] Finally, J. Brethe de La Gressaye, in a remarkably evocative article, declares: 'Cette lettre est un émouvant témoignage du coeur et de l'esprit de Madame de Montesquieu, épouse sage et fidèle, qui ne demande pas à son mari plus qu'il ne peut donner.'[5]

Was Madame de Montesquieu really the author of the letter?

For a long time little was known of Madame de Montesquieu. The first biographical account of Montesquieu was a memoir, written by his son Jean-Baptiste de Secondat shortly after the President's death. The memoir was published in 1878[6] and the manuscript is now at La Brède. A passing mention is all that is given to Montesquieu's marriage: 'Il se maria, le 30 avril 1716, avec demoiselle Jeanne de Lartigue, fille du sieur Pierre de Lartigue, lieutenant-colonel au régiment de Maulevrier, et il en a eu un fils et deux filles.'[7] The date is erroneous, and apart from correcting it to 1715 neither d'Alembert nor Maupertuis, in their *éloges*, add to the information supplied by Secondat.[8] Nor does the article which appeared in the 1759 edition of Moreri's dictionary, based largely on d'Alembert.[9] Even in 1771 the Benedictine Devienne, concluding the first and only volume of his history of Bordeaux with a note on Montesquieu, says nothing new about his wife except to introduce an error in saying that her name was Dartigue.[10]

None of these accounts makes any mention of the important and embarrassing fact about Madame de Montesquieu, that she was a Protestant. Embarrassing the fact certainly was, since it placed her under legal disabilities, and to abstain from public mention of her belief was therefore an act of civility. In 1810, however, it is referred to by two authors. Bernadau, an advocate at Bordeaux, writing on his town and its best-known citizens, alludes to Montesquieu's generosity towards his tenants, and says in passing: 'Après sa mort les secours ont été continués par

Madame de Montesquieu, qui chargea de les distribuer même des curés, quoiqu'elle fût calviniste très zélée.'[11] The other writer is an Englishman, James Caulfield, Earl of Charlemont, whose memoirs were published by Francis Hardy. Caulfield had travelled in France in 1754, in the company of Edward Eliot, later Lord Eliot. They visited Bordeaux together and in order to see Montesquieu went to La Brède: 'We . . . were shown into the drawing room, and were most politely received by Madame la Baronne, and her daughter. Madame de Montesquieu was an heiress of the reformed religion, which she still continued to profess. She was an elderly woman, and, apparently, had never been handsome.'[12]

Even after these references a discreet veil was still drawn over her religion, and even the excellent and well documented article which Walkenaer devoted to Montesquieu passes it by in silence.[13]

The second half of the nineteenth century added materially to the sum of available information about Madame de Montesquieu. In 1858 the Bordelais Gabriel O'Gilvy included in the second volume of his genealogies of the south-west of France a long article on the family De Secondat de Montesquieu, in which he reports that Montesquieu's marriage was 'contracté à l'âge de 26 ans, à Clairac, le 22 mars 1715, avec Jeanne de Lartigue, demoiselle qui eut en dot 100,000 livres, morte en 1768, fille de noble Pierre de Lartigue, chevalier de l'Ordre royal et militaire de Saint-Louis, ancien lieutenant-colonel du régiment de Maulevier, et de dame Elisabeth de Pansie.'[14] The same writer devotes a long article to the Lartigue family, of which he first produces evidence in the eleventh century. But of Pierre de Lartigue he can only say vaguely that he was descended from Antoine de Lartigue, married in 1410, without supplying the intermediate stages. Here he attributes to Jeanne de Lartigue the same age as Montesquieu, and says that she was her father's only daughter.[15]

The *Histoire de Montesquieu* by Vian comes next, Vian who, in the elegant words of François Gebelin, 'ramasse religieusement tous les racontars, faux et même vrais, sans distinction'.[16] Vian asserts that the marriage took place on 30 April 1715, not at Clairac but at Bordeaux, in the church of Saint-Michel, and that the ceremony was quiet, almost clandestine, on account of the bride's Protestantism. He scrupulously cites in proof an extract, quoted in full, from the parish register (though without saying where he saw it).[17] On the other hand, however, he describes the bride as 'une jeune fille candide et bonne, pas jolie et boitant même un peu lorsqu'on la regardait, mais riche parce qu'elle avait cent mille livres de dot.'[18] The evidence for her being 'candide' is stated to be Hérault de Séchelles's *Voyage à Montbard* —but this work does not mention Madame de Montesquieu. The evidence for her plainness is Lord Charlemont, for her wealth O'Gilvy. The fact that she is lame is said to be attested by Collé's *Mémoires* (which do not mention Madame de Montesquieu), a letter by Crébillon *fils*, and the preface to the *Lettres persanes*. This preface contains the following sentence: 'Je connais une femme qui marche assez bien mais qui boite dès qu'on la regarde';[19] a slender basis for a physical description of Madame de Montesquieu, until stronger evidence can be produced that Montesquieu was writing about his wife.

In 1888 appeared a well-informed but ill-tempered and, polemical work, which deserves more attention than it has had, doubtless through being printed in an edition of only one hundred copies. This is Jules Delpit's *Le Fils de Montesquieu*. Delpit, who was librarian at Bordeaux, does not disguise his contempt for the 'prétendu O'Gilvy' and mocks his genealogy of the Secondat and Lartigue families. Jeanne de Lartigue's father he declares to be a *parvenu*, ennobled only in 1704. He accepts Vian's physical description, adding that she was short. On the basis of archival evidence, he establishes the date of her death as 13 July 1770 and reveals that as a Protestant she was interred almost surreptitiously. He quotes also a letter which shows that she was on occasion charged by Montesquieu with his business affairs.[20]

To complete the picture of Madame de Montesquieu as she was known in the nineteenth century, the testimony of no less a person than Stendhal should be added. Stories about Montesquieu and his family lingered long at La Brède. Indeed, they are repeated to this day. In 1838 Stendhal visited the château and collected a rich harvest of anecdotes, of which one stresses the business acumen of his wife: 'Quand [Montesquieu] était absent, il n'écrivait à madame de Montesquieu que pour demander de l'argent; quelquefois un an s'écoulait sans qu'il écrivît. Quand enfin une lettre arrivait, madame de Montesquieu soupirait. En mourant, il dit à ses enfants, "mes amis, si vous avez quelque chose, vous le devez à Madame de Montesquieu".'[21]

It is the publication of the correspondence of Montesquieu in 1914 which adds most to the picture of Madame de Montesquieu. Here ample confirmation is offered of her role in managing the estates. It is made clear that she did not accompany her husband to Paris. Polite compliments are paid to her by some of Montesquieu's friends. The famous letter to Montesquieu, quoted above and to which we shall soon return, was published. Another letter, scarcely less remarkable in another sense, is published. It is from Montesquieu to the Comtesse de Grave, apparently for a time his mistress. It appears to be written from La Brède and has been editorially dated March 1725. It contains this paragraph: 'Je ne laisserois pas que de m'amuser ici. Il y a une femme que j'aime beaucoup, parce qu'elle ne me répond pas lorsque je lui parle, qu'elle m'a déjà donné cinq ou six soufflets, par la raison, dit-elle, qu'elle est de mauvaise humeur.'[22] This can refer only to Madame de Montesquieu and though a man, writing to a mistress about his wife, is not on oath, it indicates at the very least that there was friction between them. It presents the letter to Montesquieu from his wife in a poignant light.

More is told about Madame de Montesquieu in the article, cited above, which was published in 1935 by Emile de Perceval, which establishes her birth as having occurred in 1695 at Clairac and alludes to her role in Montesquieu's business affairs, and by J.-M. Eylaud's valuable study of the notarial archives of La Brède,[23] which lists the many occasions on which Montesquieu ceded to her, by *procuration*, the responsibility for managing his estates during his absence from the south-west.

It is convenient at this time to recall and correct existing information about Montesquieu's aunts and sisters. O'Gilvy's genealogy lists three aunts, Marguerite, Marie, and Thérèse, and three sisters, Marie, Thérèse, and Marie-Anne, of whom the last died in infancy. To these should be added, on the strength of archival information at La Brède, a fourth aunt called Nicole. All these ladies, except Marguerite who married Jacques Du Noyer, became nuns.

The widespread story that Montesquieu's sister Marie married d'Héricourt, *intendant des galères* at Marseille, has been effectively disproved by Céleste.[24] She was not married but a nun and at La Brède are kept records of a pension paid on her behalf to a convent throughout the period 1718 to 1740. The convent in question was that of the Paravis, belonging to the nuns of the order of Fontevrault, situated on the left bank of the Garonne and less than five miles from Montesquieu.

His aunt Thérèse was in a convent at Bordeaux. His aunt Nicole (who died in 1699), his aunt Marie, and his sister Thérèse were all nuns in the convent of Notre-Dame de Paulin at Agen. The order of the Filles de Notre-Dame was founded at Bordeaux in 1606 by Jeanne de Lestonac, who was a niece of Montaigne. The order accepted the rule of St Benedict.[25] In 1619 the house at Agen was established, and from an early date it had a close connection with the Montesquieu family. Nicole de Secondat had been Mother Superior and Montesquieu's sister Thérèse was likewise to hold that office.[26] Her tenure was famous, to the point that when she died in 1772 her successor as superior sent a letter commemorating her virtues to all houses of the order. She was regarded as one of the elect, as well as being an effective administrator of the convent's property. In the history of the house there are found members of several families allied to Montesquieu by blood, by marriage, or by affection: Sallegourde, Du Noyer, Du Bernet, Narbonne.

In the published correspondence of Montesquieu there remain one letter of Thérèse to Montesquieu, a note ofMontesquieu's daughter Denise to Thérèse, and a letter from Montesquieu to Thérèse.[27] The second and last of these are of no great importance, but the first is of considerable interest.[28] It is dated 29 November 1726. In it Thérèse speaks with sorrow of the departure of Montesquieu whose recent visit to the convent had given her great joy. There is some discussion of business affairs and some ecclesiastical gossip. There is a reference to 'la petite'—Montesquieu's daughter Marie—who enclosed a letter for her father.

The Bibliothèque municipale of Bordeaux possesses another letter of importance and relevance, signed 'Soeur de Montesquieu'.[29] This letter is unpublished. Céleste, in the last years of his life—he died in 1911—was planning an edition of the correspondence of Montesquieu. The letters were even set up in type and a single proof copy survives in the library of Bordeaux.[30]

This includes the letter in question, which Céleste attributes to
Marie de Secondat, the sister who was at the convent of the
Paravis; but Céleste's edition was not published. The Gebelin-
Morize edition of the correspondence discards the letter, probably
because it was neither to nor from Montesquieu. In the Nagel
edition, Gebelin prints eight lines of the letter attributing it to
Thérèse.[31] Here is the text, as it appears in the manuscript:

ce 10 jan. 1726

Je crains bien, mon tres cher frere, que vous aurois mal auguré
de mon cilence, et si je ne savois que vous estes toujours
équitable, et disposé a jugé favorablement de mes sentimens
pour vous, je m'imaginerois que ce retardement pourroit avoir
un peu alteré l'amitié que vous m'avés temoigné avoir pour
moy. J'eloigne volontiers ces idées qui me semblent peu con-
venables a votre scituation et je vous prie de penser sur mon
compte comme je ferai toujours sur le votre, que rien au monde
ne sera jamais capable de donner la moindre atainte au tendre
atachement que je vous ai voüé et qui ora autant de durée que
votre vie et la mienne. J'ai fait un cas infini de la complaisance
que vous avés eû de m'anvoyer votre joli compliment. Ne
croyés pas que je l'aye admiré toute seule. Je l'ai fait voir a des
gens infiniment plus capables d'en juger que moy qui en ont
esté charmées. Comme l'amitié est /p. 2/ ordinairement aveugle
je me serois meffiée de mes lumieres que j'aurois crües trop
prevenües si je ne savois que vous avés eû autant d'aprobateurs
qu'il y a de gens qui l'ont entandu ou veu. Mon oncle m'a
donné un plaisir des plus sencibles en m'ecrivant que vous
faites parfaitement votre devoir dans votre chapitre et quoy que
je n'en aye jamais douté et que ce que vous me mandés dans
votre letre m'an donne des pruves certaines je suis bien aise
qu'il en soit comptant et qu'il vous aprouve—circonstance qui
donne un nouveau lustre a votre condhuite. Cependant, mon
tres cher frere, mes interests ne s'acommodent guere avec cette
grande regularité puisqu'elle me prive de la douce consolation
de vous voir. J'espère que cette année que je vous souhaite des
plus heuruses ne passera pas sens que vous me donniés ce
plaisir qui decidera de mon bonheur, sens quoi il seroit certaine-
ment tres imparfait. Ce n'est pas, mon tres cher frere, que je

voulusse me le procurer au depens de votre /p. 3/ devoir, mais je me flate que vous menagerés les choses de maniére que vous pourrois satisfaire a l'un et a l'autre. Je vous remercie des livres que vous avés eû la bonté de m'anvoyer—ils sont tels que je les desires. La petite fille voudroit bien etre en état de vous faire son remerciement elle-meme des petittes gentilesses qu'elle a reçeu de votre part, mais elle est si malade d'un gros rhume qui la retient au list depuis plusieurs jours qu'elle me prie de le faire pour elle. J'espere que son mal ne sera pas long, quoy que violant, et qu'elle ne tardera pas a s'aquiter de ce devoir. Je crois, mon cher frere, que vous ne trouverés pas mauvais que je vous prie de m'anvoyer deux livres de café. C'est un remède dont je me sers avec succès pour soulager les grandes migraines que j'ay tres frequamant. En revanche si je puis vous être bonne a quelque chose ne m'epargnés pas, je vous conjure. J'ai esté fort surprise lors que j'ai apris le depart de mon frere pour Paris. Je serois curieuse de savoir ce qui l'a obligé de vous quiter si promptement. Je me fesois une idée des plus gratieuses de la douceur reciproque que /p. 4/ vous trouviés tous deux dans une si aimable societté. Mandés-moy, je vous prie, le motif de son voyage. Tout le monde me parle de son esprit et des aplaudissens que l'on luy donne. Je serois bien aise de savoir son adresse pour luy ecrire. Comme je ne sai point celle de Mr de Citran, je prens la liberté de vous envoyer une letre pour luy, que je vous prie de luy faire remettre; au cas qu'il soit a la campagne mon oncle aura bien la bonté de s'en chargé. Pour ma belle-soeur je ne scai nom plus ou luy ecrire, mon frere ayant changé de maison. Il y a aparence qu'elle est a la campagne et que les letres que j'adresserois a Bourdx par la poste pouroit facilement ce perdre. Voila mon tres cher frere bien des eclercissemens que je vous demande. Je vous suplie de me les donné et de me croire cent fois plus a vous qu'a moy-meme.

Sr de Montesquieu

Ma tante et nos amies vous font bien des complimens. Elles vous souhaitent une heuruse année.

The references to the writer's brother who has suddenly left for Paris and who has acquired a new address in Bordeaux are clearly references to Montesquieu. On 5 December 1725 he had sought from the parlement leave to go to Paris[32] and he dated a letter from Paris in January 1726.[33] Near the end of September 1725 he changed his Bordeaux home from the Rue de Mirail, where the *premier président* had his residence, to the house of his clerical brother, who was dean of Saint-Seurin[34]. This brother, Joseph de Secondat, is clearly the addressee of the letter.

The writer, being a nun and sister to Montesquieu, is either (as Céleste thought) Marie, who was in the convent of the Paravis, or (as Gebelin claims) Thérèse, who was at Saint-Paulin d'Agen. She conveys the greetings of her aunt, apparently a nun in the same house. Montesquieu had no aunt in the Paravis, but his aunt Marie was at Saint-Paulin. The letter appears therefore to have been written by Thérèse from Saint-Paulin, and indeed the handwriting is identical with that of the other letter, almost contemporaneous, which is attributed to Thérèse.[35]

It is now time to turn back to the remarkably touching letter with the transcription of which this article began, and to consider its authenticity.[36]

The letter is strictly undated: the year 1726, added in an eighteenth-century hand, carries no authority. The only fact which can date the letter is the inference from the postscript that Montesquieu and his daughter Denise were in Paris when the letter was sent. Denise was born on 23 February 1727. She was in Paris as a *pensionnaire* in the convent of Bon-Secours in the Faubourg Saint-Antoine from the end of 1741 to May or June 1744. Montesquieu was in Paris from May 1741 to September 1743. It is therefore appropriate to date this letter 1742-3, as Gebelin has done.

A comparison of this letter with the two letters of Thérèse (that printed above, to her brother Joseph, and that of 29 November 1726 to Montesquieu) is revealing. All three letters show in their writer a highly affectionate character. To her clerical brother, to whom she shows a little more reserve than to Montesquieu, Thérèse says that nothing will ever shake her affection for him, which will last as long as their lives. To Montesquieu she writes: '[L'amitié] que j'ai pour toi est d'une solidité à toute épreuve et il me semble que la plus grande indifférence ne saurait la rendre susceptible d'aucun changement.' This is the language of a nun whose sequestration has cut her off from ordinary male friendship. The writer of the letter of 1742-3 uses similar language and assures Montesquieu that her affection for him is not dependent on reciprocal affection from him. Thérèse looks back with delight on the visits she has received. She fears that Joseph's ecclesiastical advancement may deprive her of the 'douce consolation' of his visits. To Montesquieu he writes in 1726: 'Il s'en faut de beaucoup que j'ai le coeur guéri de la tristesse où ton départ m'a laissée, mon cher frère. La joie que j'ai ressentie de te voir a été aussi courte que ton absence va me paraître longue.' The writer of the letter of 1742-3 tells Montesquieu, 'tu m'as fait des impressions ineffaçables'.

The language of affection in all three letters is remarkably similar. Thérèse ends her letter to Joseph 'je vous supplie . . . de me croire cent fois plus à vous qu'à moi-même'; she ends her letter of 1726 to Montesquieu with the words 'je suis à toi plus qu'à moi-même'. The third paragraph of the letter of 1742-3 begins, 'Adieu, mon cher ami, je t'aime cent fois plus que tu ne m'aimes', while the letter itself ends with the eloquent formula 'Adieu, je suis à toi plus qu'à moi-même'.

There is indeed a community of outlook and expression between all three letters which suggests a common authorship and which places in doubt the attribution of the third letter to a different person from the other two. There are some specific difficulties about Madame de Montesquieu's authorship of the third letter.

The statement that Montesquieu has made on the writer 'des impressions ineffaçables' is certainly more appropriate as a comment on the effect of a short visit to a convent, than as a summary of almost thirty years of married life. The 'transports de joie' which Montesquieu's letters arouse are more compatible with Thérèse than with anything we know about Madame de Montesquieu.

The second paragraph refers obscurely to a possible approach by Montesquieu to the *intendant*. If—as is likely—the *intendant* of Bordeaux is referred to, it is frankly unthinkable that Madame de Montesquieu should have been dependent on information given to her by a friend, in order to know Montesquieu's opinion of him. Montesquieu was not well disposed towards *intendants* as a class and was particularly hostile to Claude Boucher, who was *intendant* at Bordeaux for twenty-three years, being replaced by Tourny in August 1743.[37] This letter and the lost letter preceding, in which an approach to the *intendant* was requested, cannot be squeezed into the interval of two or three weeks at most between the installation of Tourny and Montesquieu's return to Bordeaux. Boucher therefore is referred to—Boucher whom Montesquieu referred to as a beast rather than as a man.[38] Montesquieu was in conflict with him in relation to property. Madame de Montesquieu knew well the problems of her husband's estates and cannot conceivably have been unaware of his attitude to the *intendant*.

Another problem arises from the words 'mes amies' and 'ma tante' in the letter of 1742–3. What are these friends and this aunt? There is no evidence to suggest that Madame de Montesquieu was surrounded by a *cénacle* of female friends at La Brède. Thérèse, however, was a nun and her friends were her fellow-religious in the convent. In the letter to Joseph Thérèse writes, 'Ma tante et nos amies vous font bien des compliments', the aunt being Montesquieu's aunt Marie, a nun in the same house. When we read from the writer of the 1742–3 letter 'ma tante te saluent et mes amies particulièrement' we are reading a phrase which is normal and intelligible if written by Thérèse, but mysterious if written by Montesquieu's wife.

There remains the question of Mlle de Guionnet and the unnamed *comtesse*. There is little doubt that the writer of the letter is referring to Montesquieu's mistresses. Mlle de Guionnet is not certainly identifiable, but in 1732 Montesquieu bought a mill from Denise de Guionnet, dame de Pont-Castel; in 1744 he exchanged property with Marie-Denise de Guionnet in Bordeaux, and bought from her a piece of meadowland in 1753.[39] This lady or a relative is likely to have been a country *inamorata* of Montesquieu, not a Parisian; the comtesse was probably Madame de Pontac, a neighbour and a remote relative.

Is it more likely that Montesquieu's wife or his sister should write in a spirit of tolerant banter about his mistresses? Undoubtedly the words come more readily from the pen of his sister, albeit a nun. Sexual regularity was not expected of the eighteenth-century nobleman and a religious calling did not necessarily impose a higher expectation.[40]

Finally, the physical aspect of the letter should be considered. The signature is not decisive. The two earlier letters are signed 'Soeur de Montesquieu', while the later one is signed simply 'Montesquieu'. This could be explained by the fact that Thérèse had been promoted to the dignity of *Mère* and was indeed to become superior in 1745.[41] Madame de Montesquieu, on such documents as survive, signed 'Lartigue de Montesquieu' but this would not preclude the signature 'Montesquieu' on letters.

It might have been expected that the handwriting of the manuscripts would determine the question, not least since a study of the handwritings of manuscripts has, in the writer's own experience, provided a framework for the whole exegesis of Montesquieu. It is the case, however, that the hand of Thérèse and that of Madame de Montesquieu are remarkably similar—a fact which may arise from similar convent education. There are some slight calligraphic differences between the hand of the letters of 1726 and that of 1742–3. But they can easily be explained by the passage of time and the deterioration of Thérèse's eyesight. The later hand sprawls more and is less careful. It must be said that in the settlement of the problem of the authorship of the later letter the handwriting is neutral.

The arguments based on style and content are in themselves enough to shake the attribution to Madame de Montesquieu of the letter of 1742–3. Can they not be held to disprove it and to justify its attribution to Thérèse? If so, the effect of this article largely devoted to Madame de Montesquieu is to remove the one illuminating piece of evidence which was thought to reveal her character and to plunge her back into the obscurity in which she previously had lain: the obscurity of the efficient housewife and conscientious deputy to her husband in matters of property and administration.

By way of compensation the personality of Thérèse de Secondat, superior of the convent of the Filles de Notre-Dame at Saint-Paulin, is proportionately clarified and its graceful features stand out in relief. The fullest statement ever made about her is that of her successor as superior, circulated on the death of Thérèse to all the superiors of the order. What has been here said about the open, affectionate nature of her character and her tolerant kindness receives express ratification. The new superior, Mère

Narbonne, writes: 'Sa ferveur était capable d'échauffer les plus tièdes, et de porter la chaleur et la vie dans tous les coeurs . . . Elle conciliait très à-propos l'indulgence avec la sévérité, la bienveillance avec la rigueur, et possédait eminemment l'art du discernement des esprits, afin de diversifier la conduite qu'il falloit tenir, selon la variété des caractères et des tempéraments.'[42] If Madame de Montesquieu recedes into the darkness and mystery of a Protestant living in what was for her, in the eighteenth century, a religious desert, at least the transferred letter adds humanity to her sister-in-law, the nun who was held to be one of the elect.

19

Angélique Diderot
and the White Terror

JEAN VARLOOT

The biography that Angélique Diderot, Mme de Vandeul, deserves still has to be written. In spite of the place she held, both materially and morally, in the life of her father, in spite of the information given by certain archivists, her image remains vague and rather veiled, as in certain family portraits, where reality is masked. A piecemeal exhumation of some document or other is no doubt not the best means of unmasking this reality, but there are cases, none the less, where this document casts light upon one of its facets, and allows us to rectify hasty conclusions.

In the present case, in spite of the detailed and judicious criticism of his books by Jean Pommier, we still have only the monographs of Jean Massiet du Biest, *La Fille de Diderot* and *Angélique Diderot*, the second of which partly takes into account Jean Pommier's remarks.[1] But the general tone of the first book has not been changed, by which I mean a moralizing tone, dominated by the idea of a 'déchéance', which serves to explain why Angélique did not die in 'sainteté', like her mother, her uncle and her aunt, a sanctity which was her right after a life of suffering, resignation and good deeds.[2]

It is true enough that Angélique Diderot, who was a victim of childhood malnutrition, suffered from a malignant disease of the intestine which she treated with opiated drugs, but it is far from clear that this 'destruction lente' of which she complained completely eliminated the 'combativité' which she owed to an energy inherited from her parents.[3] If one takes into consideration the prudence necessitated by troubled times, and the feminine reserve which she more or less willingly imposed on herself, one finds that she did not take to religion as she grew older. H. Dieckmann was perhaps a little hasty in writing: 'A cette époque (1822), Mme de Vandeul était devenue pieuse et vivait à l'écart du monde'. The great master in Diderot studies certainly based his opinion at that time on those letters in which Mme de Vandeul gives an amusing account of her life at Auberive, playing the part of the bountiful lady of the manor, going through the motions of Catholic observance. But her life at Auberive ran in parallel with her worldly existence in Paris, where we shall find her again, and it scarcely modified, in my view, the deepest convictions of the *philosophe*'s daughter, in particular her attitude towards the clergy and religious dogma that can only, in the last analysis, be described as contemptuous.[4] Her contempt is just less lively and less gay than in the ironic remarks that she had written to her husband in her forties. But he had died in 1812, and, as was glimpsed by J. Massiet du Biest, 'les seules opinions sincères sont dans les lettres intimes adressées par Mme de Vandeul à son mari'.[5]

Unfortunately, the same J. Massiet du Biest tries, less openly, to trace an ideal model of Angélique Diderot by basing himself on the testimony of another man, Henri Meister, and on an exchange of letters of an emotional kind, where mutual feelings are all-important, and sincerity is far from total. What explains these letters is that Meister himself changed. The first Meister, who succeeded F. M. Grimm as director of the *Correspondance littéraire*, worshipped Diderot the *philosophe*, and, although he had not known him very well,[6] he lent his pen to Angélique to write the homage *Aux Mânes de Diderot*. In doing this, and in siding with her against Naigeon, he kept her under the influence of her father and of *philosophie*.[7] Angélique no doubt reacted later in life against this identification with her father, but she never abandoned her piety towards his memory nor his moral lessons.[8] In consequence, she was bound to resist the efforts of the *second* Meister, the one who, over many years, tried to convert her.[9]

Meister is then a *testis unus*, a biased witness, but, more seriously, he is not a true confidant.[10] This is the impression left by this correspondence, which is valuable for the span of time it covers and the information it contains, but which appears at the same time as an epistolary exercise, determined by convention, by fashionable themes, under the influence of English and German romanticism.[11] In the last years of the correspondence, one can sense on the moral plane, through the conventional language, the duel with sheathed swords between the confessor and the penitent. But the confessor has already been rejected. It is obvious to the reader that Mme de Vandeul's only aim was to retain the friendship of a very kind man, a long-standing and devoted admirer, of whose intellectual limitations she was well aware. One might even be tempted to believe that she had always thought him a little simple-minded. 'Il était impossible', she wrote one day to her husband, 'dans la boutique où j'ai été élevée, que je me trompasse sur les agréments de l'esprit.'[12] A man like Meister needed more careful treatment than the husband she continued to love; she remained gracious and indulgent towards him; she even played along with a certain tenderness, inspired by romantic preciosity, in her replies to the pedantic verbiage of an old man whose Germanic culture is evident in his efforts at elegance. Diderot's daughter then, as J. Massiet du Biest himself writes, 'tolère le retour de Meister à ses anciens principes religieux', and consequently his rather foolish stubbornness in trying to convert her. She remained content to avoid any meeting with him either in Paris or in Switzerland, and this allowed them to continue their epistolary game of controlled effusion.[13]

My rather lengthy analysis demonstrates, I hope, how little confidence can be accorded to the letters from Mme de Vandeul to Meister for the purpose of defining her true beliefs where delicate areas of ideology are concerned. I shall take as a typical example, or rather as an extreme and slightly paradoxical case, the sphere of politics. J. Massiet du Biest, who, to say the least, is not favourable towards the French Revolution, takes an *a priori* position: 'elle n'observait pas les événements politiques, elle a toujours préféré les affaires de sentiment et de cœur.'[14] He then makes use of those texts in which Mme de Vandeul, now in her old age, speaking of lost family and friends, recalls the harsh times her country went through, in order to show her opposed to any spirit of revolution.[15] Finally, he taxes her with 'inconstancy', and presents as a complete change of opinion those passages in which she longs for the permanence of those short periods in which history looked back, between the Empire and the Restoration.

The truth of the matter is more subtle. No more than her father was Angélique Diderot able to foresee the Revolution in its development, in the upheaval it caused, in its mistakes.[16] She nevertheless recognized in the Revolution the historical consequence of the Enlightenment, as is shown in her petition to the Committee of General Security of 18 Germinal, year II. The 'citoyenne Diderot', who 'se glorifie d'avoir eu la philosophie pour berceau et d'avoir été républicaine avant la Révolution', introduces herself as 'la fille unique de l'un des premiers et des plus courageux apôtres de la liberté'.[17]

It was indeed liberty that acted as her personal motivation, as we see in a letter to her husband of 11 Floréal, year V: 'Personne, dans la République entière, ne fait plus de cas de la liberté réelle que moi. Je n'aime pas plus à avoir un esclave qu'à l'être et je cesse de vouloir ce qui me rendrait l'être le plus heureux du monde si l'on n'a pas le même bonheur à me l'accorder ou à le faire.'[18] She desired the happiness of all, and she never changed on this point.[19]

She certainly never favoured the extremists, the 'braillards', but without defending them she speaks of the execution of the Babouvists with a concern for exact facts that characterized her whole life.[20]

What more could a nouveau-riche bourgeoise, unable to influence events, do? Bring up her son according to family precepts: Denis de Vandeul was to become a peer under the liberal monarchy of Louis-Philippe, an enlightened monarch such as his father had wished to be. Receive at her table, without any hesitation, and showing a preference totally contrary to that which her biographer attributes to her, men for whom politics is a central preoccupation: under Louis XVIII, in Paris the lady of the manor of Auberive is, as Jean Pommier pointed out so cogently, a hostess who reminds one of the world of Stendhal.

Jean Pommier does not go beyond the documents quoted by J. Massiet du Biest: 'Les citations les plus intéressantes ont trait aux passions politiques de la Restauration, ultras contre libéraux.'[21] Already incensed by the exactions of the Prussians, Mme de Vandeul was further angered by the 'horreurs commises dans le département du Gard'[22] about which she knew from direct witnesses, and regarding which she appealed in vain to the tolerance of the *philosophes*.[23] She was aware of the 'lutte enragée' for power in 1816, and this is the way she described her guests on 26 May 1821: 'Les haines politiques sont telles que c'est une affaire d'avoir quelques amis à dîner. Il faut se tourmenter pour qu'il ne se trouve pas un individu qui ne soit blessé par la violence des expressions de ceux qui ne sont pas de son avis. Toute politesse est bannie. Puis-je causer un peu avec le petit nombre de ceux qui ont des idées libérales? Impossible d'échanger deux phrases avec ce qu'on appelle le parti ultra.' This quotation comes from a letter to Meister.[24] We can see that for once even to him she reveals her opinions and the interest she takes in politics. J. Massiet du Biest glosses over this point and blinds himself to the truth,[25] whereas J. Pommier is perfectly right to say, 'cette société voulait être mieux dessinée'.

I make no claim to provide this 'dessin' here, but merely aim to contribute something for anyone who may venture to do it, in the shape of a document that seemed illuminating when I read it in the Archives de Chaumont.[26] The document is a letter by a writer who remains so far unidentified, but who is no doubt part of the Protestant milieu with which Mme de Vandeul was in contact: Pauline de Meulan, her husband Guizot, whose family left Nîmes to escape the White Terror, Stapfer, Gaspard Hess, Meister's nephew, to whom she wrote more freely than to his uncle. It can be seen that the writer is wholly committed to the liberal and republican cause. It is noteworthy, too, that he expresses his feelings with the greatest frankness, which means that he is certain of finding in Diderot's daughter, whom he treats as a man, as her father had done Catherine II, the same opinions, the same judgments on the political situation. It is striking that he, *that is to say, she equally*, does not fear the return of the Revolution, but that of the White Terror. What is more, the writer specifically attributes to her a kind of special understanding and even flair, if not of clairvoyance, in the sphere of politics. 'Je ne sais plus quel instinct', she herself wrote one day,[27] 'me faisait pressentir l'an dernier que l'on prenait un chemin mauvais.' Had she not laid bets against the return of Calonne in 1788? And on the imminence of war on 18 Fructidor, year VI?[28] Yet again this time[29]—but how many times she must have unhesitatingly evoked the future with well-informed and perspicacious guests—she was correct in her judgment. We are a very long way from the image of a sentimental and resigned old woman in her dotage, and very close, on the contrary, to that of an energetic and clear-sighted lady of the Age of Enlightenment.

Genève 4 avril 1820[30]

J'espère, Madame, que cette lettre vous trouvera encore à Paris;[31] et je désire vivement qu'elle vous y trouve bien portante; je conçois trop bien l'émotion qu'a du vous causer le crime du 13 février;[32] et d'autant plus que vous avez deviné sur le champ que les ultras se serviraient du poignard de Louvel pour égorger la charte de nos libertés. L'événement n'a point trompé votre prévoyance. En vain s'est-on trouvé dans la plus absolue impuissance de donner quelques indices d'un complot; en convenant que le crime de Louvel était absolument isolé, on a agi comme si au contraire la France entière en était complice.[33] Tout ce qui s'est passé jusqu'à présent, depuis le 14 février me semble le comble de l'injustice et de l'impolitique.[34] Assurément on ne prétend tromper personne sur le défaut absolu de motifs réels pour appuyer ce retour vers l'arbitraire, ni sur l'impudente vénalité du *Ventre*[35] de la Chambre. C'est donc sciemment, et sans daigner dissimuler, qu'on met dans les chaines toute une nation; et cela à côté des événements d'Espagne! . . . En sorte que si les nouvelles loix ne sont pas bientôt révoquées, ce sera en Espagne qu'il faudra aller chercher la liberté de la presse et la liberté individuelle.[36] Ne trouvez-vous pas cela inconcevable? . . . On répand ici le bruit que des mouvements *constitutionnels* se sont manifestés en Italie et en Suisse,[37] je ne sais si cela est; mais je parierais que cela *sera*. Le peu que j'ai vu en Italie m'a paru décisif. Le joug autrichien y est abhorré, et ce n'est pas sans cause. Il y en a sans doute de plus cruels; il n'y en [a] aucun de plus lourd et de plus humiliant. Les peuples d'ailleurs ont senti (et pour longtems j'espere) que le pire des gouvernements est le gouvernement de l'étranger. Un gouvernement national, quel qu'il soit, offre toujours une ressource. Le lieu de la naissance du chef ou des chefs. Il est difficile qu'ils ne s'en souviennent pas; et qu'à défaut d'affection, ils n'attachent pas quelqu'orgueil à la prosperité de leur pays . . . Vous m'opposerez nos *ultras* et avec raison, car le malheur de leur pays est leur seul désir. Mais ces gens-là ne sont plus français depuis 1789. Valets de l'étranger, ses stipendiés, ses adulateurs, ils ne connaissent que l'étranger. Ils chantaient et dansaient en répétant ce refrain

'Revenez, danse légère,
'Revenez douces chansons!

pendant que fumaient encore les cadavres de Waterloo; pendant que les massacres s'exécutaient dans le midi avec une effrayante regularité. Ils chanteraient et danseraient encore, s'ils pouvaient nous ramener 1815. Mais j'espère qu'ils seront confondus dans leur affreux projets . . . L'exemple de l'Espagne, et ce qui peut, d'un moment à l'autre, se passer dans des pays non moins voisins voilà des leçons, perdues peut-être pour la prudence, mais non pas pour *la peur* qui est la *sagesse spéciale* de ce parti. Espérons que la peur amènera encore un pas retrograde, et que la France ne sera pas une terre de Bastilles et de massacres à l'époque ou je me propose d'y retourner. Ce sera toujours vers le mois de septembre, ainsi que je crois vous l'avoir annoncé. Je pense, avec regret, qu'à cette époque vous serés à Auberive, et que j'aurai encore deux et peut-être trois mois à attendre, avant de vous revoir et de vous assurer de vive voix d'un sentiment que cinq ans d'absence n'auront, certes, pas affaibli.

Mr. de Stapfer a eu la complaisance de m'envoyer ici un exemplaire du proces verbal de l'assemblée de la société Biblique.[38] Le principal mérite de ce recueil, c'est un discours assez long de Mr de Stapfer. J'y ai admiré le talent de tirer parti d'un sujet assez aride; et la pureté du style et de la diction, pureté beaucoup plus grande qu'on ne devrait l'attendre d'un allemand, et que plus d'un écrivain français ne ferait pas mal d'imiter . . . Quant au fond, aux idées . . . ce sont les siennes, je n'ai rien à dire. Mais, entre nous, je le croyais plus *philosophe*. Il y a peu de logique, peu d'assurance dans le but des raisonnements. C'est la faute du sujet. Pour le traiter de bonne foi dans le sens qu'a suivie Mr de Stapfer, pour faire l'éloge des bons effets de *ce que vous savez*, il faut fermer les yeux, il faut oublier l'histoire, il faut même s'interdire les reflexions, les raisonnements analogiques, etc., etc; avec cette méthode, le meilleur esprit du monde perd cruellement de ses avantages. Je m'en suis apperçu à regret. Ces reflexions ne sont que pour vous, Madame, comme vous n'avez pas de peine à le croire. Mais j'ai vu que je n'étais pas seul à les faire. L'ami intime de Mr de Stapfer, auprès de qui sa recommandation m'a introduit à mon arrivée à Genève, m'a dit précisément tout ce que je vous dis là ... Il est d'ailleurs très vrai, (malgré les efforts de Mr. de St. pour prouver le contraire) que les *meneurs* des sociétés bibliques appartiennent à deux classes (qui peutêtre n'en sont qu'une). Ici les hommes qui, sans rien croire, veulent que les autres croyent, parce que la superstition est une bride assez commode, pour conduire le pauvre genre humain transformé par elle en bête de somme ... Là, des fanatiques pour qui toute réforme religieuse n'est qu'un premier pas; qui veulent le délire, les révélations, l'emportement, l'intolérance feroce des puritains et des méthodistes. Nous avons vu de ces hommes-là dans nos cantons ... le gouvernement d'Argovie a été obligé de leur interdire la prédication en plein air: ils fesaient déjà autant de mal ou presque autant que les missionnaires en France.[39]

Adieu, Madame, soignés bien votre santé; repoussés toutes les idées de découragement quoiqu'on soit, hélas, bien excusable d'en concevoir: donnez-moi, je vous prie, de vos nouvelles avant votre depart pour Auberive. Agréés, je vous prie, l'assurance de mon amitié respectueuse. Daignez être mon interprète auprès de Monsieur et de Madame de Vandeul.[40] Monsieur votre fils est-il plus content de sa santé.

A Madame
Madame de Vandeul née Diderot
Rue Neuve de Luxembourg
nº 18
    près la Rue St Honoré
        à Paris

(Essay translated from the French by Eva Jacobs)

Notes

1 Women and the Reform of the Nation

1 François Poulain de la Barre, *De l'égalite des deux sexes* (Paris 1673).
2 Claude Fleury (Abbé), *Traité du choix et de la méthode des études* (Paris 1686).
3 Salignac de la Mothe Fénelon (Abbé), *Education des filles* (1687), p. 1.
4 Castel de Saint Pierre, *Œuvres diverses* (Paris 1730), p. 90.
5 Philippe Joseph Caffiaux, *Défenses du beau sexe* (Amsterdam 1753), tome 1.
6 J. H. S. Formey, *Réflexions sur l'éducation en général et sur celle des jeunes demoiselles en particulier*, pp. 37–8.
7 The abbreviation *O.C.* refers to Jean-Jacques Rousseau, *Œuvres complètes*, Pléiade edition 1959–69.
8 L. A. de Caraccioli (Comte), *Lettres récréatives et morales, sur les mœurs du temps* (Paris 1767), i, Lettre XVI, p. 29.
9 Cerfvol (de), *La gamologie* (Paris 1772), Pt II, p. 63 ff.
10 This is made clear by the Comte de Luppé in his work *Les Jeunes Filles à la fin du XVIIIe siecle* (Paris 1925).
11 *Lettre sur l'éducation* (Berlin 1770), p. 29.
12 Fromageot (Abbé), *Cours d'études des jeunes demoiselles* (Paris 1772–4), p. lix. It might be possible to argue that Fromageot's emphasis on not disturbing the order of society has affinities with the use in this period of the term 'citoyen' implying 'those willing to obey a law agreed to be in the national interest' (C. A. Ottevanger, *The Idea of the Citizen in French Educational Writings of the 18th Century 1700–1789*, University of London Ph.D. thesis, 1976, p. 316). Fromageot, however, does not spell out such an advanced definition, and it would seem that he simply takes over an acceptable formula and uses it in a rather watered-down sense.
13 C. A. Ottevanger (op. cit.) discusses this development in detail. I should like to thank her for allowing me to use material from her thesis and for the help she has given me in preparing parts of this article. I should also like to thank Mme Elisabeth Netter for her help in checking some of the material available only in the Bibliothèque nationale.
14 J. H. Medlicott (Jean Bloch), *The Reputation of Rousseau's Emile in France from 1762–1790*, University of London M.A. thesis, 1964, pp. 118–91.
15 Monbart, Mme de, *Sophie ou l'éducation des filles* (Berlin 1777).
16 J. H. Bernardin de Saint-Pierre, *Discours sur cette question: Comment l'Education des Femmes pourrait contribuer à rendre les Hommes meilleurs* (1777), tome 12 of the *Œuvres complètes*, ed. L. Aimé-Martin (Paris 1818), p. 131.

17 J. S. Spink, 'Les premières expériences pédagogiques de Rousseau', *Annales Jean Jacques Rousseau*, xxxv, 97–103.

18 Jean H. Bloch, 'Rousseau's Reputation as an Authority on Childcare and Physical Education in France before the Revolution', *Paedagogica historica*, xiv, 1(1974), 19.

19 In *Woman in the 18th century and other essays,* ed. P. Fritz and R. Morton (Toronto and Sarasota 1976), pp. 127–39.

20 J. H. Bloch, 'Gaspard Guillard de Beaurieu's *L'Elève de la Nature* and Rousseau's *Emile*', *French Studies*, xxvi (July 1972), 280.

21 Mirabeau, *Discours* (fragments) and Talleyrand, *Rapport sur l'Instruction publique*, both in C. Hippeau, *L'Instruction publique en France pendant la Révolution* (Paris 1881).

22 Jean-Gervais Labène, Citoyen François: *De l'education dans les grandes républiques* (Paris l'An IIIe).

23 Dorothy Gardiner, *English Girlhood at School* (London 1929), p. 453.

2 The *Philosophes* and Women

1 C. A. Helvétius, *De l'esprit*, ed. F. Châtelet (Verviers 1973), pp. 343–4.

2 ibid., p. 346.

3 ibid., p. 493.

4 C. A. Helvétius, *De l'homme*, Section X.

5 *De l'homme, Œuvres complètes* (London 1776), iii, 49.

6 ibid., p. 50 note a).

7 ibid., p. 50.

8 ibid., p. 184.

9 ibid., pp. 184–5 note b).

10 D. Diderot, *Œuvres complètes*, ed. Assézat and Tourneux (Paris 1875–7), ii, 361.

11 ibid., p. 319.

12 ibid., p. 357.

13 *De l'esprit*, pp. 172–3.

14 *Œuvres*, iv, 263.

15 ibid., p. 264.

16 *De l'esprit*, p. 289.

17 *De l'homme, Œuvres*, iv, 347.

18 *Œuvres*, iii, 97.

19 *Œuvres*, iv, 266, 324, 591–2.

20 M.-J.-A.-N. Caritat, Marquis de Condorcet, *Œuvres* ed. M. F. Arago and A. O'Connor (Paris 1847–9), i, 219; Condorcet to Turgot, 4 December 1773.

21 *Œuvres*, ii, 294.

22 *Correspondance*, ed. G. Roth (Paris 1963), ix, 199.

23 *Œuvres*, ii, 319, 252.

24 ibid., p. 255.

25 ibid., p. 258.

26 ibid., p. 260.
27 P. H. T. D'Holbach, *Ethocratie* (Amsterdam 1776: reprinted Hildesheim-New York 1973), p. 106.
28 ibid., p. 105.
29 ibid., p. 199.
30 *Œuvres*, ix, 20.
31 *Œuvres*, x, 122.
32 *Œuvres*, viii, 141.
33 ibid., p. 474.
34 *Œuvres*, x, 125.
35 ibid., p. 122.
36 ibid., p. 129.
37 *Œuvres*, vi, 303. cf. Rousseau: 'Les femmes devinrent plus sédentaires, et s'accoutumèrent à garder la cabane et les enfants, tandis que l'homme allait chercher la subsistance commune. Les deux sexes commencèrent aussi, par une vie un peu plus molle, à perdre quelque chose de leur férocité et de leur vigueur.' *Discours sur l'origine et les fondements de l'inégalité parmi les hommes*, ed. J.-L. Lecercle (Paris 1965), p. 113.
38 *Œuvres*, vi, 263–4.
39 *Œuvres*, ix, 20.

3   The Riddle of Roxane

1 For the *Lois* (abbreviated *L.*), and *Pensées* (*P.*), references in the text and notes are to *Œuvres complètes de Montesquieu*, ed. R. Caillois, Paris,N.R.F.: Bibliothèque de la Pléiade, 2 vols., 1949–51 (abbreviated Pl.); for the *Lettres persanes* (*Lp.*), to P. Vernière's edition, Paris, Garnier, 1960 (abbreviated Gar.). Vernet compiled the Index to the *Lois* prior to its publication in 1748; see the entry 'Femmes'.
2 *Oeuvres de Diderot*, ed. Assézat (Paris 1875–7), ii, 260.
3 *Europe*, 55 (1977), 79–88.
4 C. Rosso stresses the need for such a study in *Montesquieu moraliste,* trans. M. Régaldo (Paris 1971), p. 127 n. 10. See also his bibliographical essay, 'Montesquieu présent', *Dix-huitième siècle*, viii (1976), 400.
5 In *The Political Theory of Possessive Individualism* (Oxford 1962).
6 See R. F. O'Reilly, 'Montesquieu anti-feminist', *Studies on Voltaire and the 18th Century*, cii (1973), 143–56; C. Dauphiné, 'Pourquoi un roman de sérail?' *Europe*, 55, 89–96; C. Rosso, *Montesquieu moraliste*, pp. 127–9.
7 ' "Les femmes, dit-il (Mahomet), doivent honorer leurs maris; leurs maris les doivent honorer: mais ils ont l'avantage d'un degré sur elles." ' (Gar. 83).
8 See *Lettres* LXIII, XCIX, CVI, CX.
9 On Poulain, see G. Ascoli, 'Essai sur l'histoire des idées féministes en France', *Revue de synthèse historique*, xii (1906), 161–9; for his influence on Montesquieu: B. Magné, 'Une source de la lettre persane XXXVIII?', *Revue d'histoire littéraire de la France*, lxviii, 3–4 (1968), 407–14; E. McNiven Hine, 'The Woman Question in early 18th Century French Literature:

the influence of François Poulain de la Barre', *Studies on Voltaire*, cxvi (1973), 65–79. On Fleury and Fénelon, see Ascoli, art. cit., pp. 55–6; L. Abensour, *La Femme et le féminisme avant la Révolution* (Paris 1928), pp. 35–41.

10 'Montesquieu présent', p. 400.

11 Significantly, Montesquieu includes virtually unrestricted manhood suffrage in his version of the English constitution (*L*.XI,6).

12 See Macpherson, op. cit., p. 296 n. I.

13 See *Code de la nature* (1755), ed. V. P. Volguine (Paris 1970), Intro., pp. 7–8; 'Lois distributives ou économiques', arts. I, II; 'Lois de la forme du gouvernement', I.

14 See O'Reilly, art. cit. The doctrine of physiological determinism to which he makes Montesquieu subscribe depends too exclusively on his scientific writings. The mystique of masculine potency (conveniently substantiated by the social and civic disabilities allotted *passim* to eunuchs), which issues in blatant phallocracy, emanates from a comparative study of the sexes in the *Essai sur les causes qui peuvent affecter les esprits et les caractères*, devoid, in fact, of socio-political value judgements. Montesquieu's remarks here on the mysterious properties of the seminal fluid need to be considered alongside equally extensive speculations on the reproductive machinery of the female, see *P*. Bkn. 690; 700; 702 (MS76; 1241; 16). It is easy to forget that in 1716 Montesquieu founded a prize in anatomy at the Academy of Bordeaux.

15 See J. Portemer, 'Le Statut de la femme en France depuis la réformation des coutumes jusqu'à la rédaction du code civil', *Société Jean Bodin*, xii, ii (1962), pp. 447–97.

16 For his sources see *De l'esprit des lois*, ed. J. Brethe de la Gressaye (Paris 1950–61), ii, 433, n. 49.

17 The details of Roman legislation are discussed in *L*.XXIII, 21 and correspond very clearly to the provisions of *P*.Bkn. 1966 (MS185).

18 See Brethe de la Gressaye, iv, 5–6. The text is an addition of 1757.

19 Bkn. 579–81 (MS1622, 1630, 1726). The period of composition was 1721–31, established from the graphological tables provided in the Nagel ed. of the *Œuvres* (Paris 1950–5), vol. ii.

20 See in particular *P*.Bkn. 579 (MS1622); and cf. *Lp*.CXXVI, where Montesquieu suggests that 'tendresse' promotes equality.

21 See R. Shackleton, *Montesquieu: A Critical Biography* (Oxford 1961), pp. 55–61 for Montesquieu's relations with Madame de Lambert during the period 1724–8; and Ascoli, art. cit., pp. 169–71, and E. McNiven Hine, 'Madame de Lambert, her sources and her circle: on the threshold of a new age', *Studies on Voltaire*, cii (1973), 173–91, for opinions on her circle.

22 op. cit., *Œuvres philosophiques du P. Buffier*, ed. F. Bouillier (Paris 1843), pp. 349–51.

23 *Catalogue de la bibliothèque de Montesquieu*, ed. L. Desgraves (Geneva 1954), item 691, p. 51; and *P*.Bkn.1955 (MS1207).

24 See especially, *Réflexions nouvelles sur les femmes* (London 1730) pp. 7–10; and cf. *L*.XVI, 12; XXVI, 3.

25 cf. Zulema and Anaïs in *Lp*.CXLI; the Amazonian Myrinna in *Dialogues* (P. Bkn. 486 (MS338); Pl. I, 1033); Ardasire-Isménie of *Arsace et Isménie* (1742); and see I. Maclean, *Woman Triumphant* (Oxford 1977), pp. 86; 205–8.

26 See Maclean, op. cit., pp. 79; 86; Ascoli, art. cit., pp. 50–2.

27 See *L*.XI, 15; P. Bkn. 1199 (MS1951); *P*. Bkn. 1953 (MS1540).

28 An edict of Henri II fixed a capital penalty in the event of an infant's death if the pregnancy of an unmarried woman had not been previously declared before the magistrate. It was still in force in the eighteenth century. See *L*.XXVI, 3.

4 Women in Marivaux: Journalist to Dramatist

1 P. Stewart, *Le Masque et la parole: le langage de l'amour au XVIIIe siècle* (Paris 1973), p. 140.

2 *Le Spectateur français*, 1ère feuille, *Journaux et œuvres diverses*, ed. F. Deloffre and M. Gilot (Paris 1969), p. 118. All subsequent references to the *Journaux* will be to this edition.

3 M. Gilot, *Les Journaux de Marivaux: Itinéraire moral et accomplissement esthétique* (Paris/Lille 1975), 2 vols., i, 127.

4 Gilot, op. cit., persuasively argues that irregularities in the appearance of issues of *Le Spectateur* can be directly related to the periods when Marivaux was composing his plays (i, 250–1).

5 ed. J. Dunkley (Exeter 1976), p. 19.

6 Sc. I, *Théâtre complet*, ed. F. Deloffre (Paris 1968), 2 vols., i, 89. All subsequent references to Marivaux's plays will be to this edition.

7 *Marivaux par lui-même* (Paris 1954).

8 A judicious survey, with sensible conclusions, is conducted by V. P. Brady, *Love in the Theatre of Marivaux* (Geneva 1970), pp. 15–21.

9 Divorce was impossible, but most of the leading *philosophes* claimed it as a human right: cf. L. Abensour, *La Femme et le féminisme avant la Révolution* (Paris 1923), pp. 402–5.

10 The editors of the *Journaux* document the inequality of treatment accorded to the sexes, p. 652, n. 130.

11 p. 653, n. 139; cf. Gilot, op. cit., pp. 653–4.

12 L. Desvignes-Parent argues this persuasively in *Marivaux et l'Angleterre* (Paris 1970), pp. 317–24, though she surprisingly makes no reference to *L'Ile de la raison* in this particular survey.

13 The woman in Sartre's scene, ardently pursued by her suitor, enjoys the situation because she can temporarily put off any decision and pretend to a belief in platonic love. When he takes her hand, 'la jeune femme abandonne sa main, mais *ne s'aperçoit pas* qu'elle l'abandonne' (Paris 1943, p. 95; author's italics). Marivaux is more indulgent in his comment but no less observant.

14 cf. Deloffre's comments, p. 1087, n. 43; p. 584.

15 cf. W. H. Trapnell, 'The "Philosophical" implications of Marivaux's

Dispute', *Studies on Voltaire and the Eighteenth Century*, lxxiii (1970), 193–219, which fascinatingly relates the play to contemporary social philosophy.

5 Women and Sexuality in the Thought of La Mettrie

1 The following abbreviations are used in reference to La Mettrie's writings: *DP*: *Discours préliminaire*; *HM*: *L'Homme machine*; *HP*: *L'Homme plante*; *APQM*: *Les Animaux plus que machines*; *SE*: *Système d'Epicure*, all in *Œuvres philosophiques*, Londres, Jean Nourse, 1751; *HNA* 45 and *HNA* 47: *Histoire naturelle de l'âme*, editions of 1745 (La Haye, Jean Néaulme) and 1747 (Oxford, aux dépens de l'auteur) respectively, the latter containing 'Lettre critique . . . à Mme du Châtelet'; *La Vol.*: *La Volupté*,par M. le Chevalier de M . . ., 1747 (109 pp.), with dedication 'A Madame la Marquise de xxx'; *O. Pen.*: *Ouvrage de Pénélope*, Berlin, vols. i and ii: 1748, vol. iii ('*Supplément*'): 1750. Volume i has two sets of pagination, designated here by 'A' and 'B'; *SMV*: *Système de M. Herman Boerhaave sur les maladies vénériennes*. Traduit . . . par M. de la Mettrie avec une Dissertation . . . du traducteur. Paris, Prault fils, 1735. Also referred to are: *Œuvres de médecine*, Berlin, Froméry, 1751.

2 Louise Bourgeois, *Observations sur les accouchements et les maladies des femmes*, 3 vols. (Paris 1642–4).

3 E. Bergmann, *Die Satiren des Herrn Maschine* (Leipzig 1913) passim; P. Lemée, *J. O. de La Mettrie* (Mortain 1954), pp. 202–32.

4 See *HM* p. 67 especially, and cf. the use of the word 'force' on pp. 57, 58, 63, 64 ('force de la vie'). La Mettrie would have been aware of the discussions a few years earlier in Dortous de Mairan's *Lettre à Madame [du Châtelet] sur la question des forces vives en réponse aux objections qu'elle lui fait dans ses Institutions de physique* (Paris 1741) and Abbé Deidier's *Nouvelle réfutation de l'hypothèse des forces vives*' (Paris 1741).

5 See J. S. Spink, *French Free-Thought from Gassendi to Voltaire* (London 1960), especially p. 118, for discussion of a crucial statement by G. Lamy, acknowledged by La Mettrie as source of ideas on the fire-soul and the *anima mundi* (*HNA* 45 pp. 44–7).

6 By e.g. Elie Luzac, *L'Homme plus que machine* (Leyden 1748); G. Pflüg, 'La Mettrie und die biologische Theorie am achtzehnten Jahrhundert', *Deutsches Vierteljahrsschrift*, xxvii (1953), 526–7.

7 Although La Mettrie considered that *Les Animaux plus que machines* could form a self-explanatory part of *Œuvres philosophiques* (1751), it was written as a rejoinder to B. Tralles's criticism of *L'Homme Machine, De machina et anima humana* (Breslau 1749).

8 An allusion to N. Pluche, *Le Spectacle de la Nature* (1746); cf. *HM* p. 11.

9 Diderot, *Interprétation de la Nature* (1754) in *Œuvres complètes*, (Paris 1875–7) ii, 44–5.

10 F. Rougier's edition of *HP* 48 (New York 1936) is itself fairly rare, and did not discuss La Mettrie's omissions in the 1751 text. It is therefore of

interest to list here the omitted references. La Mettrie gives only authors and abbreviated titles, so the full titles and the believed dates of the edition in question have been added in the following list.

H. C. Agrippa, 'Traité de la prééminence des femmes', probably *De la grandeur et de l'excellence des femmes* (Paris 1713, original text: 1529).

H. Boerhaave, *Institutions de médecine*, translated by La Mettrie. In 2 vols, Paris 1739–40, and in 8 vols (an amplified translation) Paris 1743–50.

D. Bouillier, 'Traité de l'âme des bêtes', probably *Essai philosophique sur l'âme des bêtes* (Amsterdam 1728 or, augmented, 1737).

J. Gesner, 'Commentaires sur les Eléments de Botanique de Linnaeus', probably *Dissertationes physicae in quibus . . . Linnaei elementa botanica . . . explicantur* (Halae propter Salam 1747).

S. Hales, *La Statique des végétaux*, translated by Buffon (Paris 1735), original text: *Vegetable Staticks* (London 1727).

Linnaeus, *Fundamenta botanica, in quibus theoria botanices tradiditur* (Amsterdam 1736).

A. van Leeuwenhoek, *Arcana naturae detecta* (Delft 1695).

M. Malpighi, *Anatome plantarum* (London 1675–9) includes 'de ovo incubato observationes'.

F. Mauriceau, 'Traité des accouchements', probably *Des* [later '*Traité des*'] *maladies des femmes grosses et accouchées* (Paris 1668).

P. Moreau de Maupertuis, *Vénus physique* (s.l. 1745)

G. B. Morgagni, *Adversaria anatomica omnia* (Padua 1719).

G. Pontedera, *Anthologia, sive Floris natura libri tres . . .* (Padua 1720).

F. Quesnay, 'Econom. Anim.', possibly *Essai physique sur l'économie animale*, 2de ed., 3 vols., Paris 1747, but probably the rare first edition of 1736, with which was published a 'Traité du feu'.

F. Ruysch, *Thesaurus anatomicus prima* [-decimus] (Amsterdam 1701–16).

A. van Royen, *Dissertatio botanica-medica inauguralis de anatome et oeconomia plantarum* (Leyden 1728), and *Carmen elegiacum de amoribus et connubiis plantarum* (Leyden 1732).

11 There was apparently a real-life original of the 'débauché': 'Vous **verrez** dans ma *Volupté* que vous en aurez fourni votre contingent, comme a fait Désormes . . .' wrote La Mettrie to Baron F. W. von Marschall, about 1750 (see Ann Thomson, 'Quatre lettres inédites de La Mettrie', *Dix-huitième siècle*, VII (1975), p. 12, cf. p. 16). The remark relates to the passage beginning 'Vous êtes Allemand, baron . . .' (*La Vol.*, pp. 58–9), and first appeared in the original version, *Ecole de la volupté* (1746), pp. 74–7 (cf. 'Discours sur le bonheur', Potsdam 1748, pp. 129f, 136f), suggesting that La Mettrie knew Marschall from that date. Désormes, the actor, was possibly the original of 'le voluptueux'.

12 See Lemée, *J.O. de La Mettrie*, pp. 23ff, 237ff. Lemée's opinion that the son was only two at the time of death is unlikely in view of the known chronology of La Mettrie's movements, and of the volume of blood-letting he prescribes (p. 240). The opinion is based on La Mettrie's near-illegible letter, and Lemée himself notes the date of birth provided by the Etat Civil as 1742 (p. 241, cf. p. 23).

6   Diderot and Women

1 See P. Le Ridant, ed. *Code matrimonial ou Recueil des Edits, Ordonnances et Déclarations sur le mariage*, avec un dictionnaire des décisions les plus importantes sur cette matière (Paris 1766), 2 pts.; Moisei Yakovlevich Ostrogorski, *La femme au point de vue du droit public* (Paris 1892), Alan Macdonald, 'The French law of marriages and matrimonial régimes', *International Comparative Law Quarterly*, 4th series, i, 1952.

2 See *Œuvres de Pothier*, annotées et mises en conciliation avec le code civil et la législation actuelle par M. Bugnet, vol. VII, *Traités de la puissance du mari, de la communauté des donations entre mari et femme* (Paris 1845). Robert Joseph Pothier's works include a *Traité du Contrat de Mariage*.

3 Among early writings on education of girls, are to be found: Poulain de la Barre, *Education des Dames pour la conduite de l'esprit dans les sciences et les mœurs*, 1673-5; *De l'égalité des deux sexes*, 1673; Mme de Maintenon, *Lettres sur l'éducation des filles*, ed. M. Th. Lavallée (Paris 1854) (also her *Entretiens sur l'éducation des filles*); Fénelon, *De l'éducation des filles*, 1687; Mme de Lambert, *Sur les femmes* in *Œuvres morales*; Charles Rollin, *De la manière d'enseigner et d'étudier les Belles-Lettres par rapport à l'esprit et au cœur*, 4 vols., 1726-8 (also *De l'excellence des hommes contre l'Egalité des Sexes*, 1675); Castel de Saint-Pierre, abbé de Tiron, *Avantages de l'éducation des collèges sur l'éducation domestique*, Amsterdam and Paris, 1740, 4 pts in one volume. See also Paul Rousselot, *La pédagogie féminine: extraits des principaux écrivains qui ont traité de l'éducation des femmes depuis le XVIe siècle* (Paris 1881); P. Rousselot, *Histoire de l'éducation des femmes en France*, 2 vols., 1883; G. Snyders, *La Pédagogie en France aux XVII et XVIIIe siècles* (Paris 1965).

4 P. Lacroix, *Dix-huitième siècle, Institutions, usages et coutumes en France, 1700-1789* (Paris 1875), p. 66.

5 cf. *L'Ingénu*, ed. W. R. Jones (Geneva 1957), p. 108.

6 *Laclos* (Paris 1975) pp. 31-8. R. Pomeau's study of Laclos' essay, *De l'éducation des femmes* is pertinent and shows that after 1770 the social and moral position of women is increasingly linked with the question of their education. Cf. Riballier, *Education physique et morale des femmes*, 1779.

7 cf. R. Mathé, *Profil d'une œuvre: Manon Lescaut*, pp. 24-5, quoted by P. H. Smith in her thesis. See below note 11.

8 *Le Siècle de Louis XIV*, ch. xxix and *passim*. For background information see E. & J. de Goncourt, *La femme au dix-huitième siècle* (Paris 1862); H. Taine, *Les Origines de la France contemporaine*, vol. i *L'Ancien régime*, 1876.

9 *Laclos et la tradition, essai sur les sources et la technique des Liaisons Dangereuses* (Paris 1968) p. 530 ff. Chapter 3, pp. 521-9 deals with the whole problem of the education of women and feminism.

10 *The Question of Feminine Liberty in the Writings of Denis Diderot*, Stanford University Ph.D., 1973. On the more general topic of feminism in the eighteenth century, see M. Y. Ostragorski, *Of Women. A comparative*

study in history and legislation . . . Translated under the author's supervision (London 1893); Léon Abensour, *La Femme et le féminisme avant la Révolution* (with a bibliography) (Paris 1923) and *Histoire générale du féminisme des origines à nos jours* (Paris 1921). See also P. Fauchery, *La Destinée féminine dans le roman européen du XVIIIe siècle* (Paris 1892).

11 *The more complicated sex: Diderot's view of the feminine universe*, Exeter University Ph.D., 1972.

12 *Lettre sur les aveugles*, ed. R. Niklaus (Geneva 1951) p. 12.

13 In D. Diderot, *Œuvres complètes* (Paris 1971) x, 28.

14 ibid., p. 32.

15 ibid., p. 39.

16 ibid., pp. 41–2.

17 ibid., p. 42.

18 ibid., p. 43.

19 ibid., p. 46.

20 Diderot, *Contes*, ed. H. Dieckmann (London 1963), p. 131.

21 ibid., p. 145.

22 ibid., pp. 148–9.

23 ibid., p. 150.

24 ibid., p. 176.

25 cf. 'L'histoire de Madame de La Pommeraye et le thème de la jeune veuve,' *Diderot Studies*, xviii (1975), 122–5, 130, 131, 132.

26 ibid., p. 122.

27 ibid., p. 131.

28 *Laclos et la tradition romanesque*, p. 180 ff.

7   Diderot and the Education of Girls

1 Diderot, *Œuvres complètes*, ed. Assézat et Tourneux (Paris 1875–7), i, xlvi–xlvii. *Mémoires pour servir à l'histoire de la vie et des ouvrages de Diderot par Madame de Vandeul, sa fille.*

2 Echoes of family discussions on this matter may be heard in Angélique's comment on her mother, ibid., p. xlvii: 'rien ne pourrait lui ôter de la tête que je dois mon existence à ce vœu.'

3 Diderot, *Le Neveu de Rameau*, ed. J. Fabre (Geneva and Lille 1950), pp. 29, 30.

4 Diderot, *Correspondance*, ed. G. Roth et J. Varloot (Paris 1955–70), iii, 300 [12 September 1761].

5 ibid., iv, 156 [19 September 1762].

6 ed. cit., p. 30.

7 ibid., p. 31.

8 *Correspondance*, iv, 166 [23 September 1762].

9 ed. cit. p. 30.

10 *Correspondance*, iv, 171 [26 September 1762].

11 ed. cit. p. 31.

12 *Œuvres complètes*, xii, 526.

13 J. Massiet du Biest, *La Fille de Diderot* (Tours 1949), p. 53.

14 ibid., passim.

15 L. Abensour, *La Femme et le féminisme avant la Révolution* (Paris 1923), p. 49.

16 *Correspondance*, iv, p. 188 [7 October 1762].

17 Voltaire, *Complete Works*, ed. Theodore Besterman, vol. 115, Best. D13898, Voltaire to Etienne Noël Damilaville, 30 January 1767.

18 *Correspondance*, ix, 127 [31 August 1769].

19 François Poulain de la Barre, *De l'Egalité des deux sexes, discours physique et moral, où l'on voit l'importance de se défaire des Préjugez* (Paris 1690), p. 76.

20 Abbé Fromageot, *Cours d'études des jeunes demoiselles* (Paris 1772), 8 vols.

21 Abbé Le More, *Principes d'Institution, ou de la manière d'élever les enfans des deux sexes* (Paris 1774).

22 Riballier, *De l'éducation physique et morale des femmes* (Brussels and Paris 1779) and *De l'éducation physique et morale des enfants des deux sexes* (Paris and Nyon 1785).

23 See G. Reynier, *La Femme au XVIIe siècle* (Paris 1929), pp. 254 ff.

24 Riballier, *De l'éducation physique et morale des enfants des deux sexes*, p. 28.

25 See *Correspondance*, ii, 50–9, A la Princesse de Nassau-Saarbruck, [May or June 1758], and XII, 36–42, A la Comtesse de Forbach [circ. 1772].

26 *Correspondance*, i, p. 190 [January 1755].

27 ibid., xii, 123 [13 September 1772].

28 This seems to be the basis, in particular, of Poulain de la Barre's little treatises on the equality of women, although he wanders off at several tangents.

29 *Œuvres complètes*, ii, 356.

30 ibid., p. 357.

31 Helvétius, *Œuvres complètes* (Paris 1818), ii, 116, n. 2.

32 Diderot, *Œuvres complètes*, ii, 319.

33 In his *Eléments de Physiologie*, on which Diderot was working at about the same time as his *Réfutation*, he expresses yet again the same ideas. A section headed 'animaux Differens par leur organisation' includes 'La jeune fille poursuit un papillon, le jeune garçon gravit sur un arbre.' (ed. Jean Mayer (Paris 1964), p. 43.)

34 *Correspondance*, xi, 211 [19 October 1771].

35 v. Diderot, *Mémoires pour Catherine II*, ed. P. Vernière (Paris 1966), pp. 86 ff. and *Correspondance*, xiv, 44–6 [June 1774].

36 *Correspondance*, xiv, 46, n. 6.

37 *Œuvres complètes*, iii, 429 ff.

8 Restif de la Bretonne and Woman's Estate

1 Réstif's thought has only fairly recently been accorded serious consideration. One aspect of it has been explored, somewhat selectively, by Mark Poster in *The Utopian Thought of Restif de la Bretonne* (New York; London 1971). David A. Coward's as yet unpublished *Social and Political*

Ideas in the Work of Restif de la Bretonne, University of London Ph.D. 1975, to which I am happy to acknowledge my indebtedness, is a work of impressive scholarship and already indispensable for any detailed study of Restif.

2 G. Guillot, 'Restif de la Bretonne par et pour les femmes', *Europe*, 427–8 (1964), 62.

3 G. Bruit, 'Restif de la Bretonne et les femmes', *La Pensée*, 131 (1967), 125.

4 D. Brahimi, 'Restif féministe? Etude de quelques "Contemporaines"', *Etudes sur le XVIIIe siècle*, iii (1976), 77–91.

5 References, given subsequently in the text and preceded by *PMN*, are to vol. 5 of *Monsieur Nicolas* (Paris 1959).

6 *Les Posthumes* (Paris 1802), iv, 17.

7 *L'Egalité des hommes et des femmes* (1622). In Mario Schiff *La Fille d'alliance de Montaigne: Marie de Gournay* (Paris 1910), p. 65.

8 *Les Gynographes ou Idées de deux honnêtes-femmes sur un projet de règlement proposé à toute l'Europe pour mettre les femmes à leur place* (Paris 1777), p. 57. Subsequent references will be given in the text in the form: (*GYN*, 57).

9 op. cit., pp. 4, 7.

10 *L'Andrographe* (Paris 1782), p. 10.

11 op. cit., p. 36.

12 op. cit., pp. 113–14.

13 op. cit., pp. 101–3.

14 *L'Andrographe*, p. 22.

15 *La Paysanne pervertie* (Paris 1972), p. 257. Subsequent references to this edition will be in the text in the form: (*Ppe*, 257).

16 Cf. 'Statuts du Bourg d'Oudun', XLVI, in *Le Paysan et la Paysanne perverties*: 'Tout homme dont la femme sera stérile ne pourra la garder plus de trois ans: ils seront publiquement démariés, avec injonction de se regarder à l'avenir comme étrangers et ordre de contracter un nouvel engagement.' (*L'Œuvre de Restif de la Bretonne*, ed. H. Bachelin (Paris 1930–2), vi, 461.

17 M. Poster, *The Utopian Thought of Restif de la Bretonne*, p. 43.

9   Women in Mercier's *Tableau de Paris*

1 *Œuvres complètes*, ed. B. Gagnebin and M. Raymond (Paris 1959–), iv, 703.

2 See C. Berkowe, 'Louis-Sébastien Mercier et les femmes', *Romanic Review*, lv (1964), pp. 16–29.

3 L. Béclard, *Sébastien Mercier. Sa vie, son œuvre, son temps* (Paris 1903), pp. 465–6. See also C. Guyot, *De Rousseau à Mirabeau. Pèlerins de Môtiers et prophètes de 89* (Paris 1936), pp. 120–1.

4 All quotations from the *Tableau de Paris* are taken from the 'nouvelle édition corrigée et augmentée' published in Amsterdam, Vols. i–viii in 1783 and Vols. ix–xii in 1789.

5 See, for instance, the *Pétition des femmes du Tiers-Etat*; *Motion de la pauvre Javotte, députée des pauvres femmes* (Paris 1790), quoted by R. Graham,

'Rousseau's Sexism revolutionized' in *Woman in the 18th Century and Other Essays*, ed. P. Fritz and R. Morton (Toronto and Sarasota 1976), pp. 130–1.
6 The standard work (O. Martin, *Histoire de la Coutume de la Prévôté et Vicomté de Paris* (Paris 1922–30), 2 vols. ii, 233) gives a very different view in the section 'Le fonctionnement de la communauté': 'Il est dominé par la notion essentielle d'autorité maritale. Sans doute, les auteurs considèrent que la communauté est une société; mais c'est une société dans laquelle les associés sont très loin d'avoir des droits égaux; le mari en est très nettement le chef, avec une large autorité, et la femme, frappée d'une incapacité presque complète, ne peut agir qu'en subordonnée.'
7 Letter CVI.

10   The *Bibliothèque Universelle des Dames*

1 Antoine Guillois, *Pendant la Terreur: le poète Roucher* (Paris 1890), p. 103.
2 Bibliothèque Nationale, Manuscrits, Fonds français 21969, Privilège général No 3334.
3 J.-J. Rousseau, *Œuvres complètes*, éd. B. Gagnebin et M. Raymond (Paris, Pléiade, 1969), iv, 736–7.
4 Cited in *Dictionnaire des Lettres françaises, XVIIIe siècle*, ed. Georges Grente (Paris 1960), under 'Roussel'.

11   Duclos's *Histoire de Madame de Luz:*   Woman and History

1 G. May, *Le Dilemme du roman au XVIIIe siècle* (Paris 1963), chap. VIII, 'Féminisme et roman'.
2 N. Lenglet-Dufresnoy, *De l'usage des romans* (2 vols, Amsterdam 1734), i, chap. II.
3 A. P. Jaquin, *Entretien sur les romans* (Paris 1755), p. 339.
4 R. Démoris, *Le Roman à la première personne* (Paris 1975).
5 R. Démoris, op. cit., p. 111.
6 J.-J. Rousseau, *Lettre à M. d'Alembert*, ed. M. Rat (Paris 1960), p. 160.
7 Lenglet-Dufresnoy, op. cit., I, 52.
8 R. Démoris, op. cit., p. 15.
9 N. Lenglet-Dufresnoy, *L'Histoire justifiée contre les romans* (Amsterdam 1735), p. 258.
10 C. R. de Caumont de la Force, *Anecdotes du seizième siecle, ou Intrigues de cour politiques et galantes* . . . (1713). For details of the various editions and titles of this work see: S. P. Jones, *A List of French Prose Fiction from 1700 to 1750* (New York 1939).
11 Mme de Tencin, *Mémoires du Comte de Comminge*, ed. Jean Decottignies (Lille 1969), pp. 60–72.
12 See M. T. Hipp, *Mythes et réalités. Enquête sur le roman et les mémoires 1600–1700* (Paris 1976), pp. 504–15, and S. E. Jones, *Ethics and the novel*

as studied in the works of women novelists, from the publication of the 'Princesse de Clèves', 1678, until the end of the reign of Louis XIV, 1715 (London Ph.D. thesis, 1961), pp. 120–3.

13 This is, of course, a generalization which fails to take account of certain exceptions, such as for instance the figure of the warrior-female or the politically active queen. In these cases, the female activity is overtly intruding on activities specifically masculine and offers a rather different problem.

14 See respectively L. R. Free, *Virtue, Happiness and Duclos's 'Histoire de Madame de Luz'* (The Hague 1974), p. 20 and J. Brengues, 'Un roman oublié du XVIIIe siècle: *L'Histoire de Madame de Luz* de Charles Duclos', *Société d'émulation des Côtes-du-Nord. Bulletin et mémoires 1969*, p. 94.

15 See *Histoire de Madame de Luz*, ed. Jacques Brengues (Saint Brieuc 1972), p. xxviii. Further references to the novel are taken from this edition.

16 The first paragraph of the novel brings together a cluster of words expressive of the besieged position of the female: 'conspirer' 'séduire', 'écueils', 'environner' and 'succomber', 'faiblesse', 'indigence'.

17 P. Meister, *Charles Duclos, 1704–1772* (Geneva 1956), p. 175.

18 R. Démoris, 'De l'usage du nom propre: le roman historique auXVIIIe siècle', *Revue d'Histoire littéraire de la France*, (mars–juin 1975, 'Le Roman historique'), 268–88.

19 See A-M Schmidt, 'Duclos, Sade et la littérature féroce', *Revue des Sciences humaines* (avril–sept. 1951), 146–55.

13 D'Antraigues's Feminism: Where Fact and Fantasy Meet

1 The writings concerned are: *Mes Soliloques* (covering the years 1753 to 1784 and 1802 to 1810), B.N., achat no. 23055; and two epistolary novels, *Talmi et Eliza* (1772–3) and *Henri et Cécile* (1784–6). These unpublished manuscripts are still in private hands.

2 See my 'Antraigues and the quest for happiness: nostalgia and commitment', *Studies on Voltaire and the Eighteenth Century*, cli–clv (1976), 625–45.

3 See A. Cobban and R. S. Elmes, 'A Disciple of Jean-Jacques Rousseau: The Comte d'Antraigues', *Revue d'histoire littéraire de la France*, xliii (1936), 181–210 and 340–63.

4 'Mais,' she adds, 'comme le dit j.j. si la patience est amère ses fruits sont bien doux.' So much for J.-J. as author of the work.

5 D'Antraigues explains his reticence as fear that representation could come to replace reality: 'Oh, amour, tu permis aux mortels de connaître tes délices, tu défendis de les dépeindre. Une telle peinture sans doute suffirait à l'imagination pour les reproduire et la vie s'éteindrait par les moiens même destinés à la conserver.'

6 Burnt down in 1792 by peasants in revolt whilst d'Antraigues was in voluntary exile.

7 His mother wrote to him on 25 May 1803: 'vous ne vous contentez pas

de mépriser le genre humain, mais vous haïssez les trois quarts de ceux que vous connaissez . . .' (L. Pingaud, *Un Agent secret sous la Révolution et l'Empire: Le Comte d'Antraigues* (Paris 1893; 2e édn. rev. et augm. 1894), p. 15.

8 art. cit., pp. 631–2, 636, 641–5.

9 *Mes Soliloques*; for her story, see my article, loc. cit., p. 633.

10 See Henry Howard, *Memorials of the Howard Family* (*c.* 1793); *Indications of the Howard Family, 1834–6*; and Papers of and re Howard Family. Arundel (Historical Manuscripts Commission, 1975 Personal Index 17614 BK.); Henry Londsdale, *The Worthies of Cumberland: The Howards* (London 1872) (on Philip Howard, see pp. 66–7). Philip and Anne frequently lived abroad, or in Bath, but lived at Corby from 1754 until shortly before 1778. I am very grateful to Mr and Mrs John Howard of Corby for permission to copy and reproduce the Howard–Coppinger letters.

11 The Potocki family was, of course, one of the most powerful of the Polish nobility. Can d'Antraigues's lady be Alexandra Potocka (1755–1821)? She inherited Wilanów from her mother, Princesse Maréchale Lubomirska. D'Antraigues's princess owns a *château* on the outskirts of Warsaw which he calls Elvankov and Elvanrov—almost an anagram of Wilanów,—a mini-Versailles which tallies closely with d'Antraigues's description: '. . . de belles eaux, des allées superbes, quelques-unes droites comme les nôtres . . .'. The park is a league across, with superb statues; the *château* 'grand et magnifiquement meublé'. D'Antraigues (forgetfully?) reveals that his princess was married to the 'grand écuier de la couronne de Pologne'—and Count Stanislaw-Kostka Potocki was in fact 'grand veneur' to King Stanislas (see J. Fabre, *Poniatowski* (Paris 1952), p. 236). This cannot be the murderous, treacherous husband of 'Sophie Alexandrie', however, for Stanislaw became President of the Council of State and a patriotic radical leader. I am grateful to Miss C. Raczynska for help in tracing Alexandra Potocka.

12 Ignacy and Stanislaw Potocki? They were in the Czartoryski faction, with which d'Antraigues had frequent contact later during his exile in Dresden (Pingaud, op. cit., p. 215; Gieysztor, Kieniewicz, et al., *History of Poland* (Warsaw 1968), p. 332). However, this Stanislaw was Countess Alexandra's husband (see n. 11). Once again, the elements are real, but transposed into fiction.

13 See J. Fabre, op. cit., pp. 299–301. Wilno could have been suggested to d'Antraigues by Wilanów—a large estate which he transforms, in his mind, into a principality.

14 Yet he is uncompromising in his hatred for Catherine II, both in his *Soliloques* and in another manuscript, *Discours prononcé par le Prince Severin Potoski à la Diétine de l'Ukraine*. Only the 'style chauffé' and references to the despotism of Louis XIV ('un roi tyran dirigé par des fanatiques') indicate the latter to be by d'Antraigues: 'Déjà se déploie au milieu de nous le rigoureux despotisme . . . de la Souveraine des Russies . . . chez elle la vertu n'habite que les déserts.'

15 'Le roman par lettres—si fréquent—ne doit-il pas une **partie** de son succès au fait qu'il donne une forme tangible à cette distance consubstantielle à l'amour romanesque?' (P. Fauchery, *La Destinée féminine dans le le roman européen du 18e siècle* (Paris 1922), pp. 293–4). As the Howard letters show, novels are but approximations to the anguish of real separation.

16 Useful summaries and bibliographies of eighteenth-century feminism are to be found in: E. R. Hedman, *Early French Feminism from the Eighteenth Century to 1848* (Ph.D. dissertation, New York University, 1954); K. M. Clinton, *Feminism: an analysis and assessment* (Ph.D. dissertation, Kansas State University, 1972); M. Albistur et D. Armogathe, *Histoire du féminisme français* (Paris 1977).

14   Cleopatra's Nose and Enlightenment Historiography

1 G. V. Plekhanov, *The Role of the Individual in History* (London 1940), p. 30.

2 R. G. Collingwood, *The Idea of History* (Oxford 1946), pp. 80–1.

3 See, for example, the Preface to C. Rollin, *Histoire ancienne* (Paris 1730), and that to A. Calmet, *Histoire universelle, Sacrée et Prophane* (Strasbourg 1735), p. xx.

4 op. cit. (Paris 1681), p. 432.

5 H. de Boulainvilliers, *La Vie de Mahomed* (Amsterdam 1731), pp. 1–2.

6 For a fuller account of these developments see J. H. Brumfitt, 'Historical Pyrrhonism and Enlightenment Historiography in France', in *Literature and History in the Age of Ideas*, ed. C. G. S. Williams (Ohio 1975), pp. 15–28.

7 op. cit. (Paris 1674), especially pp. 156–7.

8 P. Bayle, *Œuvres diverses* (The Hague 1727), ii, pp. 10–11.

9 op. cit., ed. A. Prat (Paris 1939), ii, pp. 244ff.

10 op. cit., ed. L. Maigron (Paris 1908), p. 30.

11 Fontenelle, *Œuvres* (Paris 1818), ii, p. 431.

12 *Nouveaux Dialogues des morts*, ed. J. Dagen (Paris 1971), p. 210.

13 ibid., pp. 279–80.

14 op. cit., ed. A. Cahen (Paris n.d.), p. 129.

15 Montesquieu, *Œuvres complètes* (Paris 1949), i, p. 1074.

16 See R. Shackleton, *Montesquieu* (Oxford 1961), p. 405.

17 op. cit., p. 1074.

18 G. Giarrizzo, *Edward Gibbon e la cultura europea del settecento* (Naples 1954), p. 115.

19 See his edition of *Le Siècle* (Frankfurt 1753) e.g. p. 71.

20 *Le Siècle de Louis XIV* ed. E. Bourgeois (Paris n.d.), p. xliv.

21 See, for example, J. H. Brumfitt, *Voltaire Historian* (Oxford 1958), pp. 107 ff. and 122 ff., or C. Rihs, *Voltaire: Recherches sur les origines du matérialisme historique* (Geneva and Paris 1962), pp. 141 ff.

22 Voltaire, *Œuvres historiques*, ed. R. Pomeau (Paris 1957), p. 871.

23 See Rihs, op. cit., pp. 82–4.

24 See Brumfitt, *Voltaire Historian*, p. 122.
25 See *Œuvres historiques*, ed. R. Pomeau, pp. 1302–3 and 1739.
26 E. J. F. Barbier, *Journal* (Paris 1849), i, 296.
27 See *Les Correspondants de la Marquise de Balleroy*, ed. E. de Barthélemy (Paris 1883), i, 390.
28 C. Duclos, *Mémoires secrets sur les règnes de Louis XIV et de Louis XV* (Paris 1791), ii, 188.
29 Saint-Simon, *Mémoires* (Paris 1829), xvii, 274.
30 La Mothe La Hode, *La Vie de Philippe d'Orléans* (London 1736), i, 344.
31 Piossens, *Mémoire de la Régence* (Amsterdam 1749), v, 175 ff., and V. Bacallar y Sanna, *Mémoires pour servir à l'histoire de l'Espagne sous le règne de Philippe V* (Amsterdam 1754), iii, 334.
32 A. Baudrillart, *Philippe V et la Cour de France* (Paris 1890), ii, 346.
33 H. Leclercq, *Histoire de la Régence* (Paris 1921), i, 263.
34 op. cit., *Avertissement*.
35 ibid., p. 330.
36 *Œuvres historiques*, pp. 1412 ff.
37 G. L. Renier, *History, its purpose and method* (London 1950), p. 37 quotes Collingwood as affirming that 'to know who played centre-forward for Aston Villa last year is just as much historical knowledge as to know who won the battle of Cannae'.
38 Quoted by Adrienne D. Hytier, 'Les Philosophes et le problème de la guerre', *S.V.E.C.*, cxxvii (1974), 247.

15   Voltaire and Ninon de Lenclos

1 The following books will be referred to by appropriate abbreviations, in parenthesis, in the text of this article:

T. Besterman, *Voltaire* (London 1969)	Best. V
[A. Bret], *Mémoires sur la vie de mademoiselle de Lenclos* (n.p. 1751)	Bret
G. Desnoiresterres, *Voltaire et la société au XVIIIe siècle* (Paris 1871–6)	Desnoiresterres
[Douxménil], *Mémoires et lettres pour servir à l'histoire de la vie de mademoiselle de l'Enclos* [1751] (Rotterdam 1752)	Douxménil
E. Magne, *Ninon de Lanclos. Edition définitive* (Paris 1948)	Magne
Voltaire, *Correspondence and related documents. Definitive edition by Theodore Besterman*, in *The Complete Works of Voltaire*, vols. 89–129 (Geneva, Banbury 1968–76)	Best. D (followed by the number of the letter cited)
Voltaire, *Œuvres complètes* ed. L. Moland, (Paris 1877–85)	M
Voltaire, *Sur Mlle de Lenclos*, in M. xxiii, 507–513	

2 The quotation is from the *Commentaire historique sur les œuvres de l'auteur de la Henriade*, which is almost certainly by Voltaire himself (M i, 69–70, and Best. *V*, 543).

3 My investigations were prompted by the task of editing, for *The Complete Works of Voltaire*, the *Dialogue entre Mme de Maintenon et Mlle de Lenclos* (1750—M xxiii, 497–500), and the letter *Sur Mlle de Lenclos* (1751—M xxiii, 507–13; also printed as Best. D 4456). These two texts will eventually appear in volumes 32 and 33 of *The Complete Works of Voltaire*.

4 In a note to Best. D 4456, Dr Besterman erroneously gives Voltaire's age at the time of the meeting, as twelve.

5 I have followed eighteenth-century and current usage, in spelling the name 'Lenclos', rather than adopting Magne's suggestion (p. 13, n. 1), that historians should revert to the original spelling.

6 As Magne points out, pp. 17–18, n. 2.

7 There seems to be no documentary evidence regarding the date he entered the Collège Louis-le-Grand. Desnoiresterres (p. 15) says it was October 1704.

8 Bret (p. 1) gives the date of her birth as 1615, while Douxménil (p. 8) gives 1616.

9 Magne, pp. 129, 169–70, 222–7; Saint-Simon, *Mémoires*, ed. Boislisle, xiii (Paris 1923), pp. 143–4; *Œuvres diverses de M. l'abbé Gédoyn* (Paris 1745), 'Mémoire sur la vie de l'auteur', pp. xi–xii.

10 Le Vicomte de Grouchy in *Bulletin de la société de l'histoire de Paris et de l'Ile de France* (1893), pp. 93–4 (also in Magne, pp. 300–1).

11 As suggested by Desnoiresterres (i, 34).

12 Best. D 4867, when it was printed in 1752, was given the title '. . . à un membre de l'Académie de Berlin': it is almost certainly addressed to Formey (see the Textual Notes to Best. D 4867).

13 Regarding Gédoyn and the Arouet family, see Best. *V*, pp. 27–8, and the abbé's *Œuvres diverses*, mentioned above in n. 9, loc. cit. Châteauneuf was François-Marie's godfather.

14 *Nouveaux mélanges philosophiques, historiques, critiques, &c &c* (n.p. 1765), iii, 404.

15 Formey's letter of inquiry has not survived, but its existence can be deduced from the first two lines of the letter *Sur Mlle de Lenclos*, and from Best. D 4480 (penultimate paragraph); it must have reached Voltaire before Easter, 1751; the letter *Sur Mlle de Lenclos* must have been sent soon after Holy Week (that is soon after 11 April 1751)—see the first paragraph of the letter.

16 See the article on Formey in C. Bartholmess, *Histoire philosophique de l'Académie de Prusse* (Paris 1850), i, 361–96, and Formey's own *Souvenirs d'un citoyen* (Berlin 1789).

17 Such is the impression likely to be gained from a reading of the *Souvenirs d'un citoyen*, and his moral works such as the *Mélanges philosophiques* (Leyden 1754).

18 *Bibliothèque impartiale pour les mois de Septemb. et Octobre* MDCCL, *II, ii*, 249–52.

19 See above, n. 1. There is an informative article on these two *Mémoires*: A. C. Keys, 'Bret, Douxménil and the *Mémoires* of Ninon de Lanclos', *Studies on Voltaire*, xii (1960), 43–54.

20 The first meeting took place in January 1751 (*Souvenirs d'un citoyen*, i, 232). The two men quarrelled over the König-Maupertuis affair in 1752, as well as over other matters.

21 Bret says the event took place when Ninon was about seventy (pp. 114–15); Douxménil says it happened when she was at an 'âge extrêmement avancé', but still beautiful (pp. 46–9).

22 Magne, pp. 114–17; E. Colombey, *Correspondance authentique de Ninon de Lenclos* (Paris 1886), pp. 80–138; Saint-Evremond, *Œuvres* (Paris 1927), iii, 173–98.

23 See the letter by Ismaël Boulliau, cited by Colombey in *Correspondance authentique*, p. 197.

24 See the 'Donation', cited by Boislisle in Saint-Simon, *Mémoires*, xiii, 523 (also printed in Magne, pp. 288–90).

25 See the letter to Saint-Evremond, cited in Feuillet des Conches, *Causeries d'un curieux* (Paris 1862), ii, 588 (Saint-Evremond, *Œuvres*, iii, 179–80).

26 Different versions of this story are given by Chavagnac (*Mémoires* (Paris 1900), p. 41), and Saint-Simon (*Mémoires*, xiii, 141–2).

27 That contact was maintained between Ninon and Mme de Maintenon is alleged by La Princesse Palatine (*Correspondance de madame, duchesse d'Orléans*, ed. Jaeglé (Paris 1890), i, 171–2), and Saint-Simon (*Mémoires*, xiii, 145–6).

28 As Keys points out (loc. cit., pp. 46–8), this incident has affinities with a story in *Gil Blas*.

29 Gourville himself makes no mention of the story of the *cassette* which Ninon, according to Voltaire, guarded for him so faithfully (*Mémoires*, ed. Lecestre (Paris 1894); Lecestre believes that the story is a fabrication (ibid., ii, ciii). It is true that Saint-Evremond calls Ninon 'ma belle gardeuse de cassette', but the context does not seem to refer to the Gourville episode (in Colombey, *Correspondance authentique*, pp. 107–8, and Saint-Evremond, *Œuvres*, iii, 177); Saint-Simon says Ninon 'a gardé très fidèlement des dépôts d'argent', but gives no examples (*Mémoires*, xiii, 145). Voltaire used the basis of this story about Gourville for his comedy *Le Dépositaire* (1769).

30 Huygens certainly had not seen Ninon by the end of his second stay in France (1660–61), although we know that he wished to do so (Huygens, *Journal de Voyage à Paris et à Londres*, in H. L. Brugmans, *Le Séjour de Christian Huygens à Paris* (Paris 1935), pp. 144–5 and 153).

31 *Mémoires du Duc du Luynes sur la cour de Louis XV* (1735–58) (Paris 1860–5), vi, 413–15 (22 April 1745).

32 Voltaire does not here commit himself regarding Ninon's age when Châteauneuf became her lover!

33 Regarding the criteria by which Voltaire established historical fact, see J. Brumfitt, *Voltaire Historian* (London 1958) pp. 129–47. Voltaire uses

the phrase 'Une telle sottise n'est nullement vraisemblable' to describe the story about Ninon and Gédoyn (M xviii, 354).

34 *Historiettes* (Paris 1961), ii, 440–9.

35 *Mémoires*, xiii, 140–8.

36 Though he had emphasized it earlier, in the poem about Ninon which appears in a variant to *Le Temple du goût* (1733) (M viii, 593).

37 '[Ninon] disait qu'elle n'avait jamais fait à Dieu qu'une prière: "Mon dieu, faites de moi un *honnête homme*, et n'en faites jamais une honnête femme" (*N*, 509); 'j'apprends que l'on vient d'imprimer deux nouveaux Mémoires sur la vie de cette *philosophe*' (*N*, 513). (My italics).

16   Madame de Tencin: an Eighteenth-Century Woman Novelist

1 *Mémoirs du comte de Comminge* (The Hague 1735), p. 1.

2 Described in the following terms, op. cit., p. 197: 'L'affreuse solitude, le silence qui régnait toujours dans cette maison, la tristesse de tous ceux qui m'environnaient, me laissaient tout entier à cette douleur qui m'était devenue si chère.'

3 See for instance Georges May, *Le dilemme du roman au XVIIIe siècle* (Paris 1963), p. 43.

4 *Les Egarements du cœur et de l'esprit, ou Mémoires de M. de Meilcour* (Paris 1736–8).

5 *La Vie de Marianne, ou les aventures de Madame la comtesse de xxx* (Paris (1731–42).

6 *Le Paysan parvenu, ou les mémoires de M. xxx* (Paris 1734–5).

7 *La Princesse de Clèves* (Paris 1678).

8 For a full discussion of Prévost's debt to those of his predecessors in the novel who had exploited history to differing ends, see Jean Sgard, *Prévost romancier* (Paris 1968).

9 Charlotte-Rose de Caumont de La Force, 1654–1724, related to the noble house of La Force, whose fortunes had been much impaired by having espoused the Protestant cause in the Wars of Religion. Her own life was not without its share of adventure and even of tragedy. Her novels are: *Histoire secrète de Bourgogne*, 1694; *Histoire secrète de Henry IV, roy de Castille*, 1695; *Histoire de Marguerite de Valois*, 1696; *Gustave Vasa, histoire de Suède*, 1697; *Anecdote galante ou histoire secrète de Catherine de Bourbon*, 1703.

10 Catherine Bédacier, known as Mme Durand, a lesser talent than Mlle de La Force or Mme d'Aulnoy, she did not restrict herself to writing historical novels. Among those she wrote were: *Histoire des amours de Grégoire VII*, 1700; *Mémoires de la cour de Charles VII*, 1700.

11 Marie-Catherine Jumelle de Berneville, c. 1650–1705, author of some of the best-known fairy tales of the period as well as some of the most popular historical novels of the time. She was the author of the *Histoire d'Hypolite comte de Duglas* which first appeared in 1690 and of which

twenty-eight editions appeared between then and 1804; and of *Le Comte de Warwick*, 1703.

12 Catherine Bernard, a niece of Corneille and author of some of the most touching short stories which the classical age produced; *Eléonor d'Yvrée*, 1687; *Le Comte d'Amboise*, 1689; *Inès de Cordoue*, 1696.

13 *Le Siège de Calais* (The Hague, J. Néaulme, 1739). Two further editions of this work were published in 1739. There is also a discussion of elements in this novel on Chapter 11 above.

14 Mlle de La Force was involved in several scandals, including having her marriage declared null and void by her husband's family in an episode which might interest readers of *Manon Lescaut*. She was eventually confined to a convent. The extraordinary adventures which Mme d'Aulnoy is reputed to have taken part in make it a matter for regret that she did not write an honest autobiography. Married at the age of sixteen to the debauched comte d'Aulnoy, her animosity towards him reached such a pitch that she tried, unsuccessfully, to make away with him. She is said to have hidden under the altar cloth in a church while escaping arrest; and apparently spent some years in exile.

15 For an excellent account of Mme de Tencin's life, see Pierre-Maurice Masson, *Une Vie de femme au XVIIIe siècle, madame de Tencin (1683–1749)* (Paris 1909). Society's attitude towards her is exemplified by the ignominious treatment which was meted out to her on her arrest after La Fresnaye, her erstwhile lover, had committed suicide at her house.

16 It is not possible, within the limits of this brief study, to look at Mme de Tencin's other historical novel, the *Anecdotes du règne d'Edouard II*, which, on being left unfinished at her death, was completed by Mme Elie de Beaumont and published in 1771. Although inferior to Mme de Tencin's other novels, it is a not negligible example of the use of English history as the setting for a sentimental novel.

17 See Mme de Genlis: 'Nous avons de Mme de Tencin plusieurs romans: *Le Siège de Calais* dont l'idée principale est révoltante et sans aucune vraisemblance.' *Histoire des Femmes françaises les plus célèbres et de leur influence sur la littérature française . . .* (London 1811), p. 131.

18 op. cit.

19 René Démoris, 'De l'usage du nom propre: le roman historique au XVIIIe siècle'. *Revue d'histoire littéraire de la France*, lxxv (1975) 268–88.

20 See i.a. Jean Decottignies' invaluable edition of the *Mémoires du comte de Comminge* (Lille 1964) pp. 59 ff.; Georges May, op. cit., pp. 204–45; Jean Sgard, op. cit., pp. 108 ff. The subject was initially treated over seventy years ago now, in the second of two remarkable articles by Georges Ascoli in the *Revue de synthèse historique*, xiii (1906) 161–84, 'Essai sur l'histoire des idées féministes en France du XVIe siècle à la Révolution'.

21 *Réflexions nouvelles sur les femmes par une Dame de la Cour*, nouvelle édition corrigée (London 1730), p. 30.

22 It is not without significance that Ascoli, op. cit., draws his examples of texts championing the cause of feminism from journals and plays of the time but *not* from novels.

23 op. cit.

24 Possibly the major weakness of Decottignies' argument is that it fails to take into account the prescribed aim of moving the reader by a recital of the hero's weakness, a weakness which is at the same time a strength for the prevostian hero, since it is the concomitant of a greater sensibility.

25 *Histoire de Madame de Luz, anecdote du règne de Henri IV* (The Hague 1741).

26 *Les Liaisons dangereuses, ou Lettres recueillies dans une société, et publiées pour l'instruction de quelques autres* (Amsterdam and Paris 1782).

27 op. cit.

28 *Les Amans malheureux, ou le comte de Comminge, drame en 3 actes et en vers, précédé d'un discours préliminaire et suivi des mémoires du comte de Comminge* (The Hague and Paris 1764).

29 Pierre Fauchery, *La Destinée féminine dans le roman européen du dix-huitième siècle* (Paris 1972).

30 Georges May, 'L'Histoire a-t-elle engendré le roman? Aspects français de la question au seuil du Siècle des Lumières', *R.H.L.F..*, lv (1955), 155–76.

17 Marie Huber and the Campaign against Eternal Hell Torments

1 cf. Henri Vuilleumier, *Histoire de l'Eglise Réformée du Pays de Vaud* (Lausanne 1927–33), 4 vols, iv, 249–50.

2 Vuilleumier, op. cit. ii, 131–4, 156, 467, gives an interesting view of his unorthodox doctrines.

3 Leu and Galiffe (see note 12 below) differ upon the genealogy of this distinguished family, which had branches in no less than thirteen Swiss cantons or towns.

4 *Recherches pour servir à l'histoire de Lyon, ou les Lyonnais dignes de mémoire* (Lyon 1757, 2 vols 8o), ii, 359–62. Pastor Jean Senebier of Geneva tried to be fair to her in his *Histoire littéraire de Genève* (Geneva 1786, 3 vols 8°), iii, 83.

5 Eugène Ritter, 'La jeunesse et la famille de Marie Huber' in *Etrennes Chrétiennes* (1882). (I have been unable to find a copy of this in London or Paris.) Théophile Dufour, *Recherches bibliographiques sur les œuvres imprimées de J. J. Rousseau* (Paris, 1925, ii, 83–4). Gustave A. Metzger, *Marie Huber. Sa vie, ses œuvres, sa théologie* (Geneva 1887) is a useful short thesis from the modern viewpoint.

6 For Aubert de Versé, see my article, 'A Wandering Huguenot Scholar, Noël Aubert de Versé', *Proceedings of the Huguenot Society of London*, xxi (1970 for 1969), 455–63.

7 1733 edition, pp. 36, 41, 51–3.

8 ibid., pp. 422, 435–6, 441.

9 ibid., pp. 1–16.

10 Vuilleumier, op. cit., iii, 212–36, treats Fatio's case as illustrative of the convulsions caused in the Swiss Establishment by Pietism.

11 For the position of Locke and Tillotson in this respect, see my article in *Studies on Voltaire and the Eighteenth Century*, vi (1958), 42–50: 'Pierre Cuppé's debts to England'.

12 H. J. Leu, *Allgemeines Helvetisches . . . Lexicon* (Zürich, Teil x, 1756) p. 343, and J. A. Galiffe, *Notices généalogiques sur les familles genevoises . . .* (Geneva) iii, p. 266; both refer to her without a name; Vuilleumier, op. cit., mentions her cursorily.

13 *La Nouvelle Bibliothèque*, ii (février 1739), p. 172, replying to a review; 'C'est bien définir ce genre d'écrire, l'Histoire des Idées . . . c'est tout ce dont l'auteur des *Lettres* est capable'.

18   Madame de Montesquieu, with some considerations on Thérèse de Secondat

1 *Correspondance de Montesquieu*, publiée par François Gebelin avec la collaboration de M. André Morize (Bordeaux 1914), 2 vols., i, 386–7.

2 *Œuvres complètes de Montesquieu*, ed. André Masson (Paris, Nagel, 1950–5), 3 vols. References to the text of Montesquieu are to this edition, given as Nagel followed by the volume number.

3 E. de Perceval, 'La Baronne de Montesquieu', *Actes de l'Académie nationale des sciences, belles-lettres et arts de Bordeaux*, 3e série, tome ix (1932–3) p. 37.

4 P. Barrière, *Un Grand Provincial: Charles-Louis de Secondat, baron de La Brède et de Montesquieu* (Bordeaux 1946), p. 85.

5 J. Brethe de La Gressaye, 'Sur les pas de Montesquieu', *Actes de l'Académie . . . de Bordeaux*, 4e série, tome xxix (1974), p. 82.

6 L. Vian, *Histoire de Montesquieu* (Paris 1878), pp. 396–407.

7 The particule *de* is omitted in Vian's transcription in the daughter's name, but not in her father's. It is present in both in the manuscript.

8 D'Alembert in *Encyclopédie*, v (Paris 1755), p. xvii; Maupertuis, *Eloge de Monsieur de Montesquieu* (Berlin 1755), p. 59.

9 L. Moreri, *Le Grand Dictionnaire historique* (Paris 1759), ix, 308 (*s.v.* Secondat).

10 Dom Devienne, *Histoire de la ville de Bordeaux*, première partie (Bordeaux et se trouve à Paris 1771), p. 501.

11 P. Bernadau, *Tableau de Bordeaux* (Bordeaux 1810), p. 207 n.

12 F. Hardy, *Memoirs of the Political and Private Life of James Caulfield, Earl of Charlemont* (London 1810), p. 34.

13 *Biographie universelle*, xxix (Paris 1821), pp. 501–22.

14 M. O'Gilvy, *Nobiliaire de Guienne et de Gascogne* (Paris 1856–60), 3 vols., ii, 260. Clairac is a small and attractive town on the Lot, some 12 miles from the village called Montesquieu and 16 from Agen, as the crow flies. It had an important role in Montesquieu's life.

15 ibid., p. 177.

16 F. Gebelin, 'La Publication de l'*Esprit des lois*', *Revue des bibliothèques*, 34e année (1924), p. 140.

17 Vian, op. cit., p. 27.
18 ibid., p. 26.
19 Nagel i, C, p. 7.
20 J. Delpit, *Le Fils de Montesquieu* (Bordeaux 1888), pp. 23–4, 79–80.
21 Stendhal, *Voyages dans le Midi* (Sceaux 1956), pp. 76–7. Montesquieu's children were not, however, present at his death.
22 Nagel iii, no 56.
23 J.-M. Eylaud, *Montesquieu chez ses notaires de La Brède* (Bordeaux 1956).
24 R. Céleste, 'Montesquieu: légende, histoire', *Archives historiques du département de la Gironde*, xlii (1907), 491–7.
25 Helyot, *Histoire des ordres monastiques*, vi (Paris 1721), pp. 340–55; P. Lauzun, *Les Couvents de la ville d'Agen avant 1789* (Agen 1890–3), ii, 98–129.
26 A record of pensions paid to both of them is in the archives of La Brède.
27 Nagel iii, nos 152, 389, and 713.
28 The manuscript is at Bordeaux (MS 1868, no 205).
29 MS 1868, no 204.
30 Its shelfmark is MF 478.
31 Nagel iii, no. 744.
32 J. Dalat, *Montesquieu magistrat* (Paris 1971), i, 53.
33 Nagel iii, no. 93.
34 R. Céleste, 'Appendice', in *Deux opuscules de Montesquieu* (Bordeaux and Paris 1891), p. 70.
35 Nagel iii, no. 152. The above letter calls for some explanatory notes. It is notable that Thérèse addresses her clerical brother as 'vous' while she uses 'tu' when writing to Montesquieu. The uncle alluded to is Joseph de Secondat, born in 1646, who became Abbé de Faize, near Libourne, in 1661 and who was to die in 1726. In 1724 he surrendered the abbacy of Faize to his clerical nephew, who in 1725 became also *doyen* of Saint-Seurin at Bordeaux. The 'petite fille' referred to is probably Montesquieu's daughter Marie, was sent out to board at the convent. Mr de Citran is presumably of the family of the Chevalier de Citran referred to in a letter of Montesquieu of 1752 (Nagel iii. no. 644).
36 It was with considerable hestitation that Gebelin, in 1955, attributed it to Madame de Montesquieu. Céleste, in his proof edition of the correspondence, had attributed it to Marie de Secondat; but his attributions to Marie (at the Paravis) have in general to be transferred to Thérèse (at Saint-Paulin).
37 Tourny entered office on 31 August 1743. (M. Lhéritier, *L'Intendant Tourny* (Paris 1920), i, 215).
38 Nagel ii, 405.
39 J.-M. Eylaud, op. cit., pp. 100, 105, 110; O'Gilvy, *Nobiliaire*, i, 407.
40 See for example the references to Montesquieu's mistresses in the letter written to him by Demolets, priest of the Oratory, on 23 April 1725 (Nagel III, no. 67).
41 In 1743 she had the functions of *procureuse* (P. Lauzun, op. cit., ii, 121).
42 Letter, reprinted as a single sheet in the nineteenth century.

19   Angélique Diderot and the White Terror

1 Jean Massiet du Biest, *La Fille de Diderot*, 'extraits de sa correspondance inédite avec son mari et avec Jacques-Henri Meister, de Zurich' (Tours 1949); *Angélique Diderot*, 'témoignages nouveaux principalement d'après les lettres inédites adressées à celle-ci par J. H. Meister de Zurich' (Paris 1960). Jean Pommier's review appeared in the *Revue d'histoire littéraire de la France* (1951), pp. 373 ff.

2 I certainly do not deny the positive contribution made by J. Massiet du Biest, and in particular his revelation of the social ascent of the Vandeul family. It is wrong, however, to find in Angélique, who was after all in a central position in the family, only an attitude of 'condamnation de l'esprit mercantile du XIXème siècle' (*La Fille*, p. 40, n. 2). The words *déchéance* and *sainteté* are those of Massiet du Biest (*Angélique*, pp. 57 and 65). It is wrong, too, to give to the word *cœur*, as used by Angélique Diderot, a purely emotional sense; for her, the heart remains an *organ*; see *La Fille*, p. 74. The 'conclusions' of the first and the second book do not reflect the spontaneous general direction of a work not entirely under the control of its author. The second further emphasizes the 'Meisterian' character of the first, but, contrary to Massiet du Biest's mistaken belief, does not confirm it.

3 *Combativité* is used by Massiet du Biest (*La Fille*, p. 37). *Destruction lente* is used by Mme de Vandeul (see p. 129 and especially p. 132 in her letter to Meister of 29 July 1822). On the subject of her cancer of the small intestine, see the account of her autopsy in *La Fille*, p. 220. On the 'potions un peu mêlées d'opium', see the memorandum for her doctors (*La Fille*, p. 220; Mme d'Epinay was a confirmed user of this drug, which was at the time thought to be beneficial). It certainly seems that apart from some evocations of suicide, a mood then in fashion, the 'bonasse créature', as she called herself, did appreciate the delights of peace and quiet (p. 129).

4 See *La Fille*, Ch. VIII, in which the quotations should be read as a half-ironic description of a patroness whose functions she felt to be incumbent upon her as lady of the manor, through custom and convention.

5 *La Fille*, sub-title of § IV, p. 193, bottom of page. The letters to Drevon must also be taken into account. The proportion of letters to Meister out of a relatively small total number leads to some misapprehensions.

6 Meister himself recognizes that he had had 'peu de rapports' with Diderot (letter of 25 Thermidor, year IV, in *La Fille*, p. 72; see also my edition of Diderot's *Correspondance*, xiv, 110, n. 3). Assézat's statement needs to be corrected (Diderot, *Œuvres complètes*, ed. Assézat-Tourneux, i, ix).

7 'Ne voulez-vous que la philosophie ait encore d'emprise sur moi' (letter to Meister of 1 May 1798, in *La Fille*, p. 2).

8 See what she says about her 'réaction' in 1809 (*La Fille*, p. 32). An anthology could be composed of maxims of energy and firmness from Angélique's pen. For instance: 'J'ai dans la société une espèce d'orgueil

intérieur, qui est extrêmement blessé du tort que je puis avoir à mes yeux' (*La Fille*, p. 117). Angélique had had to overcome, with the help of her father, a hot-headed disposition; she acquired *prudence* and *reason* (Diderot, *Correspondance*, XIV, 93). This is perhaps what Grimm meant when in a letter to Catherine II (*Correspondance*, XV, 239) he spoke of Angélique as an 'ex-morveuse': he only took her on as a translator of Italian when he considered that she had become docile and well-behaved. But nature reasserts itself, and later on in life she was not always able to control the scoldings that her servants deserved (*La Fille*, pp. 116–17).

9 This is the word used by Meister himself (*Angélique*, p. 92).

10 She confided only in her doctors, and even then in a manner as objective and almost technical as that of her father, when he explained his case to Tronchin (see her *memorandum* in *La Fille*, pp. 218–21). It is difficult to see how Massiet du Biest could speak of 'phobies' (op. cit., p. 219, n. 2).

11 I am thinking in particular of angelism and angelology.

12 Letter of 1786 (*La Fille*, p. 15).

13 See *Angélique*, p. 60, n. 2. On her determination to grow old gracefully, see her letter of 30 Thermidor, year IV: 'je veux, si j'ai pu être une jeune aimable, ne pas avoir une vieillesse grognante' (*La Fille*, p. 115); and on her opinion of pious persons, her letter of 19 of the same month: 'Il faut excuser la rapacité, l'amour de l'argent et de dominer chez une dévote, puisque l'on trouve quelquefois la même faiblesse chez les femmes galantes' (*La Fille*, p. 187).

14 *La Fille*, p. 56.

15 *La Fille*, p. 136, 149, etc.

16 On the disciples of Diderot during the Revolution, see my chapter in the *Manuel d'Histoire littéraire de la France* (Paris, Editions sociales, 1973).

17 Archives nationales, F 7, no 4775(39); document mentioned in the catalogue of the exhibition *Diderot et l'Encyclopédie* at the Bibliothèque nationale (Paris 1951), no 111, p. 33. Massiet du Biest (*La Fille*, p. 42) reduces the importance of this fundamental text. He mentions, however (p. 138), that Angélique attended the republican festivals.

18 *La Fille*, p. 130.

19 See her letter of 18 Fructidor, year VI (*La Fille*, p. 143), in which she imagines a happy society in a future which will justify her Jacobin friend, Dr Bacher. 'Alors, il n'y aurait réellement que nos générations de malheureuses.'

20 The term *braillards* is to be found in a letter of 9 November 1791 (*La Fille*, p. 135); it designates those who were opposed to the confiscation by the people of the lands of the Prince de Condé. The account of the followers of Babeuf is in a letter to her husband of 18 Vendémiaire, year VI (*La Fille*, p. 142). Respecting as she did social institutions (text of 1804, p. 86), Angélique was unable to accept her father's ideas on the subject of great criminals (see her letter to Gaspard Hess of 24 July 1816, on the subject of Schiller's *Brigands*, in *La Fille*, pp. 97–8).

21 These quotations are on pp. 149–53 of *La Fille*.

22 *La Fille*, p. 150.

23 *La Fille*, p. 151 (letter to Drevon, August 1816). On the idea of tolerance, see (p. 183) a passage dating from 1818 which was certainly inspired by the repressive role of the clergy during the White Terror.

24 *La Fille*, p. 151.

25 He uses the terms *radoter* and *larmoyante* (p. 151)! It is clear that his own political opinions have blinded him in the face of his own documents.

26 Massiet du Biest presumably did not know of this document, since he did not catalogue it in the series 2 E which concerns the Vandeul family. It was recently found among a collection of letters which has the shelf-mark 107 bis, and is in the last group, headed '42 lettres diverses'. I should like to thank Mlle Couvret, archivist of the Haute-Marne, for her help in letting me see it.

28 Letters of 1788 (*La Fille*, p. 40) and of year VI (p. 99).

29 Later on, the expression 'je parierais' is used again, and a contrary wager is introduced by 'vous m'opposeriez'.

30 The text, which is not difficult to decipher, is reproduced in its entirety.

31 Mme de Vandeul at this time of the year would leave Paris for Auberive.

32 On 13 February 1820, the saddler of the Royal stables, Louvel, knifed to death the duc de Berry, second son of the future Charles X.

33 Louvel denied right up to his execution that he had accomplices, and the judicial enquiry failed to prove that he had. But the government took advantage of the situation to revoke liberal measures already conceded, or promised. The reaction increased in 1821 under Villèle.

34 *Impolitique*: politically inept. The allusion is to Decazes, who was still thought to be a liberal.

35 The *Ventre* is the centre of the Chamber, whose members, often corrupt (see Béranger's *chanson*), always vote for the government.

36 The reference is to the temporary victory of the liberal movement in Spain. The French army was to re-establish absolute government.

37 In Italy, the various movements of 1820 were struggling at the same time against absolutism (for a constitution) and against the Austrians. In Switzerland, it was a question of the movement for unity against the confederation restored by the Congress of Vienna after the abolition of the Act of Mediation which had governed Switzerland from 1803 till 1814.

38 The Stapfer concerned is Philip Albert, who was born in Berne (a German-speaking canton) in 1766, and died in Paris in 1840. A Professor, who was later appointed Minister of Education, he signed the Act of Mediation in Paris in 1801. Like Meister, he was politically a liberal, but a militant in the Protestant cause.

39 The reference is to the war against the Camisards.

40 Angélique de Vandeul's son and daughter-in-law, with whom each year she spent the winter in Paris.

Index